THOMAS WENTWORTH HIGGINSON

The Story of his Life

Aet. 80

T. W. Higginson

THOMAS WENTWORTH HIGGINSON

THE STORY OF HIS LIFE

BY

MARY THACHER HIGGINSON

WITH PORTRAITS AND OTHER
ILLUSTRATIONS

BOOKS FOR LIBRARIES PRESS
FREEPORT, NEW YORK

First Published 1914
Reprinted 1972

INTERNATIONAL STANDARD BOOK NUMBER:
0-8369-6723-2

LIBRARY OF CONGRESS CATALOG CARD NUMBER:
76-37886

PRINTED IN THE UNITED STATES OF AMERICA
BY
NEW WORLD BOOK MANUFACTURING CO., INC.
HALLANDALE, FLORIDA 33009

PREFACE

THE preparation of a volume which should tell briefly and simply the story of Colonel Higginson's life, and as nearly as possible in his own words, has involved examining and sifting a great mass of manuscripts. Happily he shared with his contemporaries a reluctance, not felt by the present generation, to destroy letters, journals, or memoranda. To those who have assisted my difficult task by the loan of letters and the contribution of personal memories, cordial thanks are due; and no less to the unknown friends who have written to signify their interest and say Godspeed. Let me also express warm gratitude to those literary friends of Colonel Higginson whose sympathy, advice, and criticism have been invaluable.

M. T. H.

CONTENTS

ILLUSTRATIONS

x   ILLUSTRATIONS

THOMAS WENTWORTH HIGGINSON

Thomas Wentworth Higginson

I

INHERITANCE

THOMAS WENTWORTH HIGGINSON came from a race
of large-minded, free-handed men. Beginning with
the Reverend Francis Higginson, of Puritan fame,
and coming down through the line of his descendants, we see a striking repetition of certain traits
and habits. Confining ourselves, for instance, to the
successive Stephen Higginsons, born in Salem, —
Wentworth Higginson's father, grandfather, and
great-grandfather, — we find them all upright and
fearless, actively interested in the general welfare,
leaders in public affairs, and extending a ready and
never empty hand to the unfortunate. They were
bred to mercantile life, and two of the three met
with various reverses in fortune, which never embit-
tered their lives or made them less philanthropic.

Stephen, the grandfather, having married at the
age of twenty, and finding his income not sufficient
for family needs, embarked upon the seas, commanding one of his father's ships at twenty-one. He continued "a bold and successful shipmaster" until the

breaking-out of the Revolution, and later was a member of the Continental Congress and high in councils of state. He anticipated the literary skill of his grandson Wentworth, for he wrote for the public press, wielding a vigorous pen in defence of his political opinions. He was dimly remembered by his grandson as a dignified and benignant figure in smallclothes. His son, Stephen Higginson, Jr., Wentworth's father, was a successful Boston merchant until Jefferson's embargo deprived him of wealth. He was called the "Man of Ross" from his great philanthropy, this name having been given to a benevolent English worthy celebrated by Pope. He was prominent in civic affairs and was one of the original trustees of the Massachusetts General Hospital. His grave is in the old burying-ground on Boston Common, marked by the inscription, "In works of Love he found his happiness."

These family traits were bequeathed to Thomas Wentworth Higginson and were in no way weakened by the transmission. Combined with these was an ardent love of adventure, which may be traced in a degree to his sailor grandfather, but more directly to the grandparents on his mother's side. The career of his maternal grandfather, Captain Thomas Storrow of the British army, and his American wife,

CAPTAIN THOMAS STORROW, 1755-1795

reads like a thrilling romance. The "Grenadier,"
as he has been nicknamed in the family, seems to
have been a "gay, reckless" fellow who managed
to make away with his worldly possessions in early
youth, partly by generously endowing his brother
and sisters. He was on his way to England from
Jamaica in 1777 in a vessel which was captured by
a Massachusetts privateer; and the young officer
of twenty-two was landed as prisoner-of-war at
Portsmouth, New Hampshire. Here in "Tory
circles," says the chronicle, he fell in love with the
beautiful Anne Appleton, great-granddaughter of
John Wentworth, first royal governor of New Hampshire. Captain Storrow was presently exchanged,
and in spite of the bitter opposition of both families
married this lovely girl of seventeen and carried her
off to England to his "cold and stately" mother.
That disappointed dame, having planned a match
for her improvident son with an heiress whose es-
tate "marched with" her own, had no fancy for a
penniless American bride. The chilly atmosphere
of this English home soon drove forth the pleasure-
loving captain, and the homesick child-wife beguiled
her solitary hours, both here and in other lonely
places in which she was stranded in later years, by
reading and study. Life for this wandering couple
was a constant kaleidoscope. At one time, Mrs.

Storrow was the centre of attraction in the gay
and corrupt society of Halifax where her cousin,
Sir John Wentworth, was high in power; and again
she was undergoing great suffering and hardship
imposed by the fortunes of war. That she was a
spirited lady we may judge from a letter to her
sister, in which she speaks thus of a certain arbitrary
brother in whose house she had been staying: "I
had rather live with a Hottentot just escaped from
the Caffres coast!"

Another instance of this quality occurred after
the couple had made their home on the island of
Campobello in the Bay of Fundy, which "the Grenadier" and his brother-in-law had purchased. It happened that Mrs. Storrow was once left alone with
her little children, when a notice was suddenly served
on her that she must leave the island immediately,
as it had been sold to them under a false title. She
was at once ejected from her house. "The Grenadier's" wife then rose up in her wrath and expressed
her indignation in such forcible terms that her per-
secutors succumbed to her eloquence — restored
her cattle, and allowed her to remain temporarily
in the house. Her husband, to do him justice, was
always her ardent lover, and his dying words were,
"Nancy, you are an angel!"

The first son born to the Storrows was Thomas

Wentworth, for whom the subject of this memoir
was named. The second daughter, Louisa, mother of
Thomas Wentworth Higginson, inherited the strong
character and sound common sense with the grace
and charm of Anne Appleton. Left an orphan at an
early age, she was received as an adopted daughter
into the family of Stephen Higginson. She wrote in
1832, recalling her early life:

"When I was fourteen years of age, he [Mr. Hig-
ginson] returned from Europe, and I shall never forget the first meeting I had with him — he was then
about thirty — in the prime of his beauty, which
was then exceeding — full of youthful ardor and
flushed with success — he . . . had been eminently
successful in his commercial Speculations and he
returned from England laden with the comforts and
luxuries of that land of ease — he introduced a
degree of elegance into his own establishment which
was then unknown and abounded in all that could
adorn or embellish life."

At nineteen, this young girl became his second wife,
and stepmother to his two children. Ten children
were born of this marriage, of whom Wentworth was
the youngest.

An all-important factor in this household was
Mrs. Higginson's older sister, Anne, who was universally beloved and respected in the community,
being commonly known as Aunt Nancy. Wentworth

Higginson always spoke of her affectionately as "the aunt who brought me up." On her seventieth birthday, he wrote her, "You seem to me no older than when I used to play with blocks upon the floor of our common chamber, or when you assisted me to insert myself for the first time in nankeen inexpressibles."

Professor Charles Eliot Norton, in a letter to Colonel Higginson in 1904, says of these sisters: "They [your friendly words] bring to mind my Mother's affection for your Mother, and for Aunt Nancy, who was as dear an Aunt to us children at Shady Hill as she was to you and your brothers and sisters. What dear and admirable women! What simple, happy lives they led!"

In their days of prosperity, the Higginsons exercised a lavish hospitality. Mrs. Higginson adapted herself readily, however, to changed fortunes, and in the companionship of her children, a large circle of friends, and many books, she passed a serene and contented life. She was a deeply religious woman and bore with fortitude the sorrows that came to her, the most bitter of which was the fate of her son Thacher. This youth, whom Wentworth Higginson called his "gayest and most frolicsome" brother, went on a voyage to South America and the ship was never heard from. It was the mother's custom to retreat every evening about sunset to a certain

THOMAS WENTWORTH STORROW, 1779–1862

window to write in her daily journal for her absent son. Not for many years did she give up all hope of his return, nor cease burning a nightly beacon.

It would seem that those days must have been longer than ours when we read of Mrs. Higginson's daily doings. Not only did she care for a large household, entertain a great variety of visitors, walk from Cambridge to Boston to make calls or do errands, but withal she accomplished a vast amount of valuable reading. Of his mother, Colonel Higginson always spoke with the most tender and reverent affection. In an article of his called "The Woman Who Most Influenced Me" he says: —

"In all the vicissitudes of a reformer's career, I cannot recall anything but encouragement on her part. . . . I have thus traced to my mother's direct influence three leading motives of her youngest son's life — the love of personal liberty, of religious freedom, and of the equality of the sexes. . . . Life brought her many cares and sorrows; but it never brought the saddest of all its griefs, disenchantment."

Unfortunately, Wentworth's recollections of his father were vague. He notes in his college journal at the end of his freshman year, among other "Reminiscences of Life": "My excellent father died Feb'y 20th, 1834. I was unfortunately too young at that time to feel my loss much." But he took great pride

in his father's useful life and especially in his close
connection with the university; for not long after his
financial misfortunes, Stephen Higginson was called
from Bolton, where he had temporarily removed his
family, to Cambridge to become the steward or bur-
sar of Harvard College.   He was deeply interested
in Unitarianism and organized the Harvard Divinity
School. His personal interest in the Harvard undergraduates of his day is shown by letters written to
him by those who had gone to Germany to continue
their studies, one of these being Edward Everett.
In a poem read before the Phi Beta Kappa Society,
June, 1904, Colonel Higginson thus spoke of his
father: —

> "He planned a path to each professor's door
> And placed a gate at every footpath's end;
> Above each gate he hung a lantern o'er
> To which each pair of learnèd feet might tend.

> "He planted elms, but then there came a frown,
> And stern economy soon cast a blight.
> The frugal college took the lanterns down,
> But left the trees to flourish as they might."

It was probably during the family's stay in Bolton
that their acquaintance was made with Wentworth's
future nurse, Rowena Houghton, who left the Higginson service to become the wife of Dexter Pratt,
Longfellow's village blacksmith. From the Bolton
farmhouse came the old leather fire-bucket which

Colonel Higginson purchased and hung in his Cambridge home. It had been painted white, but the removal of the paint brought to light the name "Stephen Higginson, Jr.," and near the top of the bucket the phrase, "In suis non fallitur. 1841."

The house which the college built for Stephen Higginson on Kirkland Street, Cambridge, then called "Professors' Row," still stands; and here, on one of the shortest days of the year, Thomas Wentworth Storrow Higginson began his eventful life. To use his own words, "I was born on the 22nd of December, 1823, and had my proud birthright wrested from me when the change of dates landed the Pilgrims on December 23."

II

AN OLD-FASHIONED HOME

It is a curious fact, considering his vigorous manhood, that the infant Wentworth was at one time delicate, and according to family belief was kept alive by the juices of chicken bones. In after years, Mrs. Higginson wrote this letter, December 26, 1861: —

"Your birthday was remembered and honored by gratitude and praise, remembering as I did the poor half dead baby that I had for so long walked about in my arms and fed religiously according to direction every two hours, bearing hope in my heart when there seemed no hope, and even the most experienced doctors gave him up; how could I be but grateful and exultant when I think of my stalwart son, the Day Star of my Life!"

"Too many babies" is the concise label with which Wentworth, the man, indorsed a letter written by his Aunt Nancy in 1824, in which she says: —

"I believe I have not written you since the birth of our young Thomas Wentworth. I meant to have announced to you the arrival of the Stout Gentleman. . . . Our Wentworth grows such a mountain — that we think sometimes it would be well to ask Mr.

Perkins to invent some kind of a steam-engine where-
by to tend him this summer — for we have some
misgivings concerning the strength of our arms. . . .
Oh, dear! if this would only be the last blessing of
the sort which was to fall to our happy lot. Surely
we ought to be resigned — even if our hard fate
should condemn us to count only eleven [living]
children."

A quaint relic of those days survives in the shape
of an old English mahogany washstand, containing a
tiny concealed tub in which the Higginson babies
were bathed. This extraordinary tub is drawn out
by brass handles like a drawer, and with it come the
supporting legs. All the children who grew up under
the influence of their faithful Aunt Nancy did her
credit. Francis became a physician, but was too generous and tender-hearted to make a worldly success.
Stephen was a merchant, and the only one of the
flock who had a large family of his own. He was in
South America during most of Wentworth's childhood, but wrote charming letters addressed to "Bro.
S.'s little man." Waldo, whom the irrepressible
Thacher called a "thunderin' dandy," was the soul
of honor and chivalry, although his brave life was
partially crippled by paralysis. Neither of the two
sisters was married. Louisa, brilliant, accomplished,
and considered the genius of the family, became —

for a time — a Roman Catholic. Learning, however, that according to the belief of the Church her Protestant mother could not be ultimately "saved," she, to use her own words, "saw the door open and walked out." Anna, the self-effacing, domestic sister, outlived most of the others.

The pet of the Higginson family was — naturally — little Tommy as he was then called. Soon he was only known as Wentworth, and the Storrow was dropped. Our earliest glimpses of him are found in his mother's diary. They show how the child foreshadowed the man and also reveal the happy home in which he was reared. Indeed, we can almost breathe the atmosphere of that home when we read such sentences as these: "A large Damask rose bush sends its fragrance into one of our parlour windows and the yellow sweet briar waves its long wreaths into the other. . . . We read and work and walk and play and study German and laugh and talk and then there is nothing but smiles and sunshine to be seen."

When Wentworth was not quite four, he went to a Dame School kept by a Miss Jennison. He also went to dancing-school in a private house. His mother writes: —

"We . . . have been quietly seated at our work . . . only interrupted by little Wentworth's rampant spirits before he went to bed. He spells to me every night in sister's little book. Last night he read 'God Reigns.' He looked up at me and asked, 'What does God do with the reins?'"

At bedtime, one night, he announced, "Now I am going to d'eam something proper funny." Thus early began his lifelong interest in dreams.

Again she writes: —

"A very quiet happy day though a storm, engaged in making my little boy's clothes all day, while he [has been] by my side, reading or playing . . . he has been part of the time catching fish 'in 'ahant [Nahant].' . . . Between daylight and dark he plays Waldo is his Custard Pudding, and after beating and stuffing him, he roasts him in the oven; then after supper he takes his books. . . .

"We have been highly amused with Wentworth to-night . . . he [said he] could draw the 'Possum up the gum tree' . . . he made some marks on the paper and then showed them to me saying as he pointed, 'there's the possum up the gum tree, there's the raccoon in the hollow, there's catch-him-up-my-boy, there's give-him-half-a-dollar'; this indication of genius excited universal acclamation."

The maternal chronicle does not relate the story that Colonel Higginson enjoyed telling about one of his childhood's books which contained a rather too vivid description of a wolf's cave. The careful mamma had pasted strips of paper over the objectionable parts, but Master Wentworth succeeded in removing these precautions and the lurid words remained forever fixed in his memory.

One of his methodical habits was to make lists of his possessions, his friends, or his achievements. One cold winter night, when his brothers were wondering where an extra blanket could be found, one of them cried, "Ask Wentworth. He probably has a list of blankets in his pocket!"

The older brothers, Thacher and Waldo, went to a boy's school kept by William Wells, an Englishman, in an old colonial house, still to be seen on Brattle Street (then Tory Row), Cambridge. To this school Wentworth was promoted at the age of eight, and there he remained for five years, until he was fitted for college. His acquaintance with James Russell Lowell began here, the latter being one of the older pupils. There is an amusing letter from Lowell to Thacher Higginson which Colonel Higginson later framed and hung in his library.

"My dear Thach, —

"In the course of human events when the mind becomes indued with active spirit, with powerful imagination, with extensive enterprise, with noble designty — Then, my boy, Then! is the time to return to you this — Sallust.

"Yrs.

"J. R. L."

The first sight of "Jimmy Lowell" made a lifelong impression on the younger boy's mind as the former came galloping to school on a little white pony, although he lived only a few rods distant. Wentworth's own home was a mile away, and he often dined at the school. Afterward he recalled with amusement the fact that the old custom of serving pudding before meat lingered there. Athletic sports, as well as the humanities, were warmly encouraged by Mr. Wells, and the afternoons spent in cricket, football, and skating on Fresh Pond were always remembered with boyish glee. After leaving the school, his brother Waldo wrote thus to the younger boy about Mr. Wells: —

"There are few men that I like better, and I came to this state of feelings through some hard floggings, which I am glad your better behaved shoulders have escaped."

When Wentworth was nine, his mother recorded that he had read a great many books and was especially fond of natural history. A year later, she added that he had mastered the Latin grammar. The following summary of Wentworth's virtues from the same, perhaps not unbiased, source, may well bring the maternal records to an end: —

"He has genuine refinement and delicacy, with manliness and power of controlling himself and a

sense of right, governing his thoughts and actions —
which command my *respect* as much as if he was a
grown man. . . . I never [saw] one who was more
thoughtful and considerate of others — though he
has been the youngest and an object of uncommon
interest."

The old habit of preserving family correspondence was never abandoned by Colonel Higginson.
These little letters were written between the boy's
tenth and thirteenth years in a round clear script: —

"DEAR AUNT: —

"Henry [a cousin] left us today. The stage comes
to Davenport's tavern [North Cambridge]; so he had
to go up there and meet it. . . .

"We had [to] wait a long time for the stage and at
last it came, with 6 white horses. . . . Fast Day
Henry and me went up to Prospect-Hill [Somer-
ville]. Unluckily the mill was not going, but we ran
round and saw lots of little fortifications, and found
an old well nearly covered with a large stone which
I have heard was made in the Revolution. I brought
home two stones from it."

To his brother in Maryland he wrote when eleven
years old: —

"I have got 5 more Waverley Novels since you
have been gone: Ivanhoe, The Monastery, The
Pirates, and the 1st and 2nd Series of Chronicles of
the Canongate, besides Peveril of the Peak which
you left behind. Sunday School is in the Courthouse

STEPHEN HIGGINSON, 1770–1834

now. . . . I shall like to hear about a fox-hunt. Are
there any slaves at Mr. Martin's, and do they blow a
conch in the morning to collect them? . . . I read the
Spectator a few days ago."

Aunt Nancy received the two following letters: —

"How are you? . . . I am reading the Tales of a
Grandfather and like them very much. . . . I am
learning the conjugation of the verb parler, to
speak. . . . I think that I shall go into Cæsar, after
the vacation, at school. . . . I have seen some snowdrops already in Mrs. Carpenter's yard. I meant to
ask her for some the other day, but she was not at
home. I am learning to waltz now. Several days
ago, there was a fire here. It was at the Lyceum. As
soon as I woke up in the morning, I heard Henry
saying 'Oh Tommy there is a fire.' I looked out of
the window and saw a blaze. . . . I asked Sister Anna
if we might [go] and she said we might if we would
not go beyond the common fence. We went and
when we got there we found people in abundance.
As we were going along, Thornton [Ware] caught up
with us having in each hand one of his father's fire-
buckets. He seemed to be quite at home there.
There were a great many blankets, &c., hanging on
the fence. . . . Some burnt papers were found as far
as Dr. Holmes's. There were a great many books
thrown out of the window. . . . I suppose I have not
given you a very good description of the fire, but it is
as good as I can give. I was glad to receive your
knife, for I wanted it very much. Tell brother

Stephen that I took the schooner that I was making when he came here, to pieces. I am now making a sloop instead of it. I think this is a pretty long letter, so Goodbye. Love to all.

"Your affectionate nephew,
"WENTWORTH."

"DEAR AUNT NANCY, —
"I have just been reading 'Pride and Prejudice' and 'Horse-Shoe Robinson,' a book by the author of 'Swallow Barn,' both which are very entertaining. I have also read Miss Burney's 'Cecelia.'"

To his mother he thus recounted his doings: —

"I will now tell you of our May party. We met on the 30th of April at 5 A.M. just down by Thornton's to choose a queen. . . . Afterwards we went to Mount Auburn and walked and played until 10 o'clock when we came home. . . . I forgot to say that as [we] were going to Mount Auburn we stopped a little while at Mrs. Foster's and she gave us some cake. We found no flowers except half blown anemones."

"DEARLY-BELOVED MOTHER, —
"'The miniature tigresses' (that is Aunt Nancy, and Mrs. ——) being absent, I sit down, away from the discord of feminine voices, which there usually is when I write! What do you think of that? . . . Aunt Nancy will hardly ever show me any of your letters, for she says you always write sentiment to her, and sublunary things to the rest of us.

"I had a splendid time on the fourth of July. I

went into Boston . . . for the sake of seeing the fireworks in the evening. I walked in with Thornton, at
about 10 A.M. . . . The children were delighted to see
'Tommy,' as they both called me. I played 'me
hidey' with Lizzy for ever so long. We saw several
companies go by. At last came the grand pageant. . . .
After dinner we went down onto Long, Central, and
India Wharves, on board of a great many vessels,
and had fine fun."

And this is his comment on the fireworks: —

"Suffice it to say that I never in the whole course
of my long life saw such a beautiful sight."

To his mother he again writes at the age of
twelve: —

"The books that I have read lately have been the
'Heiress' and 'The Select British Poets,' a great
big book. . . . William —— has gone on a whaling
voyage for two years and a half, round Cape Horn.
Aunt N. thinks this is very well for him."

The last paragraph is explained by a sentence in
Higginson's "Old Cambridge" which says, "Cambridge boys were still sent to sea as a cure for naugh-
tiness."

At about this time, in 1834, Wentworth's father
died. Two years later Mrs. Higginson sold the
Kirkland Street house and removed to a smaller one
on Garden Street, which had been built by her son

Francis. This house is no longer standing, having been absorbed by Radcliffe College. Wentworth wrote this description of a visit to their former home: —

April 13, 1836.

"I went to our [old] house to see the auction. Mr. Morse begun with the dining-room, then went to the back parlour and then to the study. The champagne bottles sold for $4\frac{1}{8}$ cents apiece; the clock for $3\frac{3}{4}$; and a little table in there for 1 cent. . . . There was an old curious chair, which Mr. Morse finding he could not sell, broke. I was much obliged to him for I got a nice bat by it."

Occasionally a bit of autobiography is found among the old letters, as this: —

"I vividly remember when I first swam above my depth in the Charles River. We boys had been learning to swim at a point in the river not far from the willows where we played and read Spenser's 'Faerie Queene.' The first time I swam across from one point to another in this river was perhaps the proudest moment of my life. I had no feeling of fear, but one of great confidence. All along Mt. Auburn St. on the side bordering the river were apple trees and no houses."

At the age of twelve the boy kept a diary of his own, from which it appears that one of his amusements was attending lectures on such subjects as these: The French Revolution, Ancient History, the poet Southey, and miscellaneous lectures by "Rev. Waldo Emerson."

The habit of omnivorous reading, which clung to him through his long life, can always be taken for granted. At this period he read "Philip Van Artevelde," always a favorite, for the third time. A little later he speaks of spending many half-days in bookstores.

During all these evidences of unusual maturity, compared with the slower juvenile development of to-day, the record shows a healthy interest in boyish amusements and activities. For instance: —

"Went to see Signor Blitz the juggler, Court House; produced 2 rabbits, guinea pig and cat from a tin."

He was fond of visiting the ruins of the Ursuline Convent in Charlestown, the burning of which had made a great impression on his youthful mind, and which seems to have first aroused his love for religious tolerance. He walked often to Boston and spent a good deal of time at Mount Auburn or "Sweet Auburn." In his Decoration Day address at Sanders Theatre, in 1904, he thus alluded to the old playground: —

"I remember our great cemetery, Mount Auburn, when it was not yet a cemetery, but was called Sweet Auburn still; when no sacred associations made it sweeter, and when its trees looked down on no funerals but those of the bird and the bee."

In the boyish record of walks and games, girls of his acquaintance are often mentioned, and not always with deference, as when he lost a philopena to Henrietta B—— and exclaimed, "Confound her!" These girl friends seem to have been known by symbolic names, as he often speaks of meeting "Poetry," on the street, or walking with "Sensibility" or "Spinster." The boys also rejoiced in nicknames, for "Soap" and "Broadsides" are frequently mentioned, and it is stated that "no one danced with Sensibility except Broadsides."

These were happy, care-free days. But a new and thrilling experience was at hand. It was a proud day in Wentworth's life when, at the age of thirteen (1837), he began a student's life at Harvard, entering the freshman class which contained forty-five members, of whom he was the youngest.

III

In his college days, Wentworth Higginson was uncomfortably tall, shy, and reserved. He presented a curious combination of qualities—intellectual precocity with immaturity of character, and a marked love of study with great fondness for athletic sports. He was given to self-analysis, inclined to be somewhat sentimental, and, partly owing to his extreme youth, was not popular among his fellow-students. His only intimate friend in the freshman class was Francis E. Parker, who always held the place of first scholar, and who later became a prominent Boston lawyer. The two boys were rivals in rank and two years apart in age. Under date of May 22, 1839, Parker wrote of his young classmate, then a sophomore: "I like Wentworth rather, quite well. He is now young but a good scholar — tolerable looking, awkward."

There were other members of the class of 1841 who attained distinction in later life. Among them were the Boston physicians, Dr. Edward Clarke and Dr. Francis Minot. Two of the men took high rank as officers in the Union army; and the list of those who made their mark includes Henry F. Durant, the founder of Wellesley College. An intimate friend who entered college two years after Wentworth was Levi Thaxter, later the ardent student of Browning and FitzGerald. He did much to guide wisely young Higginson's literary tendencies.

The lifelong friendship between Thomas Wentworth Higginson and Edward Everett Hale also began while they were undergraduates. In some of the former's unpublished notes is this comparison: —

"There was a curious parallel in some respects between the life of Edward Everett Hale and my own. He is nearly two years older than myself, graduated at Harvard College two years before me (1839); each of us having the second rank in his class, a time when much more was thought of college rank than now. There were analogies also in physical matters between Hale and myself in some directions which had perhaps a bearing on the later problem of old age. Each of us was six feet tall; each of us combined the love of three studies which are rarely combined — Greek, mathematics, and natural history — and had on this last point the invaluable influence of Dr. Thaddeus William Harris, librarian, botanist, and entomologist. Each of us, therefore, was tempted out of doors, a very desirable temptation to naturally studious boys, and likely to strengthen their constitutions."

From the same notes the following reminiscences
are taken: —

"When I entered Harvard College an 'Abstract
of Laws and Regulations' of the University was given
me. The one thing that now seems of peculiar interest
in that circular is an item headed, 'Dress. On Sab-
baths and Exhibition days, and on all public occasions,
each student in public shall wear a black or black-
mixed coat, with buttons of the same color.' What
would a student think, today, of this regulation!

"While in college I took an active interest in all
athletic exercises, kicked football assiduously in the
autumn on the so-called Delta where Memorial Hall
now stands. We also played cricket of the old-fashioned kind with large bats and heavy balls, an outfit
now stowed away by gift of the class in some unseen
closet of the Harvard Union. The few who could
afford it rode on horseback; in winter Fresh Pond
afforded relays of beautiful black ice [for skating]
after each ice-cutting.

"I had invitations to join several of the college
clubs, but declined membership in all but the I. O. H.
which my elder brother, Waldo, helped organize and
in which I was very much interested; and also the
Institute of 1770 which was of elder date and of more
permanent fame. Here the members had frequent
debates."

Through the four years of college life Wentworth
kept a minute account of all his doings in the form of
a college journal. In these records are preserved, not

only lists of books read, but of "books I want to read," "of pieces I can repeat"; of bouquets (always composed of wild flowers he had gathered), with dates of presentation to his friends; of calls he had made, of drives and walks he had taken; and of the engagements and marriages of friends, as, "Dr. Howe and Julia Ward of New York"; "Mr. Longfellow and Fanny Appleton." He was equally careful and minute about all his expenditures, the latter being a lifelong habit. At one time he seriously thought of making the law his profession, and with this end in view he made an inventory of all the lawyers in Boston, and of various law books.

He was always a great pedestrian, often walking nine or ten miles a day, and taking evening walks with Parker far into the "gloomy and desolate" country, after which he sometimes sat up reading into the small hours. His walks were varied by wanderings in old graveyards to study the quaint epitaphs. The daily rambles were, however, confined to no locality, as this note testifies: —

"Walked to Charlestown through Lechmere Point [East Cambridge] and thence to Bunker Hill. Charley stumped and we rushed up the monument with a lantern. A weary distance, but finally got to the top. Splendid view all around. Counted 24 inward-bound schooners in the harbour."

The boy's frequent walks between Boston and Cambridge were interrupted at the Port to refresh himself with cream-cakes, and he seems to have been unmolested by the "Portchucks" (the Cambridgeport boys) in spite of the rivalry existing between the youth of the latter place and that of Old Cambridge. The journal also mentions "a pleasant time" at a horse-race, frequently sailing round on a raft at Fresh Pond; playing leap-frog, hockey, "pirate," and rolling ninepins at the same place, winding up the report with "had first-rate fun." In his elation at having recited ninety-five lines of Latin without many corrections, he records that he kicked football by moonlight; and he sometimes speaks of two hours spent in the water, once climbing a ten-foot fence to reach the wharf. In spite of his strenuous evenings, he usually rose at five to study. Living at home the first year, he found various ways to make himself useful. He chopped wood diligently, sometimes by candlelight; recorded transplanting clematis from the Norton place, and once gathering six dozen water-lilies at Fresh Pond. One day he was "engaged about $\frac{3}{4}$ hour in driving a strange yellow cat out of the cellar," and in the afternoon making rat-traps. He took boxing-lessons, played chess and backgammon with his mother, recited poetry and read aloud. Another amusement was firing the cross-bow with his cousin Farley Storrow "at bottles in the closet. Broke 5." He also speaks of "shooting with same at a phrenological bust. *Smashed !*"

Later he wrote to a friend, —

"It is dreadful to me to see a woman kill an insect."

Although his strong aversion to giving pain kept him from joining shooting expeditions when older, he says in his youthful journal: —

"Went to shoot peeps with Thacher's gun. Something was the matter with the gun, however. It would not go. In the evening F. and I fired at a mark in a field, with pistols."

He was fond of visiting the Botanic Gardens (a habit he never abandoned), and was president of the college Natural History Society. Such notes as these often occur in his journals: —

"Caught a little green snake and afterwards killed and preserved it.

"Skeletonizing a toad.

"Talking with Dr. Harris, I was seized with a larva-mania and hunted for them. Obtained a variety of ugly worms which I am going to keep through vacation till they turn to chrysalises. I feel more entomological than oratorical just now.

"Tried to draw some insects — particularly a beautiful Papilio Philenor Harris had given me. Succeeded quite well."

That he had a boy's healthy appetite we may judge from these statements made in his freshman year: —

"Thanksgiving Day. Dinner, walked into the turkey, ham, pudding and pie!" — "Eat 2 quarts of cherries with P. at noon, his treat." — "Eaten 12 ices in 3 days. Tuesday, Wednesday, & Thursd: 4 each day." — "Home at XI & made half a pitcher of *iced molasses & water* — molasses not very good — drank some, however — reading Ladies' Magazine, &c., until dinner."

Occasionally he went to an evening party. After one of these gatherings, he reports: "Played backgammon. Danced. Had a miserable time." Those who knew him only in later years find it hard to comprehend how great a social stumbling-block was the youth's early diffidence. Improvement soon began, as the next year he wrote, —

"Went at 9 P.M. to a party. Had a decent time. Splendid ice-cream."

The following extracts are taken from his freshman journal, showing what an intimate relation existed in those simple days between President and student: —

"President Quincy was present at our Livy recitation. Lucky. I never recited better." — "President Q. was present at our recitation in Herodotus. Got along decently." — "Went to President to get my marks. He wants me to behave well, so he says at least." — "Deaded in Geometry for the first time." — "Cut both recitations for amusement. Spent some time in the library [a favorite place of refuge]."

On his fourteenth birthday, December 22, 1837, he found that he was the youngest undergraduate. Two months later his journal records some of the lively scenes then witnessed at prayer-time: —

"Many of the class having become slightly boozy, made somewhat of a noise in prayers."

And again: —

"What a sight the Chapel presented at prayers this morning! About 200 panes of glass blown up, the hands of the clock taken off, and the dial stove in. The front panels of the lower part of the pulpit removed, and all the damask between the pillars torn away, and 'A Bone for old Quin to pick' written on the wall."

On another page he exclaims: —

"I have most indecorously omitted to mention one event . . . my receiving a Detur, Coleridge in 3 volumes, 12mo, college seal and all. 24 were given. Mine is pretty fair."

These volumes in the original handsome bindings are still on the shelves of the Higginson library.

In after years he often alluded with amusement to his youthful susceptibility, and wrote: —

BIRTHPLACE OF THOMAS WENTWORTH HIGGINSON, KIRKLAND ST., CAMBRIDGE

"I don't believe there ever was a child in whom the sentimental was earlier developed than in me."

When a freshman, he records meeting an old friend, "now a fine-looking girl of sweet sixteen. I think I will fall in love with her in vacation!" Of another damsel, met when away from home, he says: —

"It is not exactly love I feel towards M. C. D. — it is rather a *Platonic* affection, if there is any such thing — or a *connubial* one."

When he was introduced to Mr. Papanti's "best scholar and very agreeable girl," he escorted her home from dancing-school and then wrote: —

"To bed at $11\frac{1}{2}$. Smitten."

Apparently the impression lingered as this reproach follows later: —

"Felt sentimental and loafing. Oh M. C.!"

and

"Dulcinea absent for which I am glad, for to have seen her would have used me up for some days."

Then he confides to his journal: —

"By the way, I am getting quite susceptible to female charms."

Again, he reports. —

"Had a glorious flirtation with H. & P. in the Study, first reading sentiments in the parlour, &c."

This letter to his boon companion, Parker, has no date, but was undoubtedly written somewhat early in his college career: —

"Oh be joyful — hooray — hooray — Interviewed the eccentric brick this morning and he informs me that the term begins '*three weeks from next Monday*' — id est, the 2nd Monday after Commencement. Glorious, glorious — engage the horse & wagon, get a fresh supply of powder & shot, have your duck pants washed, brush up the Eminent, sharpen the knife and Jack, — and please the pigs we'll be off yet. . . .

"I cut my oration Monday and devoted the day to botanizing, which cheered me wonderfully and I feel quite nice now."

At the end of his sophomore year, he resolved to be fourth or fifth scholar, and a month later his diary contained this caution: —

"Look out, Higginson, or your resolution, top of page 13, will go to grass!"

The college term closed on July 19, and he wrote on that day: —

"My Sophomore year is now over, this day concluding the second term. My rank during this term has been pretty satisfactory (v. p. 8 [of journal]). I must beat Hoffman, however, if possible."

When, early in the following October, he went to the President, the latter said to him, "You stand

very well. I could n't wish you to stand much
better." To the account of this interview, the young
student adds, "If I only could be 3rd scholar." Two
days later he speaks of lounging on the grass of the
Delta with various friends, and exclaims, "I 've given
up all hopes of keeping above Parker." A little
earlier in that year, Professor Felton had required
the youth to translate the soliloquy of Henry V into
Greek iambic verse, which the victim pronounced
"A terrible visitation!"

Of the occasion on which this translation was presented to the public, Higginson wrote in later life: —

"There lies before me a printed programme, entitled 'Harvard University, Cambridge. Order of
Performances for Exhibition, Wednesday, July 17,
1839.' It must have been a great day for me, for
this is the first exhibition in which I took part. . . .
I have somewhere, among my papers, my first efforts
at that Greek poetic translation which was practically rewritten by Professor Felton and recited on
the actual occasion with a dignity that I did not forget for a long time. My two nearest rivals in rank at
that time spoke a Greek dialogue, a thing not done
for many years, I believe, in the college."

The same event is described in his college diary: —

"I spoke excellently, my friends say so, remembered my part and was much applauded. I felt perfectly comfortable & cool on the stage but badly

before going on. Drank 7 or 8 glasses of iced lemon-
ade of which Sedgwick made *a bucket* & brought it
up to Mason's room!"

He also mentions his attire on this important day,
when he escorted his mother and sisters to the
chapel wearing "black coat, new pants, dark 'ves-
kit,' blk stockings & pumps."

His report of a later exhibition is not quite so
creditable: —

"Oct. 2. Had the pleasure of finishing my oration & rewriting a good deal of it, wh. delighted me &
I spent the rest of the day in reading Rookwood —
also the eve'g—comfort, fire, 3 candles, rock'g chair."

"Oct. 20. Exhib. passed off well. . . . I was perfectly self-possessed, but owing to looking round on
the audience &c. did n't know what I was saying,
made mistakes, hesitated & omitted — but they
did n't perceive it & thought it good."[1]

The next interesting event seems to have been
Wentworth's admission to the Phi Beta Kappa. In
an address before this society, many years later, he
said: —

"I was chosen into it at sixteen, for we graduated
from college earlier in my time than now; I took
active part in later years, under strenuous opposi-

[1] In order to save time, Mr. Higginson constantly used abbrevia-
tions as above. Such words are henceforth given in full to avoid
confusion.

tion, in expanding it into a national organization; I was President of this chapter for 3 years and of the national organization at the same time and helped build the latter up when it was so sought after that we had one application from a Southwestern college which said that they had heard of Φ. B. K. and as they already had nine Greek letter societies it would be nice to have ten!"

In the college journal, the event is thus recorded:

"August, 1840. Φ. B. K. day — the greatest of my life so far. Rushed round till 9 on committee business — having carried the ribbons to Wheeler's room and put on my medal. . . . I went in [to dinner] later than was necessary — Judge Story and the grandees sat at the raised West end. First course I had was roast beef carved by 'White' Simmons. 2nd, plum pudding and apple pie, then wine, fruit and segars — Passed a charming afternoon, lots of wit — the Judge always ready and always witty, as President."

In the spring of his Junior year, Wentworth wrote: —

"Such a smile as today's! The 2nd English Oration, a first Bowdoin prize and good pieces accepted in the magazine — and I am for the present perfectly happy."

During the senior year he roomed in a dormitory, and enumerated for his mother's benefit these modest wants: —

"3 chairs of a uniform pleasing pattern. I should prefer 2 uniform to 3 miscellaneous. 1 Washstand, 1 Bedstead and bedding, 1 Bureau."

Soon after leaving home, his mother wrote to him:

"Your study and chamber look so forlorn I cannot bear to go near them — The Study particularly ... presents a scene of desolation and *order*, so opposed to that beautiful confusion in which you keep it, that I find myself sighing for the odd stockings, shoes, gloves, coats, and waistcoats that whilome adorned the floor — and look in vain for the odds and ends of insects — bottles of gum — dirty boxes, and scraps of paper that reposed on the table —"

and continues: —

"How thankful I and you ought to be, my beloved Son, for the pure and firm health which has enabled you without interruption to give yourself to your College Studies."

Judging from the next report, he could hardly have posed for a "grave and reverend senior": —

"The Prex sent for me. . . . He found I'd cut 17 prayers. . . . I must look out. Rather a bore, for I shall have to cut some more for skating. . . .

"I went to see Fowler, the Phrenologist at the Marlboro' . . . said I had 'splendid talents' but no application. . . . Lovering says I'm the greatest trouble he has in recitation, and has deducted for whispering frequently."

At this age, as well as in maturer years, Higginson was easily lulled to sleep by monotonous lectures or sermons. His college journal reports: —

"Slept thro' sermon, hymn, prayer, read'g proclamation and blessing. Pleasant! Fellows laughed at me a good deal."

And of a lecture, he says, —

"Snoozed thro' it all comfortably."

In the winter vacation of his last year he made a visit to his Southern cousin, Farley Storrow, who was a fellow-student. In anticipation of this visit he wrote: —

"If I go, I intend to have a good time . . . and *certainly* not fall in love."

In his minute account of this journey the young traveller even gives the number of his berth on the Norwich boat. At New York he was pleased to see "Mr. Higginson's arrival" announced in a newspaper; and while at the Astor House, he wrote thus to Parker at Cambridge:

"As I must . . . miss the class election, I write to give you my proxy and charge you not by any means to let the Bird of Paradise be chosen Poet!"

From Philadelphia, he wrote to his mother: —

"I was at the hotel there with H. W. Longfellow, Esq. . . . He introduced me to the great Charles

Sumner who was with him, for which I was duly grateful."

At Baltimore, he saw for the first time a sign, "Negroes bought and sold," and noticed the difference in appearance between the "gloomy dull-looking" Baltimore negroes and a lively colored waiter whom he had made friends with at the New York hotel, and added, "Slaves and a freeman is the difference, I suppose."

While in Virginia, Wentworth received this letter from his mother, with its pathetic reference to her son Thacher's fatal voyage: —

"Now for news — Thacher sailed yesterday for Rio Janeiro. . . . He took out Books of all kinds, Scientific and literary. Theology, Law, History, Poetry, Philosophy, French, Spanish and English — he expects to be home in July. . . .

"I hope you will be able to come to some determination during this pilgrimage — what you would like best to do after you leave College. . . . At any rate the next term had better decide the business as it is very important that from the time you graduate you should be able to support yourself independently and be able even to lay up something to carry you through your Profession or to help you along during the first years of your setting out."

From the autobiographical notes made in later life we take the following: —

"During my senior year in college, I had under my charge a young fellow of the well known Perkins family, who with his elder companions, after a party, had sung a song beneath the window of the President's wife. So he was put in my care, although we were of much the same age and I needed supervision as much as he. My room was his headquarters, although he went to his home in Jamaica Plain every night. Later, when I lived at Newport, he and his family came there to live and his children were very anxious to see me, because they had heard so much about their father's guardian."

Continuing these notes about his college career, he says: —

"My greatest peculiarity was an inordinate passion for *books* — of any sort — great and small, heavy and light, useful or useless, nothing came amiss and I probably accomplished, in the first 13 years of my life, more miscellaneous reading than most youths of eighteen."

In 1906, Colonel Higginson wrote on the fly-leaf of one of his old textbooks (Professor Peirce's "Elementary Treatise on Curves, Functions, and Forces"): —

"When I left college at graduation in 1841, a few months short of 18, I was the best mathematician in the class, and Prof. Peirce ... had me placed at once on the examining committee in that department. We studied this book in sheets as it came unbound from the press and I enjoyed it, and used to give my elder brother Waldo (Harvard, 1833) who was a practicing engineer, lessons out of it. . . . Now, at 83, I cannot comprehend one word of it. Do I know more or less than then?"

IV

THE YOUNG PEDAGOGUE

SHORTLY before graduation, Wentworth Higginson began looking about for employment, and in June, 1841, was engaged by Mr. Samuel Weld, of Jamaica Plain, as assistant in his school for boys, at six hundred dollars per year. In August he wrote Parker, "I succeeded in getting a good room [at Jamaica Plain] for $25 the year and board from $3 to $4 [per month]." Settled in this new room, he began at once another journal. He was at first in a quandary as to whom it should be dedicated to, but finally decided on three girl friends and added, "Now to business." Homesickness assailed him at first, but after a few days he "got rather more comfortable, reading 'The Flirt' and those beautiful poetical passages in the 'Devil's Progress.'"

Apparently the "young pedagogue," as he calls himself, had no trouble in teaching the boys or making friends with them. He took them with him on his long rambles in search of flowers, and describes a tramp around Jamaica Pond in cloth boots in "a pouring rain and furious cold gale," adding, "these walks are nothing." But he was criticized by Mr. Weld for being on too informal terms with his pupils, and the necessary school discipline proved a hard problem. School began at half-past six, with an interval for breakfast, and then continued until eleven. There was also an evening session from seven to eight, described in the journal as the "cursed evening school," which prevented other more attractive plans. His favorite pupil, out of school hours, was Daniel Curtis, whose brilliant witticisms were often quoted in after years. Although Curtis was studious, he gave a great deal of trouble to his boyish preceptor. He was probably the author of this clever description of the young teacher which the latter captured as it was going the rounds of the school: —

"Our tutor feeds
At Madam Leeds,

"And is none the thinner
Postquam dinner

"Est semper clever,
Morosus never.

"Et nunquam hollers
At the scholars,

"But whenever they caper
Transcribes them to paper."

The friendly teacher sometimes took Curtis with him to make evening calls on young ladies. Returning quite late on one occasion the daring pupil reached his room by way of the waterspout, for which adventure his tutor was reprimanded. Another imprudent action on the part of the boyish teacher which naturally aroused criticism was riding on horseback with one of the girls from the opposite boarding-school, this damsel quietly climbing out of the window to take these rides in the early morning, while her schoolmates were still asleep.

In these years Wentworth Higginson seems to have been somewhat of a dandy, rejoicing in what bits of fine apparel his scanty means allowed him to lay hands on. For he reported himself once as "strutting" after church to display the "combination of gaiters and high heels"; and said also that he had his hair cut and curled which improved it. He sometimes went to parties and was fond of playing whist. After one of these gatherings he wrote, "By the way, nudity was rather the rage." He also recorded the possession of "a sudden entire confidence" in his conversing powers; and on the arrival of visitors he "talked with calm miscellaneousness till tea-time." His family were a little uneasy about him at this time, and his sisters found fault with him for being frivolous, whereupon he wrote in his journal: "I had

never thought of it before — but I think it is so. . . .
How I prize every moment taken from my occupation which I believe I shall be perfectly sick of
before the year is out." To add to his discomfort, he
once when in Boston missed the omnibus on account
of having spent ten minutes in a bookstore, and
walking rapidly to school, he arrived late and recorded that Mr. Weld received his apology in ominous silence. The next day he wrote, "Sleepy and
homesick all day."

The young teacher continued ineffectual efforts
to like smoking, which he had decided in college
days was a necessary accomplishment. His diary
says, "Got quite enthusiastic in reading about Student Life in Germany, got a pipe and smoked it as
well as I could, and determined to get a meerschaum."
But the experiment was a failure and later smoking
was wholly abandoned. He added, "Read Italian,
having brought over [from Cambridge] my books
and resolved to set about it resolutely. Read poetry
by a moonlit window." Another evening after the
pangs of toothache, genius burned, and he sat up
until three in the morning writing blank verse. He
read one of his poetical effusions to his family and
"they laughed at its sentimentality, which enraged
me . . . went to bed angry and feeling unappreciated.
Resolved to show them no more poetry."

The youth's imagination was as vivid as a child's, and after reading "Undine" he wrote, "Just now I heard a noise outside the window and looked up in hopes it was Kühleborn — oh, how dreadful it is to be in a land where there are no supernatural beings visible — not even any traditions of them!"

Christmas evening of that year was spent in serenading a Cambridge belle; but his companion, Levi Thaxter, escaping at a critical point, Wentworth, according to his journal, broke down in the song "Love wakes and weeps," and "made an absurd exit, scrambling over fences. . . . Home and gladly took off my horridly pinching boots — spent the evening sociably, reading Brother Jonathan and eating burnt almonds."

In addition to school perplexities, the unfortunate tutor's serenity was sometimes disturbed by the state of his purse, for he wrote, "Grumbled over my accounts. My affairs'll go to the devil if I don't economize." After six months in this unsatisfactory position, Higginson decided to leave the school and to become a private tutor in the family of his cousin, Stephen H. Perkins, of Brookline. The last days at Jamaica Plain he thus describes: —

"February 28. School for the last time — . . . Bid the boys good-bye quite satisfactorily — they are really sorry to lose me, and I felt so too. . . . Had a delightful evening till near 11 packing — then home and worked like a horse till 1 — taking up the carpet and everything else.

"March 1. Rose before 6 and fixed things. . . . We got Mrs. Putnam's ladder and the wardrobe slid down very easily."

Wentworth now went to his mother's in Cambridge for a few weeks, whence he wrote, "An exquisite soft spring day which would have cheered the soul of a lobster — and it did mine." A few days later he added, "Assumed my Cambridge state of mind. . . . I certainly intend to try — and not give way to the causeless melancholy I have occasionally fallen into heretofore," and "resolved to wake up from my dreams and work."

All through these early years, one finds allusions to a habit of indulging in occasional despondent moods, when silence and sadness cast their spell over him. These visitations lasted into middle life, but were eventually outgrown. In a letter written a year after leaving Jamaica Plain, Wentworth said: —

"You will be glad that I got hold of a stock of spirits this evening that may last me thro' some days, who knows. But that's always the way with me — the grasshopper is a burden to me, but I can carry a hippopotamus and dance and sing."

MRS. STEPHEN HIGGINSON (LOUISA STORROW)

He wrote his mother: —

"I always must envy these thoroughly intellectual men who go on so regularly with neither passions nor feelings to interrupt them — I shall never be so, I fear — for every now and then comes something and upsets me. Either a cloud that will pursue me — or sunbeam that I must pursue . . . and I sometimes sigh to see that I do not become calmer as I grow older."

Even at this early age he declared, "My great intellectual difficulty has been having too many irons in the fire." This was a trouble with which he was destined to contend always.

A month later, in April, 1842, about the time that his mother and sisters removed to Brattleboro, Vermont, Wentworth transferred his belongings to Brookline where he was to teach the three sons of Mr. Perkins. He took with him a quantity of books which were throughout life inseparable companions in his wanderings. In preparation for this new position he had purchased a new "flash vest!" and reports, "Promenaded the [Boston] streets in my silk attire till 7." Again, "Took a walk after church — my new pants perfect. . . . Walked out from Boston to Cambridge. My new boots pinched my feet so I could hardly walk. What did I do thereupon! Stopped at the Port, sat down, pulled them off, and walked home barefoot. It was dark, remember."

As to his school duties, the tutor wrote: —

"I am getting on nicely in my parental relations. Order of performances thus. Rise $6\frac{1}{2}$–7, bathe, dress and see that the boys have dittoed by $7\frac{1}{2}$ — up stairs till breakfast at 8 — school 9–11 . . . dine at 3. From 4 to $8\frac{1}{4}$ my own master — $8\frac{1}{2}$ to 10 three-handed whist with the venerable, and to bed $10\frac{1}{2}$ – 11 regularly. Thus you see our life is systematic and simple — the aforesaid three-handed whist is as great a blessing as Homeopathy."

The Brookline stay was eventful, because under new influences Wentworth Higginson rapidly developed and matured. There was a large circle of relatives within a radius of a few miles, and he took part in their frequent meetings and merrymakings. It was in Brookline that he first met his second cousin, Mary Channing, daughter of Dr. Walter Channing, and sister of the Concord poet, Ellery Channing. A few years older than himself, unworldly, intellectual, and brilliant in conversation, she proved a congenial companion. She was a frequent visitor at the Perkins homestead, and after an acquaintance of a few months the cousins became engaged, Higginson being then a youth of nineteen.

One of the absorbing interests of his little world at this time was magnetism, various members of the circle trying experiments upon each other. "Nothing is spoken of here," he wrote, "but the Community and Magnetism." The group of Brookline cousins often exchanged visits with the young people at the Community, or Brook Farm, in Roxbury, where in modern parlance the experiment of the simple life was being tried. Wentworth thus describes his first drive thither: —

"I had to ask the way to the Community — but we came in sight of it at last, and a pleasant looking place it was. We passed some young men belonging there with long hair, who had just been gathering flowers and looked happy as possible. . . . I was delighted with the appearance of everything — and was especially aroused by hearing that young Dana [later editor of the New York Sun] formerly of the Junior class, was a great gun there. . . . We saw genteel looking men too, painting a boat outside — and altogether the combination of gentlemen and laborers was perfect."

At another time, he spoke of again meeting "Community Dana, the handsomest fellow I know and an excellent, cultivated one too." A later visit seems to have given a somewhat different impression, as he wrote, "At the Community we saw a variety of dirty men, boys and girls; and one or two clean ones."

It was during the Brookline stay that Wentworth wrote and published what he called his first poem, the one on the Sistine Madonna, and he now began to feel some of the thrills of successful authorship. He quotes from a friend's letter: "Ma wishes me to enquire with more remarks than I have room for who wrote the Madonna and Child. It is much admired and copied here and is said to be by some one of the name of Higginson." The young poet adds, "It's quite exciting, is n't it?" Some months later, Rev. Samuel Johnson, then a divinity student, said in reference to these verses, "Then you did write that beautiful thing." Going to the Craigie house one day he saw Mrs. H. W. Longfellow, who "said more things about the Madonna," and looked "things unutterable out of her unfathomable eyes"; and when Mr. Longfellow included the poem in his volume called "The Estray," the youth's cup was full.

In Brookline, the young man had plenty of leisure for his favorite pursuits, for he wrote: —

"I have taken up reading very strong, — am much interested in Carlyle's Miscellanies and have quite a fancy for German — have begun to dabble a little in the study of it — next winter I shall go into languages wholesale."

And in one evening he perpetrated "four sonnets to Longfellow, Motherwell, Tennyson, and Sterling, — good — the best things perhaps I've written."

From Ellery Channing he gleaned some items about
the profits of literature: —

"Ellery has just been telling me about Hawthorne
whom he thinks the only man in the country who
supports himself by writing. He is enabled to do this
as his expenses are very small. Ellery says he [Haw-
thorne] might live for $300, as he does at Concord
— there his farm gives apples enough to pay his
rent, $75. He sells these and fishes in the river in
summer. His magazine articles are paid higher than
any one's except Willis who gets $5 a page. He could
get what he chooses, probably $30, $40 or $50 an
article. He is to be a regular contributor to three
magazines — the Pioneer, Sargent's, and the Democratic Review. This of course would give him $1000
to $1500 a year. He writes very slowly and elabor-
ately. Willis probably can get $50 for an article."

In planning his future, the young tutor wrote: —

"Spent the whole morning at home — reading
Richter's Life and meditating and made the day an
era in my life by fixing the resolution of not studying a profession. . . . The resolve is perfectly settled
and perfectly tranquil with me, that I will come as
near starving as Richter did — that I will labor as
intensely and suffer as much — sooner than violate
my duty toward my Spiritual Life" and "to do my
duty to the world at large, in whatever manner I
can best use my talents. . . . For myself I believe
and trust that I have got *above* following Ambition as

the leading motive. . . . For neither Wealth nor Fame will, I trust, make me happy or satisfy me."

He exclaimed that summer, "Give me books and nature — and leisure and means to give myself up to them and some one to share my ideas with, and I think I should be perfectly happy." And later, "I feel overflowing with mental energies — I will be Great if I can."

While in Brookline, Higginson tried to live freely and simply like the birds and squirrels, declaring that "The only true free man is he who can live on a little." In after years, he called this stay the May-time of his life, which he, however, qualified by adding, "The present is not beautiful until overhung with the mosses and veiled in the shadows of the Past. . . . I think the free communion with Nature in past years has done much for my mental health. Those long afternoons in the woods with no care, no solicitude as to time and place, no companion but my tin box. . . . That Bigelow's Botany of mine is the most precious book I have — not a page of it but is redolent of summer sounds, senses and images." But he never became reconciled to his work, and wrote in November: "To Teaching I have an utter and entire aversion — I love children passionately and am able to attach them and to discipline them, but I am not fitted for an intellectual guide and I hate the office"; and added "I read the Theory of Teaching (which put me in despair)."

The school was often held out of doors, and one of the features was a course of talks to the boys on animals. In 1852, Higginson wrote to Harriet Prescott: —

"When I was of your age and had scholars like you, — or as you will, — I used to take them long walks and teach them to use their senses. We used sometimes to have school in a wood beside the house or in a great apple tree; and once on a rock in the wood there came to us a new scholar, a little weasel who glided among us with his slender sinuous body and glittering eyes, while we sat breathless to watch him. I fancy the boys will remember that little visitor longer than any of their Natural History Lessons."

But in the Brookline period Wentworth was still a boy himself as this note from his journal shows: —

"I made an Excursion (about $\frac{1}{4}$ 12) & attacked the 4 steel signs in the neighborhood — no one suspecting but the girls. No danger — in spite of the $50 reward."

Truly history repeats itself, for a few years ago, Colonel Higginson's doorbell was tremblingly rung by a young relative, then a Harvard student, who confessed that he also had been "attacking signs" and in consequence had just passed the night in the police station.

Mr. Perkins, whose three sons were under Wentworth's care, was absent part of the time, leaving
the young tutor in charge, and then his duties included tending fires and pumping water. He never
objected to manual labor, but wrote, "I always love
to do any work — digging paths or chopping wood.
I think I should always like to do both for myself,
and feel thus far at least independent of other's
hands." In the spring of 1843, he was urged by his
employer to stay another year, at a salary of $250 in-
cluding board and lodging. In the letter which Mr.
Perkins wrote about this project, he praised him
highly, and said that his devotion to the boys was
only equalled by theirs to him. But the young man
could not be induced to remain longer and wrote: —

"Much as I am interested in the boys . . . and
sorry as I shall be to part with them, my removal
from the responsibility of their *intellectual* Education
will be a very great relief to me. I shall never love
teaching — anybody."

V

THE CALL TO PREACH

WENTWORTH HIGGINSON wrote to his mother, August 25, 1843: —

"If fortune offers nothing better I mean to do this: Go to Cambridge. Take a proctorship. Live with the strictest economy. I can place my minimum at $300 — $100 to be got by my proctorship and the rest by literary labors — . . . So I may regard it as from this day settled!

"That I need not study a Profession. No Law! Hurrah!"

And this is his estimate of necessary expenses: —

"Board, not over	$120
Clothes	75
Washing	25
Incidentals	30
	$250 "!

Continuing his meditations upon the proposed Cambridge move he again wrote to his mother: —

"I don't want to keep up the dignity I must there as proctor — I want to be a boy as long as I can. . . . This brings another Evil as regards dress. Could I, in proctorial dignity, figure round in blouses and bobtailed frocks? If not it would affect my finances much. . . . To be elegant, or even *genteel* in dress always, I will not undertake. . . . I have been brought up poor and am not afraid to continue so; and certainly I shall be *glad* to be so, if it is a necessary accompaniment to a life spent as I wish to spend it. . . .

"By the various old gentlemen who ask me every time they see me what my profession is to be, I do not expect my plans to be understood or approved; I shall expect to be frowned at by many and laughed at by some. But I do not wish to be frowned at or laughed at by you. . . . I can never be happy myself or feel that I am doing my duty, if I neglect a single bright flower that I might plant in your evening days. And to you in return I look for sympathy and interest."

This beautiful tribute to Wentworth's mother is taken from a letter to Miss Channing: —

"I think mother is one of the most fascinating persons I ever saw. She enjoys nature with a freshness more unalloyed than I ever saw in anybody. I wish all the world could have a chance to know her loveliness before she passes away from it. She is the most wonderful being I ever knew. There are no bounds to my enthusiasm about her."

And on the back of one letter his mother wrote these touching words: —

"He is the star that gilds the evening of my days — and he must shine bright and clear — or my path will be darkened."

Soon after announcing his new plan, Higginson moved to Cambridge and wrote to his betrothed: —

"I shall live very unobtrusively and probably have no intimates, but I shall have a world made up of you and books and nature and myself and a great touch of unknown human nature in the streets of Boston besides. Oh it will be nice — so free.

> " 'Life went a Maying
> With nature, love and liberty
> When I was young.' "

In this hopeful spirit, the young emigrant loaded his traps upon a wagon and led the horse over muddy roads to the room he had chosen in the first building called College House. The new quarters he described in a letter to his Aunt Nancy: —

"Here I am very nicely fixed, Madam; a very pleasant place is the Old Den, I assure you, particularly this room, North East third story — commanding a pretty view of the College Yard, especially neat in the morning — dew — grass — trees — library ground-glass windows — sunshine and so on — overlooks the street too very nicely — Brighton cattle — enthusiastic pigs — agonized maternal cows — heartrent filial calves and all that, very enlivening. Oh it is the nicest room I know anywhere in its situation . . . the back part veiled into a bedroom by tall curtains a la Greque (secondhand — the gift of our liberal fellow citizen L. L. Thaxter, Esq.) — and the rest of the room filled up with superb furniture, among which shine pre-eminent two sulphur

colored chairs, a contribution from Brattleboro'
— white curtains veil the windows, ditto the book-
case. Over the floor spreads a many hued carpet,
put down by the fair hands of Mr. T. W. Higginson. . . . Parker is the only person I see — there are
only one or two others of my class here, and no
others I care much about — though I have half a
dozen visiting acquaintance. . . . I lead a nice
oysterlike life with occasional trips to Brookline and
Boston. . . . Commons I like very much."

To his mother who was anxious about her son's
frugal diet, he wrote: —

"As to commons you must be satisfied too, you
rebellious little thing — don't I tell you that we have
an unlimited supply of good milk and excellent
bread, and have n't I lived the greater part of my life
on bread and milk? There is no *stinting;* whatever
we have at all, we have an unlimited quantity of:
vegetables every day, potatoes, beans, squash, tomatoes: — nice Indian and tapioca puddings: meat
every other day very good and well cooked — nobody complains of anything. . . . With regard to
going to a boarding-house I should not like it now
at all. . . . I have never liked the relation between
boarder and boardee and never should wish to try
it."

Later the faithful son reported: —

"You will be sorry to hear that I have been disappointed in getting a Proctorship. There were a few
vacancies and a great many applicants. I was sur-

ANNE STORROW (AUNT NANCY)

prised and provoked at first; and Mr. Channing who
told me seemed surprised and sorry at my appearing
so. The reason the others were appointed I suppose
to be that they were considered more *needy* characters than I — so much *for dressing like a gentleman*,
my dear. . . . It will not alter my plans and may be
useful to me as obliging me to pinch, etc., more than
I otherwise should. . . .

"My life here is dreadfully prosaic — that is, in
many respects I often feel as if I would give heaps of
gold to be able to see something from my window
that imagination can rest on — the view of the college yard was sweet to be sure. . . . If I could go into
the woods and see a single flower I should n't care."

"I have sighed, and sighed in vain," Wentworth
confided to his journal, "considering the expense,
for a *tin hat* [bathtub] and a big sponge." When
Aunt Nancy sent him five dollars for clothing, he
noted, "Determined to apply it to a velvet waist-
coat"; but he thought better of it and said, "I am
using part of Aunt Nancy's $5 to buy a tin hat —
$3." This luxury being secured, he went still further
and wrote: —

"To-day I have taken quite a step. Resolved to go
to the gymnasium. For $3 I can go three months.
This is more than I like the idea of paying, but still
it is worth it. I have considerable strength and activity to start with, and by 3 months' daily practice
I can strengthen my constitution for lifelong use."

Poverty possessed no terrors for this independent youth, and only when he thought of marriage did he sigh for the traditional rich uncle. He wrote: "I think I could bear and even enjoy poverty were I alone. I mean real, pinching poverty." And again, triumphantly, "I am an independent individual with a clear income of $60 to be doubled after this year." But he soon found ways to increase this incredible income by copying, making profiles (perhaps the black paper silhouettes then in vogue), doing work connected with surveying for his brother Waldo, and teaching a private pupil in town for half an hour daily. He wrote to his mother: —

"I purpose giving the morning to study (par excellence), i.e., at present, languages — German, Greek & Italian, and the afternoon to other reading of various kinds — the evening when at home to reading, writing and so on. I am in my room all day pretty much, and find no difficulty in applying my mind — and no irksomeness, but rather a pleasure in reading and studying. . . . Although I need daily excitements, I can get along with very small ones — the post office, the reading room, the library at their regular hours each day are an all sufficient variety to me."

But soon Higginson mentions a more momentous interest: —

"I had the excitement of the great Abolition convention which I several times attended. Got some settled views about abolition, and all but made a speech."

And later, —

"I have got the run of slavery argumentation now and can talk Abolitionism pretty well."

When the youth's anxious friends sought to restrict his movements, he burst out in his journal with this protest: —

"It seems that the interesting pack of bloodhounds denominated 'my friends' have reopened their musical mouths. . . . Oh confound the whole set of wretches — if they could get me stuck to a polar iceberg for five years surrounded by seals, penguins, and law books, they might perhaps be satisfied. . . . Oh words cannot express how intensely I sometimes wish I could be put into a tin box and rolled away under a barberry bush!"

Wentworth continued the habit of taking long walks, seventeen miles after supper being once recorded; and he returned to his old pastime of kicking football in the evening, pleased to find that his running powers had increased. Skating on Fresh Pond still attracted him; coasting was always to be had in Brookline; and there was the same fascination in having long evening talks with Parker (now a law student) as in undergraduate days.

Another diversion was attending mathematical

examinations at Harvard, being still on the Examining Board (at nineteen), and occasionally dining with the committee. In describing the committee examinations, the young visitor says: —

"There are probably half a dozen in the present Senior class who know more by a good deal than I do now, or shall when I examine them. So I must go to the examinations and be satisfied with looking learned, which after all is all the Committee ever did when I was in College."

The journal records: —

"I am studying away at a great rate and enjoying it especially. I do seek to gratify this craving for knowledge which will not let me rest. No kind of studying is anything but a pleasure to me."

And in the student's enthusiasm, he exclaims: —

"Oh the delicious pleasure of learning whatever there is to be learned."

He continues: —

"I am delighted to find my memory is becoming more retentive than ever before. The last year at Brookline gave me time to digest the immense weight of miscellaneous matter heaped on it from my earliest boyhood, and now I begin to study to very much more advantage and feel my powers of retention to be relied on."

But in spite of his enjoyment of this solitary life, Wentworth occasionally mused: —

"I think on the whole that this life is not the right one for me — I cannot live alone. Solitude may be good for study sometimes, but not solitude in a crowd for a social-hearted person like me. Here in my own pleasant room I seldom feel it, but when outdoors I constantly feel the unpleasantness of having no common interests in the life I lead and that of others."

Again he chides himself for being too much of a recluse: —

"What I want now most urgently is more of a controversial spirit, the will and the power always to pitch right into people and show 'em how foolishly they are thinking and acting, instead of my present spirit of being willing people should think what they please if they'll only leave me alone. The latter spirit will never do any good to the world and I hope it'll wear off."

This anxiety would seem to have been needless, in the light of Higginson's later career.

What his future might be was a fascinating if troublesome problem, and he often made such notes as these: —

"What destiny is intended for me, I cannot tell — not to go in the beaten track I am sure. I cannot express how strongly I long to come out and obtain a working place among men. How my ability will second my wishes I know not, but some things are in every one's power — to live a true, sincere, earnest, independent life. Of this I think daily and hourly. . . .

"I feel there is no man too small to be useful so he be true and bold. . . . I am an enthusiast now, I know. So much the better. Whoever was in the highest degree useful without being such?"

In these years of thought and study, Wentworth wrote many verses, some of which were published in periodicals. This led to the dream of being a poet. His few hymns which are included in American and English collections of sacred song and are still sung in churches were written at this time. One day, many years later, he met his Worcester contemporary, George F. Hoar, on the street, who asked him if he was the author of the hymn containing the lines —

"And though most weak our efforts seem,
Into one creed these thoughts to bind."

Upon Mr. Higginson's assenting, Mr. Hoar said that he considered this hymn "the most complete statement of Christian doctrine that was ever made."

In that early period the young man exclaimed, "Oh, heavens, what would I not give to know whether I really have that in me which will make a poet, or whether I deceive myself and only possess a mediocre talent." But later the dream vanished and he wrote: "The idea of poetic genius is now utterly foreign to me and I cannot conceive at all now the feeling that underlay my whole life two years ago. I must be content to enjoy instead of creating poetry."

On the eve of his twenty-first birthday, Wentworth wrote to his mother: —

"I have repented of many things, but I never repented of my first poetical Effusion. If you are not familiar with the poem, I will sometime give you a copy. . . .

"The only additional 'great truth' that occurs to me is this which it is strange I mentioned not before — that on Sunday next you will lose your last baby. Your youngest son will attain his majority! Shall you not have an ox roasted whole at Boscobel?"

This was the name of the Brattleboro house.

The poem referred to, written at the age of eight, ran thus: —

1.

"How sweet the morning air
To those who early rise
To gather flowers for their hair
Before the sun is in the skies!

2.

"The waterman waits, the waterman waits
For somebody in his boat to glide: —
A gentleman from Santa Fe
Says, 'I'll go in the boat with thee,
If you with *cents* will contented be
Then I'll go in the boat with thee!'"

The plan of reviewing a book by Lydia Maria Child occurred to Higginson one winter evening.

He got home late, and without a fire sat down and wrote until midnight. His satisfaction was great, for it seemed to him that he now saw the way to gratify his "longing to do something for the world," and wrote, "I feel as if a new world were opening before me and my work were now beginning." Afterward he met Lowell who told him what he was earning by writing: —

"Soon after the Year's Life was published, Graham wrote to him [Lowell] offering $10 per poem if he would publish there — This was afterwards raised to $20 and then $30 — now he thinks he could get $50. This encouraged me considerably."

Once, the young critic sent "a box of gentians to Mrs. Child and carried a fine bunch up to Mrs. Maria Lowell in the evening. Spent an hour there. James and she are perfectly lovely together — she was never so sweet and angel-like in her maiden state as now when a wife." And again, describing a walk, he writes that he met "James Lowell and his moonlight maid — how closely I felt bound to them through the sonnets." Of a later visit at the Lowells', he wrote (September, 1846): —

"The angel is thinner and paler and is destined to be wholly an angel ere long, I fear, but both were happy. . . . We talked Anti-Slavery and it was beautiful to see Maria with her woman angel nature plead for charity and love even against James, that is, going farther than he, and as far as I could ask. This was delightful, but it was sad to me to feel we must lose her. . . . I do not suppose there ever was known before anything so beautiful as this union. There have been many loving couples but never any where both units and union were so wonderful in character and mind. They excite in me a perfectly chivalrous feeling. I . . . should delight in . . . being where I could constantly watch them."

To Miss Channing Wentworth dedicated his journals and wrote her letters full of his thoughts, struggles, and aspirations. Having never had a brother or sister near enough in age to himself to be a confidant, he found this outlet a great relief. In his gratitude he called his *fiancée* his "Commonplace Book," and was surprised that this epithet did not seem an endearing one to her.

During the four years of their engagement, although it was suspended for one year, on account of Higginson's straitened finances, and while he was feeling his way into the future, their correspondence was voluminous, in spite of the fact that they often met. In one letter Wentworth thus warns the young lady against the difficulties she may have to encounter as his wife: —

"Setting out, as I do, with an entire resolution never to be intimidated into shutting either my eyes or my mouth, it is proper to consider the chance of my falling out with the world."

He adds: —

"I have been worrying a great deal lately as to what is to be done for this preposterous world. . . . "The great reason why the real apostles of truth don't make any more impression is this — the moment any person among us begins to broach any 'new views' and intimate that all things are n't exactly right, the conservatives lose no time in holding up their fingers and branding him as an unsafe person — fanatic, visionary, insane and all the rest of it — this has been the case with all reforms great and small and moreover there is often some ground for it because it is the enthusiastic (i.e. half cracked people) who begin all reforms. Mrs. Child you know has long been proscribed as an entirely unsafe person and as for Mr. Emerson and Mr. Alcott, it does n't do for a sober person even to *think* of them."

Miss Channing was a disciple of James Freeman Clarke, and Higginson was thus led to attend his church. There under Dr. Clarke's influence he began to think of studying for the ministry. But he deprecated haste and wrote to his betrothed, "I have declared my independence of this invariable law of our young men's sacrificing everything else to going ahead quick."

Over this new project, Wentworth pondered long, now rejecting the plan as impossible, and again reconsidering. "How long halt ye," he despairingly asked himself, "between two opinions. O, I am sorely puzzled and know not what to do. I cannot in action any more than in thought bear confinement — How then can I settle down into the quiet though noble duties of a minister. . . . I crave action . . . unbounded action. I love men passionately, I feel intensely their sufferings and short-comings and yearn to make all men brothers . . . to help them to strive and conquer." And he sometimes wondered if choosing the Ministry at Large would solve the problem. Another stumbling-block was theological doctrine, and he hoped to find light by studying Swedenborg.

However, the die was presently cast in favor of the church, although Higginson still announced himself "a seeker and entirely unsettled." His family were delighted at the decision, and he found satisfactory quarters in a quiet corner of Divinity Hall, looking toward the sunset and close by the Palfrey woods. Here he boarded himself, having contrived a wire and tin cup arrangement for boiling water over his study-lamp in order to wash his breakfast and tea dishes. "I feel very proud of it," he wrote to Miss Channing. "You should hear the water sizzle! I could brew rum punch with ease."

He rejoiced in his leafy surroundings, there being

no house visible from his room, and wrote in March, 1845, "I am so impatient for spring that I keep my windows open perpetually though it is generally cool, but the birds do pipe surpassingly. Soon the anemones will be here and my summer joys begin."

One of Wentworth's summer joys was a visit to Niagara with his mother and sisters. Before his first sight of the falls he said to himself, "There is more in this one *second* than in any other second of your life, young man!" But after looking at the cataract, the only words he could use were Fanny Kemble's, "I saw Niagara. O God, who can describe that sight!"

While he was a divinity student Higginson's expenses for food were surprisingly small. His pencilled accounts report one dollar spent on food in a fortnight. He usually dined on Sunday at Dr. Channing's in Boston, but bread and milk formed his principal diet the rest of the week. Books were more attractive than food, and he wrote: "I am longing much for money to buy books [this was a lifelong want]. Books I want to read thoroughly I always want to have for my own, to annotate and mark."

It was a relief to find that "the bonus to poor Divinity students amounts to almost as much as the proctors get, $100. This being the case, I need n't

take a proctorship. Just what I wanted. . . . At 20
before 6 A.M. the bell ding-dongs for prayers. I shall
probably go to bed early and get up ditto."

As the young man looked forward to the duties
of the ministry, a feeling of despondency sometimes
came over him.

"A pure earnest aim is not enough. Intellectual
as well as moral armor must be bright for I know I
shall have to sustain a warfare. I feel that if I do
justice to my own powers (i.e., if I do my duty) I
cannot remain in the background. . . . Preaching
alone I should love, but I feel inwardly that something more will be sought of me — An æsthetic life
— how beautiful — but the life of a Reformer, a
People's Guide 'battling for the right' — glorious,
but, Oh how hard!"

In these moments of doubt his ever solicitous mother exhorted him to fresh courage and persever-
ance.

Through these years of study in Cambridge,
Wentworth made frequent visits to Brattleboro,
kept the family supplied with books, and suggested
lists for the village book club. He was constantly
adding to his own collections of books, and wrote,
"My library is now becoming rather imposing."

His principal companion in the school seems to
have been Mr. Samuel Longfellow, brother of the
poet, who was one year in advance of Wentworth.

About this friend he said, "He is a beautiful soul, though there is a certain shadow of reserve about him. He spoke of his sister 'Mrs. Fanny' [Mrs. H. W. Longfellow]. I got a charming idea of the household goddess. She was just Wordsworth's 'phantom of delight,' he said." While living in Divinity Hall Higginson formed a romantic attachment for a brilliant youth named Hurlbut, who was also a theological student. This friendship was destined to make a permanent impression on Wentworth's life, being freighted with much joy, but ending in deep sorrow.

During his first year in the school, our young theologian came into contact with an older student named Greene who had great influence over him.

"Now has this man of real genius come to be with me, to teach me humility, even toward my fellow-creatures. He has shown me the difference between real genius and a self-confident talent and the lesson though useful is severe. I do not believe a vainer person than I ever existed. I have never really felt that anything that a mortal can reach was beyond me. It was negative rather than positive. What my mission was to be I never knew. I only felt assured that

'Despair! thy name is written on
The roll of common men!'

was *not meant for a lesson for me*."

In his long letters to Miss Channing, Higginson freely expressed his opinion on public questions, having already at twenty-one taken his lifelong stand as to the position of woman.

"I do go for the rights of women as far as an equal education and an equal share in government goes. . . . I think it a monstrous absurdity to talk of a democratic government and universal suffrage and yet exclude one-half the inhabitants without any ground of incapacity to plead. This is theoretical — practically I have no doubt we should have much more *principle* in politics if woman had more share from her standard of right being higher than that of man. I think there is no possible argument on the other side excepting prejudice."

He was also then interested in the perennial problem of the workingman and wrote, "I have read the articles on the organization of labor and were I a rich man would have 30,000 printed and distributed." In the autumn of that year, 1845, he shared in the popular excitement about the proposed admission of Texas to the Union, attending meetings in Cambridge and at Faneuil Hall. He composed in verse a Texas rallying cry which appeared in "The Liberty News," in "The Free State Rally," and in "The Liberator." He joined others in getting signatures to a petition called "Remonstrance against the Admission of Texas as a Slave State from 764 Inhabitants of Wards 1 and 2 of the Town of Cambridge, Mass. (known as East Cambridge and Cambridge Port)." He records spending Sunday morning at home, the first time he had missed church-going for a year and a half, to prepare the petition. One hundred and sixty-six of the signatures were feminine and he pasted them all on a long strip of cloth and pressed them with a borrowed flatiron. Somewhat later he reported to his mother: —

"At Cambridge we are in peace since the Texas petition thirteen feet long, double column, went off. . . . I have pretty much concluded that a consistent Abolitionist (which last every person who thinks and feels must be whether nominally or not) must choose between the Liberty Party and the Disunion Party. I don't like the dilemma at all, but fear I must come to it. . . . In the Liberty Bell which appears in a week at the Faneuil Hall Anti-Slavery Fair will be a sonnet of mine which may rather astonish some of my friends. Do not be afraid of seeing my name [signed] to pieces in papers."

In the midst of these absorbing public interests the young student was agitated by personal problems; and when his first year at the school was nearly over, he wrote this startling letter to his mother. It must have fallen like a bomb into quiet "Boscobel": —

"That the cup of your joy may not be more full than is good for you, I write to say that I have finally made up my mind that I must leave the Divinity School. Entirely apart from the fact that instructors, companions, and course of study have failed to interest or satisfy me — I am now convinced from a longer trial that I cannot obtain the equilibrium and peace of mind I need while I remain a member of it.

"My faith in God is unshaken — as of Festus — 'with all his doubts he never doubted God' — but God gives to some people a temperament much harder to deal with than others and while nineteen persons are going quietly on their way the twentieth is working hard under ground to make his way up to light and sunshine. . . . It is now as impossible to tell what the course of my life will be as when I was a babe and this is no subtile repining, but plain and simple."

Higginson's plan was to resume solitary studies, thus escaping the routine of the school, but still living on in the same room, and this project he successfully carried out. During this period of self-banishment, he yet expected to make preaching his profession and sometimes cried out, "Oh, I keep asking who is there to go on with me to the aid of liberal Christianity."

In this mental perplexity, he wrote to his fiancée:—

"I feel that I have a right to some means of influence. I should prefer poetry or in general, literature — because that lasts the longest, but should be content with blacking boots, if I could only feel that to be the thing for which I was intended."

The student's interest in political questions never flagged, and in January, 1846, he thus commits himself to the disunion project: —

"I might have recorded on my birthday or New Year's Day, my final self-enrollment in the ranks of the American Non-Jurors or Disunion Abolitionists and my determination not only not to vote for any officer who must take oath to support the U. S. Constitution, but also to use whatever means may lie in my power to promote the Dissolution of the Union. . . . To Disunion I now subscribe in the full expectation that a time is coming which may expose to obloquy and danger even the most insignificant of the adherents to such a cause."

In the following spring, describing to his mother a series of meetings, "Unitarian, Anti-Slavery, and Association," of which he had chiefly attended the Anti-Slavery ones, Higginson said: —

"The most interesting and moving speech of all I have heard this week was by an old colored woman, Mrs. Thompson of Bangor, at one of the Anti-Slavery meetings in Faneuil Hall. This old lady rose among the crowd and began to speak — all stood up to gaze on her, but she undaunted fixed her eyes on the chairman and burst out into a most ardent, eloquent and beautiful tribute of gratitude from herself and her race to Garrison 'who came truly in a dark hour' she said; her style was peculiar, tinctured strongly with methodistical expressions and scripture

allusions, but her voice was clear and her language
fluent and easy; and if ever a speech came straight
from the heart of the speaker and went straight to
the hearts of the hearers that was the one; no one
could resist the impression and the tears came to
many eyes; there was a perfect hush while she spoke
on without a single pause or taking her eyes from the
chairman — and when she sat down there was a
spontaneous burst of applause. It was a truly beautiful and noble scene, one which opened to one's view
the prospect of a future when American Brother-
hood shall be a reality of daily life and honour and
respect be given where they are truly due."

Wentworth now reported himself as peaceful and
industrious, and "delving away at the Old Testa-
ment" about which his mother had anxiously asked
his opinion. He was still addicted to evening plunges
in the river, and describes swimming at half-past
eleven when it was high tide and he "found it beautiful to lie back on the water and gaze at the sky."
So unconsciously he was even then preparing for his
"Night in the Water" many years after when in
command of the black regiment. The student wrote
his Aunt Nancy: —

"One feels strangely lingering on here in Cambridge after one's time is up — mine has been just
ten years; I have staid here longer than any of my
contemporaries — yet never have felt before as if I
had staid too long, but now I do; people look at one

with a kind of surprised glance — 'Well, are you *still* here? Is there no end to you?'"

As the year of solitary study drew to a close, the young recluse began to consider the importance "of being regularly authorized to preach and the desirableness of being associated with a special set of young men." These views were reënforced by a strong appeal from his class to rejoin them. He heard the class exercises when his special friends, Johnson, — whom he calls "my young hero and prophet," — Longfellow, and O. B. Frothingham were graduated, and Johnson's oration on this occasion had a profound effect upon him. He felt a strong desire to speak himself on next "Visitation Day" on the "Relation of the Clergy to Reform."

In August, 1846, Higginson had a long talk with Dr. Francis, then dean of the school, about reëntering his class, which resulted in a letter to the Faculty of Theology, applying for readmission. In this the writer, speaking of himself in the third person, explains his reason for withdrawal — the need of perfect freedom: —

"This freedom might have been destructive to others: it was the breath of life to him. He has now built up a *Credo* for himself, whose essential and leading points are so strong and clear that he can patiently leave minor ones for a time unsettled. He

has abandoned much that men call belief . . . while
at the same time his confidence in mere intellect has
waned and he has grown more and more disposed to
see in Love and Spiritual Trust the only basis of
Christian Life within or Christian Union without and
he feels now that for himself he has a gospel to preach
and is ready to preach it. He feels more and more
each day the call upon the minister; and this makes
him feel he has been best preparing himself by learning to live. . . . Thus the result is to ask not 'Have I
learned?' but 'Have I grown?'"

In the autumn, Wentworth writes to his mother: —

"Am very glad to have rejoined the school. I find
it altogether improved in the year of absence, a
higher tone of spiritual life and more mental activity
. . . a fine liberal spirit such as has never before
prevailed. . . . I am the only one who reads German. . . . Am busy on two dissertations — one on
the erroneous views of the Scriptures — the other on
the early history of the Trinity — both of which
give an opportunity for original and 'unsound' views.
. . . Nothing keeps a man so fresh as abolitionism
and kindred propensities, I observe."

In a December letter he continues: —

"I wrote an elaborate essay on the true use of the
Scriptures — against attributing (practically) literal
infallibility to any part of them, or setting them up
as absolute Master of Reason and Conscience; this excited interest and we brought it up at the Friday evening debate where it was discussed for four evenings

with animation; one evening Elder Holland a Christian minister from Buffalo was present and spoke. . . . He is considered one of the ablest men in the body, reads Emerson, etc. After the debate he inquired with some anxiety whether 'that young man' (meaning me) 'ever expected to find a pulpit to preach in?' . . . I look forward to preaching with great interest, it will be a serious work to me if I do it. But I have several doubts as to practical success — whether my view of Christ as in the highest sense a *natural* character, divine as being in the highest sense human, sent to aid men by living a higher spiritual life, not in the character of an infallible teacher of any truth to the intellect, — working wondrous works by virtue of this inward spiritual energy — whether this will be acceptable to people. . . . As for my particular poetical studies I never write a sentence without experiencing their benefit and look back with inexpressible satisfaction to one morning last spring when I shut Ecclesiastical History in despair (which I have often re-opened with pleasure) and rushed into the woods to read Browning's 'Paracelsus'! . . . The Browning gospel is flourishing — my Bells and Pomegranates are half with Mr. L. [H. W. Longfellow] and half with —— the former is very ardent and has agreed to try and get Ticknor & Co. to republish them, which I before attempted."

Again: —

"I have been *writing* more in these two months (or six weeks) than in the previous five years — I had begun to doubt whether I should ever feel the *im-*

pulse to write prose — now I have been manufacturing sermons and essays (to be read before the class) with the greatest readiness — all being crammed with as much thought as I can put into them. . . . I have a dozen subjects or so marked out — on all of which I have thoughts — but how will it be when these are used up? Will new ones come? How will it be when I have to write two a week and shall not be willing to dilute any?"

The young thinker naturally felt some solicitude as the time approached for new responsibilities; and the thought of being obliged to write weekly sermons — forcing himself to write when not feeling inspired — filled him with dismay. He also dreaded the necessity of preparing his graduation theme or "Visitation Part." In February, he preached two sermons at Walpole, New Hampshire, which met with much favor. The minister borrowed one of the sermons for his wife to read, and she gave it her highest endorsement, pronouncing it a "real Parker sermon!" His clear enunciation and expressive way of reading the hymns also won praise. About this time he had an invitation to preach at Newburyport. His mother was overjoyed at these successful beginnings and congratulated him on the "happy opening of his career."

Wentworth was now reading Emerson's "Essays" and sometimes wondered why he read any other book. "I can't make up my mind," wrote the youth in one of his moments of doubt, "whether my radicalisms will be the ruin of me or not." At any rate, these "isms" caused much dismay among his more conservative brothers and sisters. The question what the baby of the family might do next gave them many an uneasy moment. His brothers represented the old-fashioned type of Unitarianism, and, though sympathizing with his abolition views, shook their anxious heads over his theory about women. The independent and sympathetic mother did her best to keep up with her younger son in the path he was striking out for himself; but even she asked in bewilderment, "You don't want women to vote, do you, or be lawyers, or go to Congress!"

The son, never daunted, thus expressed his taste for individuality: —

"I do not like family characteristics to prevail very strongly among brothers. Now the B——s are not regarded as individuals, but as a batch of brothers and sons of Dr. B."

Early in this year, Higginson had written to Samuel Johnson: —

"I have made my début at West Cambridge. I pleased the audience, I heard and did something towards satisfying myself that the pulpit is my vocation."

After delivering his visitation address on "Clergy and Reform," 1847, he wrote Miss Channing: —

"I cannot tell you what a sensation my yesterday's words made — nor how exhausted and weary of soft speeches I got before night. All sorts of men from Dr. Parkman to Theo. Parker introduced themselves to me (some of them knew father) — and said all manner of things. . . . With Mr. Parker I had some excellent talk — he came out to hear me principally he said and was not disappointed — and he said some wise words of sympathy and encouragement. . . . The Reformers were delighted. . . . One candid man . . . said . . . 'I must *thank you* for your sermon to us, though I feel that in so doing I condemn myself.' . . . Edward Hale came up . . . and said he had missed hearing me, but he was glad to hear there was somebody who was going to electrify the world. . . . Finally *Uncle George [Channing] has offered to insert it whole in the Christian World.* . . .

"When I got through I felt entirely uncertain what would be thought of it — it seemed tremendously severe as I spoke it and I put in my fullest energy — but I have not heard a single complaint of it or objection of any sort!"

Somewhat late the young reformer learned that his visitation speech had been, after all, "a rock of offence" to many. Yet this disapproval did not injure his prospects, as a pulpit was already awaiting him.

VI

IN AND OUT OF THE PULPIT

IN the summer of 1847, Wentworth Higginson, being then twenty-three, accepted an invitation to become pastor of the First Religious Society of Newburyport. He wrote a friend: —

"I think the pastoral relation will be interesting to me — and if I fail in it, it will be for want of time or skill, not of inclination. . . . Now I have fairly shaken myself free of the too fascinating home of all my past years — I do not believe any one ever clung to Cambridge as I have done."

But the following extracts from another letter show that he soon became reconciled to the change: —

"I do think we need transplanting, sometimes even I, — I grow tired of things and people. . . . I think all we have to do with, houses, rooms, towns, &c. should have perpetual slight changes going on, that we may feel that they live and grow with us. . . . Aunt S.'s everlasting parlors are a weariness to my spirit — even pretty engravings do not bear the same places and the same cords for years."

And his natural buoyancy, which never deserted him through life, led him to moralize thus: —

THOMAS WENTWORTH HIGGINSON, 1846

"It does require a great deal to live in such a world — but the way to prepare for the worst is not to be constantly expecting it, but to be constantly sensible of the superabundance of beauty and good in the universe, a thought which is never for an instant out of my mind, and in view of which I cannot conceive of being overcome by anything."

In this courageous frame of mind, Mr. Higginson was ordained September 15. His friends Johnson and Hurlbut wrote hymns for the occasion. His cousin, Rev. William Henry Channing, preached the sermon, and Dr. James Freeman Clarke gave the charge. While the latter exhorted his young brother to reform by construction, not destruction, he urged him to speak scathing words of rebuke against the sin of slavery. Thus was the path marked out in which the new minister was not reluctant to walk and which finally made his position too hot to hold him.

His marriage to Miss Channing took place September 30, 1847, he having previously convinced the young woman that two healthy persons could keep house perfectly well without servants, and that housework would never destroy real romance; and they began housekeeping on this plan. The economy practised by the newly married pair was amazing, and the following year Mr. Higginson summed up their financial status in this wise: —

"We have now no bill over $3 in Newburyport. We are amply provided for this year and the next must take care of itself. . . . On looking back at our expenses, the clothing account surprises me most — our united expenses have never gone beyond $80, which is very little."

These frugal habits pleased the young clergyman's mother and she exhorted him: "Rise up moralist and preach frugality to the age!" And the son responded, "The most trying thing is this great big house. I pine for a nutshell." Yet he determined to make the best of unwonted luxury and wrote to his brother: —

"I am fairly settled now in a lovely house, with a noble-hearted wife and a marvellous parish. . . .

"You can hardly imagine how far off my dreamy Cambridge life now seems to me."

In the spring, they rejoiced in a garden: —

"Our sunny little garden is insane with tulips everywhere — appearing in the most unexpected and improper places."

Of his parish, he wrote: —

"They [the parishioners] manifest regard for us only by full and attentive presence at church — certainly the most agreeable way, but queer. Not a particle of *petting*. Rather afraid of us, in fact, Mary thinks — as if we were handsome spotted panthers, good to look at and roaring finely — something to be proud of, perhaps — but not to be approached incautiously, or too near; except by a few familiar ones. . . .

"I find less to complain of and far more to enjoy in the ministry than I have ever anticipated: my people are thus far willing and impressible at least; I say whatever seems right, and they listen; I preached yesterday to about 400. . . . If I can do my duty, there is much to be effected here. . . .

"We met Mr. —— the richest man (about) in the Society . . . he ere long proceeded to compliment me on 'the good whipping I gave them Sunday afternoon on Freedom of Speech.' . . . I have not yet found one who approves the war or disapproves free speech on the minister's part and I begin to feel somewhat confident that they will stand the trials I have ready for them. . . . I have talked very plainly in private."

But in the midst of his satisfaction doubts occurred, and Wentworth wrote to his mother: —

"Strive as I may, I still feel myself in a position to some extent artificial. . . . I cannot reconcile myself to the recurring *forms* even of worship, still less those connected with church organization. I find no outward difficulty, but only inward; this may decrease, but it looks more like increase."

To his Aunt Nancy he confided that he sometimes felt "terribly false, . . . like Mr. Emerson with a hole in the heel of his stocking. (He refused to go to pay a visit on this account.) 'Why, nobody will know it,' urged his friend. 'I shall know it,' replied the sage, gently." With prophetic foresight he added: "But as regards *preaching* proper, I have no sort of doubt of its being my mission — in some form or other — that is *speaking* to men, in the pulpit or elsewhere. . . . But enough of churches and preachers and future botherations; what trifles they all seem when Spring is opening and the tardy blue anemones are almost ready to open their blue eyes."

Of his work outside the parish, he wrote: —

"We are becoming somewhat more acquainted with the poor people here, which is to me very painful work — *unnatural* I think, this charity — though necessary in our present imperfect state. It seems so much easier to prevent than to cure. This necessity of entering into the concerns of so many families (in sympathy if not in act) which is part of a minister's duty is trying to me, — it is as much as I feel fitted for to steer my own course. It is n't because I sympathize too little but too much."

This sympathy led him to take an active interest in the working-people and to concern himself about the long hours of labor of the factory girls. At the same time he interested himself in a magazine for their benefit with a title which he pronounced somewhat uncouth, "The Mirror and Casket of Female Industry."

Besides this local work, Mr. Higginson often preached and lectured in other places, spoke at anti-slavery and temperance meetings, and wrote for various newspapers. He was also drawn into politics. In the autumn of 1848, he accepted the nomination of the Free Soil Party for Congress and wrote thus to his brother: —

"You have probably seen my nomination for Congress. I did all I could to get Whittier nominated, but he obstinately declined, and it was he who proposed my name. . . .

"Perhaps I should not have started my [local] newspaper column had I expected this nomination — but now I am in for it, I have no thought of flinching. It will hurt my popularity in Newburyport for they call it ambition &c. — but I trust that time will do me justice. . . . I expect to 'stump' a little and but little."

To the same he wrote, October 11, 1848: —

"I shall be glad when the Presidential Campaign is over. I spoke at Haverhill last Monday to a fine large audience — the best I have seen, and the best speech. I always knew I had a fountain of extempore matter in me somewhere — but did not expect to find it tapped so suddenly. . . . I am getting used to seeing my name at the Corners of the Streets. In juvenile days that would have seemed beyond the horizon of earthly ambition, but it don't seem to tell for so much now. I don't think Morleena Kenwigs herself would be tempted to be proud, could she actually have the experience.

"Free Soil does n't prosper much just in this

town — it will take longer than in most places. My good people have not yet uttered a croak — nor will they," a prediction which was not realized.

The young politician, in gauging his prospect of success wrote, "There is of course no chance of my being elected; but I am sincerely desirous that Mr. —— should be defeated." And he recalled with some amusement "how carefully good President Quincy used to forbid our showing any political preferences on public occasions, even on the popular side."

The watchful mother, who had warned her son against Theodore Parker's radical sermons, thus wrote of his activity in politics: —

"And so you are fairly entered again on a political career — safe — because on the unpopular side. Therefore I don't complain."

And later she wrote to his wife: —

"I have been thinking of him this winter going from Dan to Beersheba on his Mission and concluded [that] with his utter contempt of all wrappings he must freeze."

"I am engaged in several new enterprises," wrote Higginson to Samuel Longfellow who was abroad; "one is or was the attempt to bring back the Free Soil Party to self-control and consistency from the more fascinating paths of coalition and conquest; this has failed already; and I have only seen my name in many newspapers, with unwelcome Whig compliments and melancholy Free Soil ones; and no good done but warning and reproof. The other may be more successful — it is to induce Massachusetts to follow the example of Maine, and either have laws that can do something, or none at all, in the way of checking the liquor traffic. But as you are now in England where all teetotallers take to drinking, and going soon to the Continent where all forget that they ever were teetotallers, you will not care about this, though we are really entering on a very important revival."

Temperance was one of the vital causes in which the young minister interested himself with some practical results. His wife wrote: —

"W.'s Temperance Sermon which he repeated last Sunday eve — has already done good — *three* establishments are to be closed in consequence."

Of this interest Mr. Higginson wrote to his mother in 1851: —

"I have been persuaded to speak on Temperance Every Sunday for a few weeks to come and after Christmas shall perhaps take the offer made me by our State Central Committee and become their Secretary for a month or so, during the agitation of the Maine Law ... the Committee are ready to take me at any time on handsome terms, and but for the Evening School and a small piece of literary work I have for this month, I might perhaps go at once. . . .

"Last Tuesday and Wednesday I went to the State Temperance Convention; the best part of a Convention is in the preliminary meeting when the wires are pulled and all the real fighting done. I was in the thick of it."

He adds: —

"A week ago to-day I lectured at Concord on the Maine Laws. . . . I had a queer time going to Concord — part in stage and part in sleigh and was upset once in each, together with a slight concussion on the railroad, coming back."

The clergyman's pen as well as his voice was busy and he never lost an opportunity to help what was called the "woman question." One of the prominent workers in this cause wrote to him, in later years, that he had "done great service by bringing to the necessary hard work of unpopular reforms the urbanity of literary culture and social talent," and he has been called a "harbinger of successful causes." In 1849, at a meeting in Boston of a society of literary men called the Town and Country Club, he nominated a woman for membership, and gave as his reason, "Because it seemed a rare opportunity for asserting a valuable principle, viz., the union of the sexes in all intellectual aims and instrumentalities." This club, as Mr. Higginson wrote later, was "valuable as an attempt to organize intellectual Boston in the days of its most seething mental activity"; and "died, like so many other good things, in endeavoring to be born." The effort to include women members failed, but he persisted in similar cases, as when much later he accomplished the admission of Julia Ward Howe to the Academy of Arts and Sciences.

Of all the movements which claimed the young reformer's support, that of anti-slavery was nearest his heart. He wrote to his mother: —

"We have had another interesting beggar, viz. a colored brother of gigantic proportions, named Foster, who is raising money for an excellent Manual Labor School he has started (for fugitive slaves and others) in Michigan. He spent the night here and was very good company; told plenty of stories about slaves and slave-catchers; a man of superior intelligence, information and humor. . . . I entirely forgot he was black, — (though I never have much colorphobia)."

Later, when the prejudice against the race seemed increasing, he wrote, "The worst trait of the American race seems to me this infernal colorphobia."

Mrs. Higginson always regarded her husband's philanthropies with whimsical — if sympathetic — amusement, and once exclaimed, "Why do the insane always come to you!"

As to Mr. Higginson's sermons, his wife wrote to the family at Brattleboro: —

"The Parish are really beginning to appreciate W. somewhat. His last two Sermons were so much liked they insisted upon their being published — and he gave his consent. They are upon *The Tongue*."

Another sermon on "Merchants" attracted much attention, and a friend begged the preacher to write and print a lecture on the same subject and "sow it broadcast." This advice was taken, for later he said, "I have just had one of the most real honors I have ever had; the reprinting of nearly all my Lecture on Merchants in Hunt's Merchant's Magazine."

To the children of his parish, the minister preached sermons once a month, writing to his mother, "I want to do something for them and this is much easier to me than Sunday School addresses. The little things seem to listen and enjoy it."

A letter recently received from one of these very children, now a wife and mother, says that Mr. Higginson was connected with many of the most joyous experiences of her childhood; "for while he was an inspiration to the young people of the town, he was a genuine playmate to us. Many were the bright winter afternoons when we went coasting together on the long hills back of the town, when we had no doubt he enjoyed himself as much as we did." She adds that the children listened with delight to the juvenile sermons, feeling that they were spoken to them by a comrade, and she gives a vivid description of a Christmas tree which he had for poor children, an unusual and exciting event in those days. One small child who had spent a day with the minister told his parents that Mr. Higginson was a "real boy"; which meed of praise the latter reported with glee to his mother.

The young clergyman gathered around him also a remarkable bevy of maidens who studied English poetry with him and for whom he planned a course of Shakespeare readings. These young girls assisted him in the evening school which he established for working-people. This evening school was one of the first in the country, and the experiment led to similar schools in other States. Some of these Mr. Higginson aided in establishing, as the one in Dover, New Hampshire. In his carefully kept records of the evening schools of Newburyport are the names of "male" and "female" pupils with their various employments and the factories where they worked. Even then most of the men were of foreign extraction, and instruction seems to have been given principally in the three "R's." One of the young teachers who helped in these classes was Harriet Prescott, now Mrs. Spofford. She writes, "Mr. Higginson was like a great archangel to all of us then and there were so many of us! Coming into the humdrum life of the town, he was like some one from another star"; and incidentally she speaks of his great personal beauty. This last impression was confirmed by Wendell Phillips, who, while listening to a lecture by Higginson, said to his companion, "Is it not glorious to be handsome!"

Among other things it fell to the lot of the clerical pair to entertain various men and women of note who came to Newburyport to lecture. In the winter of 1848, Mr. Higginson wrote to his mother of Professor Agassiz: —

"He is a charming companion, very joyous, gentle and modest, always ready and willing to communicate his endless information about all invisible things. . . .

"Mr. Emerson comes on Friday and will stop here — as will also probably the minor star, Dr. Holmes, the week after. 'T is a nice way of seeing great people, for they can't well be otherwise than complaisant when you rescue them from a dirty tavern and give them hominy for breakfast."

And Mrs. Higginson added: —

"Friday night that enormous Charles Sumner stretched his ponderous form of seven feet in length under our roof. He has not very good manners — he always sits in the rocking chair, gapes almost constantly without any attempt at concealment. . . .

But he is a true *moral* reformer which is a good thing."

Apropos of these visitors the following extracts are taken from Mr. Higginson's letters to his mother: —

"I had the pleasure week before last of making acquaintance with Henry Ward Beecher who came here to lecture. . . . Something very fresh and noble about him, and he showed vigor and richness of mind, rather than subtlety and refined culture; perfectly genial and simple and practical too. It was so much pleasanter to see him in this informal way. . . ."

"A most charming individual has been here in the shape of a female Anti-Slavery lecturer — Miss Lucy Stone by name — a little meek-looking Quakerish body, with the sweetest, modest manners and yet as unshrinking and self-possessed as a loaded cannon."

"At Plymouth I heard some pretty things. One is about Laura Bridgman — that a lady whom she visited in Duxbury read her the whole of Evangeline on her fingers! Laura enjoyed it excessively and has talked about it a great deal. She wants to be as good as the heroine and wonders whether Evangeline would have *kicked a cat* — that animal being her aversion."

After hearing Kossuth, he wrote: —

"No such series of speeches was ever delivered in so short a space by one man, since the world began; and when you add the fact of the foreign language, it becomes so astonishing that you cannot remember

how astonishing it is. There seems absolutely no
limit to the resources of his eloquence, his mastery
over language, or his power of meeting the occasion;
his career from the moment he landed has been one
long intellectual triumph. It seems more like the
Chronicle of the Cid than any more modern story —
a prolonged tournament in which the victor is always
the same."

And after meeting Thoreau: —

"In Concord I went to see Thoreau; he is more
human and polite than I supposed, and said he had
heard Mr. Emerson speak of me; he is a little bronzed
spare man; he makes lead pencils with his father on
Monday and Tuesday and was in the midst of work.
On other days he surveys land, both mathematically
and meditatively; lays out houselots in Haverhill
and in the moon. He talks sententiously and originally; his manner is the most unvarying facsimile of
Mr. Emerson's, but his thoughts are quite his own.
. . . He does not seem particularly affected by applause, but rather by his own natural egotism. I
find nobody who enjoys his book as I do (this I did
not tell him). . . . I saw his mother, a gaunt and
elderly Abolitionist who had read my Thanksgiving
sermon with comfort, and told me anecdotes of
'Henry's' ways which are more domestic and filial
than one would suppose."

While at Newburyport, Higginson renewed his
acquaintance with Whittier, having first met him
when a boy of nineteen.

"I spent a day in Amesbury and saw Whittier. . . . Dark, slender, bald, blackhaired, kind, calm, flashing eyed, keen, somewhat narrow; not commanding, but interesting. Evidently injured by politics, easily content with limited views; yet sympathetic and (probably) generous. Lives in an appropriate cottage yet very simple. A queer compound of Yankee-Quaker and Yankee-hero and Yankee-poet; the nationality everywhere. He would whittle, no doubt. But his eye gleamed with a soft, beautiful tenderness as he came to the door and remarked on the cold sunset sky. . . . He lives with an odd Quaker-dressed mother, who haunted the back room with knitting and spectacles; — square and mild, as the elderly of her persuasion always are. Also his sister who talked with us, a queer little sprightly woman, reputed very brilliant and looking so. We laughed a good deal, (he has much humour) and she was funny; for she has, you see, a tremendous *nose*, very solid and peculiar, and her wits seem all to be dodging behind it and when you look into one eye that seems very demure they are all sparkling in the other — and vice versa. She is half an invalid."

Boston was near enough for occasional visits, and after attending a concert by Jenny Lind, Mr. Higginson wrote to his mother in November, 1851 : —

"I was very ardent at the time, partly because the Boston audience seemed so peculiarly icy. There was not a spark of enthusiasm from beginning to end. . . .

"There she stood and looked out over the people

in a half-smiling, thoughtful sort of way, swaying herself a little to and fro, not graceful, but sweet and gentle, tall, slender, with a very unbecoming white dress, and white roses in her hair, — face like *all* the pictures. I could conceive what a 'new sensation' she might have been to hacknied opera-goers in London. . . . [She sang] a wonderful Bugle Song, the notes dying away in the distance. This last was perfectly incredible — you listen and listen and at last become perfectly bewildered and decide that the notes will never end but go with you always."

One of the valuable friendships formed at this period was that with David Wasson, whom Mr. Higginson dubbed "the most interesting person I know." This radical young parson had recently been ordained at the neighboring town of Bradford (or Groveland), to Mr. Higginson's surprise, who thought Wasson too heretical for any council to admit. Mr. F. B. Sanborn remembers encountering in that region a country youth who summed up the two independent clergymen thus: "Wal, he's [Wasson] a sort of infidel; *he* says he don't take much stock in th' old saints; Mist' Hinkerson [Higginson], daown t' the Port, 's the sweetest saint I ever knew."

After attending some of the May anniversary meetings, Mr. Higginson reported that he had spoken his mind freely about the emptiness of Unitarian gatherings. Some present did not approve, and other elders who were there said it "should have been said long ago and had been long felt. I am very sure that good will come of what I said: they need a note of discord to break the general monotony of the meetings." To Mr. Wasson he confided some of his professional anxieties: —

                                        "Nov. 17, 1851.

"Something must be done with this great Orthodox church; no question of that; the *how* and *what*, alas, are more difficult of decision, and beyond my gifts and training at least. . . . Who is to pilot the ship, pray, if each Palinurus jumps overboard and strikes out for shore on his own account. . . .

"I wish you would go and see . . . Sam Johnson of Salem, . . . who can help many troubles by his sheer unconsciousness of the possibility of having them."

Doubts as to his own success in his chosen profession sometimes recurred. In his second year of preaching, he mused: —

"I am weary of these lives that end early and leave only blossoms, not fruit, for a remembrance. Unless it is worth while to have me stay long enough on earth to produce something, it is not worth while to be remembered at all. Was this in Keats' mind, when he chose his epitaph 'Here lies one whose name was writ in water'? Should I go before I have borne not flowers only but fruit, I would have no biography written and have my epitaph

> ''T is not a life!
> 'T is but a piece of childhood thrown away!'"

Later, after one of the annual family Thanksgiving parties in Brookline, Wentworth thus defined himself to his mother: —

"If not exactly one of the Hans Andersen's ugly ducks, I have always been an odd chicken. I have always been at other people's Thanksgiving parties and not my own. I have been a snubbed little boy among an elder cousinly circle, I have been a Lord of Misrule among a younger; but not until we are all born again into some sphere of Saturn or Uranus shall I find a Thanksgiving party of contemporaries. Still I am not sure but this office of connecting-link has as many pleasures and as few pains as any other."

At this time, Mr. Higginson wrote few letters, except these filial ones and said to a neglected correspondent: —

"People don't lecture and edit and keep school for 135 factory girls for nothing, and cannot expect to have much time left afterwards to answer bright letters."

He reports clearing about twelve dollars from a lecture, and consenting to have some of his sermons printed because the people wanted them, and adds, "My lecture arrangements, poor people, etc., have kept me going down town so much that M. thinks I have begun to practice physic."

"All is prosperous thus far," wrote the hopeful son. "I preached my most (preachable) theological heresies yesterday and have heard nothing yet but applause. . . . It is the place for me and I think there is now but a small chance of a reaction against me — as I have already taken ground against the War (they say) and my next Sunday's blast will be but a following up of that."

The preacher evidently did not foresee that these frank utterances would antagonize his hearers. In reference to an anti-slavery convention at Newburyport, he wrote: —

"I read the notice of the Convention and said I should preach on Slavery in the afternoon — in connexion with it — which I did, on the text, 'Behold the men who have turned the world upside down are come hither also' giving a free spoken blast, showing . . . the apathy . . . and the duties of the North — and finally recommending (indirectly) my hearers to go to the Convention in the Evening — which many did. . . . There has been much discussion on the subject this week and I feel entirely satisfied with the success of my effort — which has not, so far as I know, excited any opposition. At all events I have defined my position."

The pro-slavery sentiment was very strong in Newburyport, and Mr. Higginson's parish contained sundry sea-captains who saw no sin in returning fugitive slaves to their owners. Later one of these very men took Sims, the runaway slave, back to Savannah. Mr. Higginson's frequent sermons on the abolition of slavery and his activity in furthering the crusade caused growing discontent in the parish; although it is said that even these unwelcome sermons were so intensely interesting that the dissatisfied members of the society were his most constant hearers. But the opposition to his political views finally led to his resignation, after preaching for two years. " An empty pulpit," he said to his people, "has often preached louder than a living minister." He thus stated the event to his mother (September 6, 1849) : —

"The case was perfectly simple. Mr. W. distinctly stated that they had no fault to find with me personally, they liked and respected me; they were always interested in my preaching; they had no complaint as to pastoral matters; the only thing he had ever heard mentioned was Slavery and Politics; my position as an Abolitionist they could not bear. This, he admitted, could not be altered; and he tacitly recognized that I had but one course to pursue."

To his old friend, Sam Johnson, he wrote at the same time: —

"Dear but agitated Brother, —
"I intended to write you, but for procrastination and the knowledge that ill news travel fast. Mine is good though. I *had* resolved to release myself from the whole thing next year, for various reasons. But the discontents of the Pleasant St. 'upper ten' . . .

have led to it now. I said so Sunday before last, to the surprise of many and the tears of all women, poor men, young men, Democrats and Come-outers. A kind of reaction has followed since, and now all the rest are shedding tears — still they have accepted my resignation only not to take effect for 6 months. With a free church I could carry off half the society and many urge it — but I will not . . . I intend to give lectures here by and by or something of that sort. We are never going to leave these parts and are to board for the present at Mrs. Curson's, Artichoke Mills, 3 miles from town and the loveliest place on earth. . . .

"Not a dozen are really opposed to me, but they have all the *wealth*. Oh Christian Church!"

One member of the congregation wrote (November 7, 1849) these words to a relative of the dislodged pastor: —

"After hearing his two exquisite sermons — in the morning 'Rejoice in the Lord' — in the afternoon 'It doth not yet appear' I felt profoundly sad at the thought of his leaving the pulpit. . . . We cannot spare such gifts."

During the last six months of his stay in the parish, Mr. Higginson wrote to a friend: —

"The beautiful words 'pastor' and 'minister' have become almost offensive; but the good thing they used to denote has not. . . .

"These last months have something of pain for me, though they go very fast."

When this trying period was over, the Higginsons removed to a charming rural spot embowered in trees where the Merrimac and Artichoke Rivers meet. Here they shared the home of certain distant family connections who held their right to the place as long as they ground corn once a year. In this retreat the banished couple not only produced their own butter, but even sent some to Brattleboro, for Mr. Higginson wrote to his mother: —

"This is not my first churning, nor did I do all of this, for it took a great while and I had not time, but week before last I did it *all* and this time most of it, so you may safely call it my butter with some twirls of the crank from M. likewise.

"You don't see such butter every day!"

Soon he added: —

"It is quite as beautiful here as was reported and our feet are fast growing to the ground." From this earthly paradise "in the ecstasy of June" he wrote: —

"The soft west wind blows into my window, rich with lingering apple blossoms and half blown clover . . . thrushes' and bobolinks' and robins' notes. . . .

"In these lovely Spring days with the blue Merrimack waves dancing before me, the world seems very young, and all evil short-lived."

It is said in Newburyport that the young minister on leaving there burned all his unpublished sermons. However this may be, he preached in a hall after he had, to use his own words, "preached himself out of his pulpit." One of his Newburyport friends says that the majority of his parish, those who agreed with him, followed him to this hall, and those who remained in the church went to his evening meetings. This lady, who was then one of the adoring young people, says, "We sat on the steps of the platform from which he spoke, and worshipped him instead of God."

"It is pleasant to me to feel," he wrote, "that I have resumed my post of public scold. I have announced about 12 lectures, on every other Sunday Evening."

He remained in Newburyport two years after his resignation, interesting himself as before in the welfare of the people. He kept up his evening classes, walking back and forth to the town, made frequent visits to the public schools and served on the school committee. The pupils looked up to him with great reverence and accepted his advice as final. He was one of a committee of three which offered a prize of ten dollars each for the best essay and the best poem. Harriet Prescott wrote the successful essay on "Hamlet," and remembers how she retired to her room in deep emotion after receiving from Mr. Higginson's hands her gold eagle in a little mesh purse.

His practical interest in libraries seems from this record to have begun here.

"We have about $1250 subscribed and hope to get $1500 in town and $500 to $1000 out of town — besides books. By January 1 I hope the Library will go into operation; but we have a temporary place of deposit now."

In answer to his mother's entreaties, he wrote:—

"Thanks for your letter and its excellent advice. Certainly I shall never edit a paper — not go *solely* into politics; and as for companions I am always too thankful for real ones to care what garments they wear, — '*Bob*' my principal crony, at the Mills, has rather nondescript ones at present, but will probably come to pantaloons in time. . . . Did I tell you of seeing them (the Whittiers) at the Mills with Miss 'Grace Greenwood' the poetess &c. whom I had the privilege of rowing on the Artichoke?"

While in Newburyport, he renewed his intimacy, begun in college days with Levi Thaxter. The latter had announced that he was looking for some lonely place where he could, like Demosthenes, declaim to the waves. "I have suggested," said Mr. Higginson, "the Isles of Shoals. They are peopled by a queer race of fishermen." Neither of the friends could have foreseen that the result of this suggestion would be

the discovery of Thaxter's future wife. Later Wentworth wrote to his mother:—

"We had a nice visit from Levi, he brought the
loveliest seaweed and gave a glowing account of
Appledore."

But Mrs. Higginson's version of the visit was
somewhat different, for she declared:—

"Last Wednesday Levi appeared with a cod and
several Salt Mackerel (awful things); we are trying
to give them away."

After an expedition to the Isles of Shoals, where
he met for the first time the fair young Celia Leighton, with her necklace of sea-shells, Mr. Higginson
wrote:—

"There is no passion so beguiling as boating and
I could sympathize with Levi in that; Levi has still
his beautiful boat The Lady of Shalott. . . . As to his
other Lady I grew more and more attracted to the
sea maiden; Celia has a lovely nature, simple, true,
confiding, brave and of perfect serenity of temper. . . .
And the more I think of her, and remember that she
is but fifteen; the more I feel that there is no predict-
ing what she may not turn out."

In writing nearly a year later of the Thaxter marriage, Mr. Higginson said:—

"Characteristically enough the great event was
decided on, the priest sent for to the mainland and
the ceremony performed all in one day!"

The interludes of play, however, were brief and infrequent, and the days more than full of manifold tasks. To his over-anxious mother, the dutiful son reported his doings thus: —

"I have just been writing a sheet of Maxims for Maidens going to Normal School. Two of my children — they were little girls when I came here — are bound thither in a fortnight . . . to let two such locomotives as these two girls go off to one small town . . . without any manual of wisdom would be obviously unsafe; so I have written them a series of little Maxims like General Washington's. This I say partly to frighten you, because you believe such singular things about me that I have no doubt you suppose that I advise them to take boxing lessons every Sunday morning . . . but I don't."

Again he wrote: —

"I was amused yesterday by reading in a note of Dr. Young's Chronicles that when Francis Higginson, the ancient, became a non-conformist 'he was accordingly excluded from his pulpit; but a lectureship was established for him, in which he was maintained by the voluntary contributions of the inhabitants'; so I have good precedents."

Having given up his editorial column in the Newburyport paper, Higginson undertook to write two articles a week for the "Commonwealth" to appear as editorials, for which he was promised two dollars and a half per column. His early connection with this paper was brief; he was impatient at the misprints in his contributions, and complained:—

"This makes five articles of mine in your unhappy paper and there has been some diabolical erratum in each one. I shall try no further."

It is needless to say that these *diaboli* continued to annoy the author through life.

It was while in Newburyport that, with the coöperation of Samuel Longfellow, Mr. Higginson undertook to edit a volume of sea poems called "Thalatta." The editors apparently thought of bringing this volume out at the same time that "Uncle Tom's Cabin" appeared, as Higginson wrote, "Thalatta is at a standstill because Mrs. Stowe exhausts all the paper mills."

The young author was aroused from these peaceful pursuits by the enactment of the Fugitive Slave Law, September 18, 1850. After reading the details of what he called "this most cruel and unrighteous bill," he appealed to his old schoolmate, Charles Devens, United States Marshal, writing a burning letter of expostulation from which this passage is quoted:—

"NEWBURYPORT, Sep. 29, 1850.

". . . For myself there is something in the thought of assisting to return to slavery a man guilty of no crime but a colored skin [at which] every thought of my nature rebels in . . . horror. I think not now of the escaped slave, though he has all my sympathies, but of the free men and women who are destined to suffer for this act. And I almost feel as if the nation of which we have boasted were sunk in the dust forever, now that justice and humanity are gone; and as if the 19th century were the darkest of all the ages."

In April, 1851, Mr. Higginson, as a member of the Boston Vigilance Committee, received a summons to aid in rescuing Sims, the first fugitive slave captured in Boston and returned to slavery. Higginson was at this time a stockholder in the yacht Flirt, which was nominally for rent, but actually kept cruising about the coast in readiness to rescue slaves from incoming vessels or to kidnap their pursuers.

A crowded meeting was held in Tremont Temple, where Higginson made a vehement speech urging instant action. To this advice a subsequent speaker, Charles Mayo Ellis, strongly objected. Apropos of these speeches, Mr. Higginson's sister-in-law, Miss Barbara Channing, wrote: —

"I went to see Anne Phillips [Mrs. Wendell Phillips], who is enthusiastic about W. [Wentworth] — she said her hopes of Sims' rescue rested upon him, and if he had not been followed in his splendid speech at the Temple by a man who threw cold water upon his coals, he would have sent hundreds to the Court House."

Reporting the comments upon this eventful meeting to his mother, Wentworth quoted Anson Burlingame, a prominent politician, who said: —

"It [Higginson's] was the most remarkable speech he ever heard; it held the audience spellbound; it was more remarkable for what it kept back and hinted at than what it said; there was a fire in the eye that made him tremble.

"W. Phillips said that Dr. Howe said 'we were on the eve of a revolution with that speech — nothing but Ellis's speech saved us.'

"Yet it was very short and I was conscious of no such effects. In fact I walked in a dream all that week, but it tested me to the utmost. . . . Meetings where every one present had to be identified and every window closed; and plans that involved risking one's life and reputation solitary against law, state and nation."

From an account of the attempted rescue, written by Mr. Higginson in 1890, these extracts are taken:

"All projects for the rescue of fugitive slaves were embarrassed in those days by the fact that the most trusted abolitionist leaders were largely non-resistants in principle, and were unwilling to take part in any actual outbreak, while other well-wishers, such as Horace Mann, were utterly opposed to any violation of the law. . . . A plan was hastily formed by four or five abolitionists for the rescue of Sims. The plan was to communicate with the prisoner through a colored clergyman, and get him to consent to jump

from his window in the third story upon a pile of mattresses to be placed below, a carriage being placed in
readiness to take him away. . . . We were not sure
that Sims would have the courage to do this, rather
than go back to certain slavery. . . . At any rate
the mattresses were got and placed in a lawyer's
office in Court Square. Great pains were taken to
keep the plan a secret and I well remember the sinking of the heart with which I saw, on walking
through Court Square on the evening planned for
the enterprise, that masons were at work putting
iron bars in the window of Sims' cell. The whole plan
was thus frustrated."

In this despairing mood the ardent young Abolitionist found some comfort in the attitude of his
fellow clergymen, for he wrote: —

"I heard from Sam Longfellow a few weeks since
that he was thinking of leaving Fall River. Among
'settled' divines the game of Puss-in-the-corner
seems growing harder and hotter. The Fugitive
Slave Law has mightily stimulated it. But how finely
our 'Unitarian' brethren have done and are doing,
on that point. It shows the clergy to be a grade above
politicians, after all, that the capitalists have less
power to muzzle the Reverends than the Honorables.
Perhaps you read an editorial of mine in the 'Commonwealth,' some 2 months ago, on Sims' case. It
was Dr. Walker who said to me, apropos de Sims,
that if these things continued 'the pulpit would
become a *refuge for scoundrels*'! Don't of course

imagine my mind at all anxious or perplexed. I have plenty to occupy me and the current of thought may float me as it pleases."

Although Mr. Higginson had fancied his preaching days were over, he received in 1852 an invitation to take charge of a Free Church in Worcester, an organization which the influence of Theodore Parker had just brought into existence. This society was composed of radicals of all descriptions and as a whole was imbued with strong anti-slavery sentiments. Mr. Higginson wrote to a friend: —

"They want me to stay at Worcester where there are 600 come-outers and a very thriving city and a clear Free Soil majority and no anti-slavery preaching, and 40 conventions in a year."

"Rather to my own surprise," he wrote from Worcester in May, 1852, "I find myself likely to assume the charge of a new Free Church in this city, on a plan resembling Mr. Parker's in Boston more nearly than any other. This is a very thriving and active place, materially, intellectually and morally; there is as much radicalism here as at Lynn, but more varied, more cultivated, and more balanced by an opposing force; a very attractive place, and this free church movement a very strong one. I feel a sort of duty toward it, because I see clearly the need and the possibility of infusing more *reverence and piety* into this *comeouterism* of New England, to which I belong by nature; and this seems a good place to do it. The congregation is very large and they desire very much that I should come. And it will very probably be so."

Later he told his mother: —

"I was yesterday offered $1200 to give up Worcester and be Secretary to the Temperance Committee for another year. . . . There is a feeling of the necessity for a vigilant superintendence while the law is being enforced. I of course declined."

His mother replied that she would let him choose his own way of doing good, not even saying, as Judge Story's mother did: "Now, Jo, I've sat up and tended you many a night when you were a Baby, and don't you *Dare* not to be a great Man." She added that she did not even care to have him a "great Man," except as greatness was achieved by interesting himself in the good of those within his reach. "Steer clear your own way," she exclaimed, "and the result I am sure will be right. . . . You object to beginning Life anew — remember you are not yet 30!"

VII

THE FREE CHURCH

ON the eve of Mr. Higginson's departure from Newburyport, this resolution was adopted at a Free Soil
caucus in that town: —

"Resolved, That in the departure of one from this
community whose purity of life, earnestness of purpose, restless energy, and remarkable abilities are
universally acknowledged, we suffer a severe and an
irreparable loss, and that our regret at the removal
of the Rev. T. W. Higginson to Worcester is relieved
only by the consideration that wherever he may be
he will not cease in his efforts for the elevation of
mankind."

Shortly before removing his household goods the
faithful chronicler reported: —

"Here we are still, wind and water-bound. . . .
We are thoroughly packed and living on two or three
chairs and a borrowed plate. M. thinks it is like
a picnic. But I feel more as if it were a part of a
menagerie, waiting to be transported across the
country, when the great wagon is ready. We are
exhibited in Worcester next."

The Higginsons were accompanied on their journey by "kit in a basket" and a stout Irish damsel

who had been accustomed to doing housework for twenty-three truckmen, and who it was thought could probably take care of "kit and us." The new abode, which commanded a view of Wachusett, was not in the most select part of the town, nor was the new congregation drawn from circles of the élite. But undisturbed by these facts Mr. Higginson thus described the Worcester home: —

"Nice little house, in a charming part of the town . . . nice tangled jungle of a small garden, with peach trees that carry one nearer the Mills than anything else. . . . I never knew what the love of one's own vegetables might be. I have a great dislike to tomatoes and yet I linger over the great red creatures, and nip off leaves to give them sun and treat them as tenderly as kitty.

". . . Close by us . . . is Mr. Brown, a *tailor*, quite a remarkable person I think, very original and agreeable, and rather the wit of the city; I have ridden, walked, and sailed with him with great satisfaction. In fact I find the merits of the masculine side of human nature rather coming uppermost here, quite unlike Newburyport. . . .

"People look busier and happier here . . . there is much more air of country too, the main street is filled all day with country wagons, and you buy your fire wood from the carts. . . . The Hall [Horticultural] is nearly or quite as large as the Universalist Church in Newburyport and is always well filled in the morning and crowded in the evening;

everything prospers in the Free Church and I like it very much. The people are a very wide-awake set; and we have a neighboring parishioner in Bloomer dress who sends us squash pies and alarms Mrs. H. continually. . . . Indeed the recognized respectabilities of the town are quite willing to honor us occasionally in the evening."

"Sept. 23. To-day is cattle-show. I have always wished to live in a town where this happened and have been wandering about this morning and enjoying the country people. . . . More country people than I knew existed, enough to farm the whole solar system, I should think!"

The new minister preached his own installation sermon and wrote to his mother in reference to it: —

"The 1300 copies have been scattered far and wide, and met with favor [here] and elsewhere among various people. . . . The Boston Universalist Trumpet has denounced it violently and then eagerly borrowed all its Anti-Orthodox thunder. . . .

"I have just had a singular epistle on my sermon from a Dr. —— of Philadelphia, a distinguished Anti-Slavery man and writer generally; his wife charitably adds at the end that her husband is slightly delirious when he is feverish, and M. thinks the explanation was quite needful."

About this sermon Mr. Higginson received letters from all parts of the country and newspaper notices of equally miscellaneous origin. His mother was somewhat aghast at the radical views propounded in the discourse, and wondered what would be said of a document "so bold, original, and independent." Early in his new career, she offered her son this bit of advice, — "As to your admiring females, don't let your head be turned!"

Mr. Higginson's intense love of children enabled him to reach the little people in unusual ways. His Worcester Sunday-School is thus described in a letter to the writer by an eyewitness: —

"It was unique, not at all modelled after the conventional type where the scholars are divided into classes and recite lessons to the teachers. He was himself the only teacher. He told them stories illustrating some simple moral principle — Truth, Generosity, Love, and Loyalty; talking familiarly with them of the perplexities which even children often suffer from, in deciding between Right and Wrong. These little talks were delightful to listen to, they were so simple and clear and impressive."

But companionship with the children was not confined to Sundays, for he "enticed a select circle of pet little girls to play Puss-in-the-corner on the green after tea." "I am plunging," he told his mother, "into parish visiting with great pleasure. It is rich to see the small children." In referring to one child, he said, "The little darling . . . showed me her dolly, with both legs broken off. It was a

young lady doll, but 'He's broken his legs,' said she
— '*he has to walk on his drawers.*' . . . 'But,' she
added hopefully — 'one of 'em is growing out again
— *I* saw it!' Her name is Alice and she and her
sister *play Mr. Higginson!*"

The young clergyman recorded in his Worcester
journal that his only sorrow was "the absence of
children to one whose passion for them is so rare
and profound. . . . I try to pass for a sober and
respectable man, but there is really no sentimental
school-girl whose demand for being loved is greater
or more comprehensive than mine — it makes me
uncomfortable to be for five minutes in the room
with a strange child without winning it to love me."

The project of a Christmas tree delighted the Free
Church people, and Mr. Higginson appealed to one
of his former Newburyport parishioners for help:
"I thought perhaps your mother and E. would gild
some eggs for me and send them to Boston by and by.
I shall want all manner of little duds for the children." After this successful event, it was found that
"There were over 150 children (including about 20
colored children — invited guests). Where they all
came from I don't know, but everybody who could
claim eleventh cousinship to the Free Church came
in. . . . Ever since that Tree we have been the
most sociable parish in town."

"Would you like to look in at the Free Church?"
wrote Mr. Higginson to his young friend, Harriet
Prescott, May, 1854. "The people are bright and
earnest, rather than cultivated. There is a tradition of a progressive improvement in the *bonnets*, o'
evenings, since the first summer; but I doubt if we
can bear this test of increased social distinction.
Worcester is a great thoroughfare, and there are
always many strangers, and many Nicodemuses
there are, who come by night only." — "We are
well," he reported to his mother, "and I am only too
busy; too busy to read, which is the greatest trial.
. . . And inwardly, my transplantation to this new
soil has enriched and strengthened me immeasur-
ably; and given me many steps toward maturity."

He always craved books and more books, but the
actual purchase of one was a luxury. With a little
money sent him by his Aunt Nancy, he bought Mrs.
Jameson's "Commonplace Book of Thoughts, Memories, and Fancies," and told his aunt, "I shall write
very carefully in the beginning that it was a present,
so that my parishioners and friends may not think
it my own extravagance, in these hard times." Certain favorite books, such as Jane Austen's novels,
Scott's "Pirate," and Thoreau's "Week on the Concord and Merrimack Rivers," Mr. Higginson usually
read once a year.

Four years of his ministry at the Free Church had gone by when the president of the organization wrote to the clergyman's mother, that, after listening to his preaching, "common sermons appear weak and stale, and our people will not go to hear them." He added that something in her son's appearance and manner "called out the masses."

As a matter of course the newcomer interested himself in the schools, and was placed on the school committee. Reporting one of the meetings of this body he said triumphantly, "We raised all the female teachers' salaries." But for defending the right of a Roman Catholic pupil to use the version of Scripture approved by his parents he was dismissed from the board. He wrote to his mother, "I am half glad and half sorry that the Know-nothings have dropped me from the School Committee." Public opinion changed, however, and he was not only reinstated, but one of his companions on the later board was a Roman Catholic priest.

Never in Mr. Higginson's long life did he abandon his custom of fearless protest by voice or pen against anything which seemed to him wrong or unjust. Anonymous letters of abuse were speedily consigned to the waste basket; words of criticism or rebuke he received calmly, and kept on his chosen course. His equanimity was seldom disturbed, but when confronted by what he considered a great wrong or injustice, anger could come in a mighty flash.

In his journals of that period, Mr. Higginson speaks of the "untamable gipsy element in me which gives me instant sympathy with every desperate adventure. . . . Never did I hear of anything dare-devil without wishing to leave all else and do it. . . . I never read of but one thing which thoroughly came up to my idea of enjoyment, and that was the Charge of the Six Hundred. All the rest of existence would I freely give for one such hour." This was written soon after the actual event. Thirteen years later, Colonel Higginson added this pencilled note to the above: "The war slaked this appetite to some extent — but it will never die out."

An occasional note of discontent appears in the diaries, as when he complains: —

"All I ask of fate is — Give me one occasion worth bursting the door for — an opportunity to get beyond this boy's play. . . . Till then my life, frittered away in little cares and efforts for the sick, sad and sinful, is not worth the chronicling. . . . I never remember to have rested my cares on any earthly being — all with whom I have ever associ-ated have rested theirs on me."

But the habitual frame of mind of this "incorrigi-ble optimist," as he was called in later life, was expressed in a letter to his mother when he was thirty-three: —

"My birthdays pass by almost uncounted, for I never feel any older; indeed in these last years I feel a sort of exuberance of life, and love of action and adventure, which seem more like 23 than 33. I think the one great possession of my life has been this sunny vigor of nature and unfailing animal spirits, which have carried me buoyantly over everything so far, and which I am sure I inherited from you. And many as are my other causes of gratitude, this seems the greatest."

The ardent friendship between Higginson and Hurlbut, begun when they were both theological students and continued into these Worcester years, was destined to end in sorrow. After coolness began to separate the friends, Mr. Higginson still wrote to Hurlbut once a month, but scarcely ever received a reply. "Still, O changing child," he exclaimed, "out of the depths of my charity I still believe in you and out of the depths of my heart I still love you." Their letters were more like those between man and woman than between two men. Hurlbut's letters — still preserved — are always brilliant, often affectionate, sometimes full of rollicking fun. One of them begins, "The unfaithful to the unforgetting—greeting." In answer to a young friend's question, Mr. Higginson wrote this account of the romantic friendship: —

"[I have had] one terrible disappointment. You asked me, a while ago, and with some apparent shrinking, if I had ever had any very intimate friend. I do not wonder that you ask, for you have seen so little evidence of such intimacy. My child, I have never had *but* one; all others have been only acquaintances, though I have always had a profusion of those. But I never loved but one male friend with passion — and for him my love had no bounds — all that my natural fastidiousness and cautious reserve kept from others I poured on him; to say that I would have died for him was nothing. I lived for him; it was easy to do it, for there never was but one such person; never have I met such another all gifted, all accomplished, all fascinating person; some men were jealous of him, some women distrusted him; all the rest he fascinated. . . . He knew everything in advance of study, he could do everything at the first trial. In travelling I have been waylaid by utter strangers who saw me with him, and who having talked with him five minutes could not rest without learning who this wondrous creature was. To everybody he was an astonishment — to me he was a delight — we lived together at Cambridge like Warrington and Pendennis (for he was younger than I, and yet how barren I seemed compared to him!). To me, moreover, he was always noble and sweet, he loved me truly and generously — and I on the other hand when clouds came around his good name and at last utterly swallowed him I clung to him — for *years*. . . . My eyes were opened — too late to save him — and he was lost to me forever.

. . . And yet all his crime is an utter moral weakness, joined with gifts too brilliant for anything but a strong moral nature to carry steadily. . . .

"One good which I have gained even from this loss [lack of intimate friends] is that I have learned to stand alone, free from cliques, and parties, taking my own responsibilities and keeping my own counsel."

Apropos of this independence of outside sympathy, he wrote in the diary of 1860, "While I have M.'s unequalled brilliancy for a perpetual stimulus, I need none from others."

"Hurlbut's downfall is the hardest thing of all," Mr. Higginson once said when alluding to the privations and disappointments of life. In happier mood, he wrote: "For myself, the universe is all clear and sweet; nor do I see why it should not be so, to all healthy natures. . . . My own faith is simply and solely Natural Religion. To me Jesus is a brother and the Bible a book."

The craving for larger opportunities was somewhat relieved by lecturing in other towns; and besides these outlets, Mr. Higginson frequently made stirring speeches at Free Soil, Temperance, and Anti-Slavery conventions. In his regular chronicles to his mother he reported that Worcester was very gay, but that his own evenings were engaged in public speaking. He also preached in pulpits other than his own. These trips often took him some distance from home, and he wrote from Niagara: —

" . . . My Congregation was good, including Mr. *Barnum*, whose autobiography I came very near unconsciously referring to. In the afternoon I spoke at one of a series of remarkable meetings for free talk on theological subjects which Mr. May started in a public hall. All sorts of persons take part, Methodists, Jews, Catholics, &c. and no one can speak but ten minutes."

These absences from home not only gave a needed change, but took the young man among various interesting people. He wrote to his mother, after lecturing in Concord, that he had Mr. Emerson for an auditor "which made me nearly dumb at first. . . ."

"Last Saturday I was in Boston [Jan. 1853] and went to see no less a person than Mr. Thackeray — not as lion but as lecturer. We wanted him here for a new association and offered him $500 for 6 lectures — which he declined; he was very frank about it, saying it was more than he could get in England: but he could get more in other cities; in Providence $800 for three lectures!

"He is six feet four, at least, very sweet and manly, with a large head and bushy gray hair, almost white; looks 55. He has very little English hoarseness or awkward *breadth* of voice; a very good voice and enunciation; and no hauteur or coldness; was laboriously anxious to show me that he meant me no discourtesy by refusing our offer."

He adds that Thackeray's greatest desire in this country was to see Theodore Parker.

A saving quality through life was Mr. Higginson's keen sense of the ludicrous. He wrote to his Aunt Nancy: —

"WORCESTER, June 29, 1858.

"I spoke in Springfield on Sunday, to the Spiritualists so called. My name was paraded in the streets in the largest capitals I ever had as the Rev. T. W. H. 'the eminent clergyman, popular author (!!) and eloquent lecturer.' Directly over it were the remains of a theatrical handbill in large letters 'The Fool of the Family.'"

Describing a pilgrimage of young men to Concord, he says: —

"No one had any acquaintance with Mr. Emerson except a certain Frank Sanborn, a remarkable young poetic youth, formerly farmer and shoemaker, more than six feet high. . . . He is a Junior and one of those who walked to Watertown when I preached there."

And again: —

"Last Friday night I went to Concord to an Anti-Slavery tea-party, where I spoke, together with the Lieut. Governor. Mrs. Emerson was there with her fine daughters — (R. W. E. being at the West) — Elizabeth Hoar, looking very noble — Thoreau and his mother and sister, and many other people of more or (especially) less note. . . . The Lieut.

Governor . . . said . . . slavery was a subject to *which he never had paid much attention* — see what it is to be absorbed in the larger interests of life."

To Worcester there came from time to time people whom it was a delight to meet. "Last week," wrote Mr. Higginson, "Mr. Emerson was here and gave óne of his old style of lectures, rich and delicious, he staid here, and I never liked him so much; he had all his invariable gentleness and graciousness."

At another time he writes, "To-day I have had a tolerably good time. Tea with Alice and Phœbe Cary, the latter a dumpy jolly milkmaid, the former rather fine and superior."

Of the actress, Charlotte Cushman, whom Mr. Higginson introduced to a Worcester audience by reading a letter describing her, he wrote to Harriet Prescott: —

"What a wonder she is! That magnificent vigor and vital heat of hers is enough to redeem her native land forever from the charge of producing sickly and lifeless women. . . . I was careful what I read, but there was one little sentence which described her so perfectly, I read on, but first I asked Miss ——, 'Will she blush?' and the good great creature broke in herself in her hearty uproarious way, '*Nary blush*,' quoth she, shaking her wide brows merrily at me. . . .

"Her acting affected me infinitely beyond Rachel,

though I thought the latter beyond anything; perhaps I saw C. C. in her greatest part — Queen
Katherine; but I remember Rachel's death scene as
the climax of acting, while in the last scene of this,
it was as if my own mother was sinking and dying
before me; if I had another thought it was of the
wickedness of having a crowd of people to see all
this. Where she put her person and all the abundance of her life and left nothing but that frail wasted
shell of humanity, no thought could tell; she was
seventy years old and reduced to the weight of a
child. I felt as if I would have given worlds to be
able to look away for a moment and yet I could not.

"Then I saw her in comedy . . . the fun was on
the same large scale with everything else, and carried
every one along irresistibly."

One day the young clergyman encountered Henry
Ward Beecher on the street "looking fresh and wholesome as a great Baldwin apple. . . ."

"I had in one hand," wrote Mr. Higginson, "a
box of strawberries, a large box, and 2 pasteboard
boxes, and in the other an umbrella. He said, 'You
are as badly off as I was in Boston t'other day, when
I met Wendell Phillips. I saw a great red lobster on
a stall — a thing I had n't seen since I was a boy'
(as if he had ever ceased to be), 'but in N.Y. they
are not sold boiled. So I bought it and carried it
with me to the Railroad Station, but presently I
saw a much bigger one and bought that too. It was
so big the claw would n't hold it and it dropped, and

then I held it by the other claw and that broke too and it dropped again and as I had just succeeded in picking it all up, two lobsters, two claws and all, I looked up — and there was Wendell Phillips and two ladies!'

"He says he repays himself for overwork during the rest of the year, by six weeks of total inaction in the summer — no man is saved, he says, except by his inconsistencies. I told him he had laid up a large assurance of salvation in that line, to which he heartily agreed."

In 1855, Mr. Higginson ventured on an unusually extended lecture trip. He reported to his wife: —

"I am too soft-hearted for a Lecturer and cannot bear to take money out of people's pockets. I wish I were as tough as old John Pierpont, who never relents, and insisted on $10 more than the $30 paid at Rochester; while I refunded $5 — my audience being about as large — but not worth the money they offered me. . . .

"An Anti-Slavery Lecturer is better off than a mere Lyceum lecturer in this — that he is greeted with an enthusiasm of the heart and not merely of the head. . . . I have also seen rather a queer placard from Skaneateles which announces me as 'leader of the forlorn-hope from Worcester.'

"I had a pathetic scene at Syracuse with the dearest little pair of quaint rosy German children. . . . I bought a ball of parched corn and molasses candy . . . for them and they looked demure delight, trying in vain to discover how to eat it — I watched them till their wicked father came along, as ignorant as they were, and examined it in vain till at last it broke in his fingers and he threw it down and trotted them hastily away! I watched it from a distance, powerless and desolate, till the queer little antiquities disappeared."

In Syracuse he encountered Horace Greeley, who "was observed by all, and people tried to make the newsboys sell him his own life." In a letter from this place, Mr. Higginson says: —

"I am writing on the office desk and am constantly taken for the landlord. A man has just come up and whispered confidentially, 'A lot of first rate segars I'd like to sell you, Sir.' 'Thank you, Sir, I don't smoke,' I said without looking up. '*Ah,*' said he rather astonished, 'ain't you the landlord of this here house?' '*No,*' said I, shuddering. — Next a man indignant at not having been waked in time for his train — but happily the real landlord has just come in — a man in ruffled shirt and *two* seal rings."

Although his lectures at that time could not have been very remunerative, he rejoiced in working, and in working all the time. He wrote to his wife while on this very trip: —

"Like your father, and other very busy persons I suppose, I have the most intense dread of *ennui*. I very seldom suffer from the thing itself — but when I look forward and see a space of time which I cannot easily use to advantage, it gives me a sort of suffocating sensation."

Lecturers in those days were apt to encounter hardships and discomforts — snowstorms delaying trains and preventing the keeping of engagements. Once Mr. Higginson wrote from Toledo in a most perplexed frame of mind, after missing various connections and mourning the loss of twenty-five dollars: —

"Here I am spending Sunday in a city of absolute strangers in a wild snowstorm, in a rather forlorn hotel from whose windows no house is visible, but only a few sheds with a dirty pig or two, then a frozen river and a bleak uninhabited shore behind. . . . I doubt not that here also there are Abolitionists and Women's Rights people who would welcome me, could I only get at them."

At another time, when attending certain suffrage meetings in New York city, he wrote: —

"This morning our Woman's Suffrage Convention began — I being President thereof; think of me in that big Hall! We had a very successful beginning — large numbers. . . . Rev. Antoinette [Brown] is a soft, gentle-looking person, youthful, and 'nervolymphatic' — quite unlike most of the Woman's Rights women. Lucy Stone is staying in the house with me and more charming than ever. . . . I am willing to have women preach, if they will do it as much better than average men as she [Antoinette

Brown] does. As for Lucy Stone, I admire and love her more every day."

Of the success of this convention, Mr. Higginson's mother wrote: "And altogether you have been decidedly the great gun of the New York meeting. What a singular position for a Higginson!!"

From Philadelphia, where he attended a similar convention, he wrote to his wife: —

"We have had a very good meeting so far. I am staying at Edward Hopper's, a sturdy son of old Isaac (Mrs. E. H. being Lucretia Mott's daughter). I wear dear old Isaac's slippers and dressing-gown when I go to the bathroom in the morning and shave with his razor afterwards. . . .

"There is a medical student here named *Ora Moon* who beats Hattie Hosmer altogether. She is a Virginian, wears pistols and smokes; has a season ticket at the theatre and the pistol-gallery; rather a formidable result of the business — yet such there must be."

About this visit, one of his letters says: —

"I have really had a most charming time. . . . Plain Friends by the dozen, male and female, would come up and say, 'Well, Thomas Higginson, I am glad to see thee at last, I have often heard of thee and read thy words.' . . .

"How shall I describe to you Lucretia Mott . . . the most brilliant eyes. Such a face and such a regal erectness! Nobody else ever stood upright before.

She said but little in the meetings, but that so clear and sagacious and wise; and there was such an instinct of her superiority, that she ruled like a queen on the platform, and when she looked as if she desired anything we all sprang to see what it might be. Then to see her at her house — at her long table in the great dining-room, eighteen at table (and filled twice over, one day) — she at one end and her quiet, sensible, manly husband, James Mott, at the other; a perpetual Thanksgiving Day; her children and their partners beside her, and all looking up to her so admiringly. . . ."

To his mother he wrote: —

"Lucy Stone of course was the real presiding genius [at the Convention], dear little stainless saint that she is; but I was very much struck with the character and ability shown by the women."

When this lady was about to lecture in Brattleboro, Mr. Higginson thus besought his family: —

"My principal object in now writing is to beg all of you, who will, to go and hear Lucy Stone speak. . . . She is simply one of the noblest and gentlest persons whom I know; with her homely face and her little Bloomerized-Quakerish person — and her delicious voice. . . . Lucy wears them [bloomers] for health she avers, being exposed to storms and wind and snowdrifts in her wanderings."

At the time of the gentle reformer's marriage in 1855, Mr. Higginson wrote to his mother: —

LUCY STONE, 1855

THE FREE CHURCH

"Guess what wedding we are going to next — on
May Day . . . dear Lucy Stone's!! . . . I am glad
the world should see her as a wife and mother. Still
there was something so powerful and beautiful in
that lonely life of hers, nothing in history more so.
. . . I spent several hours with her in Boston last
week. . . . She said, 'You will laugh when I tell
you what I came to Boston for, to buy a wedding
dress and to put my little property into the hands
of trustees, so that my husband shall not control it;
think what a thing that is, for a woman to have to
do! But I am determined that it shall be held by
a married woman in some way, so my sister is a
trustee.' Then she added, 'Harry says (Mr. Black-
well) that I ought to be very thankful that a woman has thus much freedom, but that is like telling a fugitive slave to be thankful there is a Canada,
when he knows he ought to be free without going
there.'"

Mr. Higginson officiated at the wedding and
heartily approved the protest made by the newly
married pair against the existing laws which did not
allow a married woman to own even her own wardrobe. This protest was read and signed as a part of
the ceremony.

One of the many instances in which Mr. Higginson
defended the equality of the sexes is preserved in an
old newspaper account. He had been asked to serve
on the committee of credentials at a temperance

convention in another State. In explanation of his failure to do this, a speaker at the convention, who called Mr. Higginson the heart and head of the temperance cause in Massachusetts, said, "He came here at the call, but declined to serve on a committee that could not recognize his sister as well as himself."

With all this remarkable activity, the indefatigable pastor did not neglect outdoor exercise and recreation. His love of boating found a happy outlet at Worcester where he was instrumental in organizing a boat club for young men and also one for girls, the latter being practically an unheard-of thing in those days. These novices he patiently and enthusiastically coached, to their own great delight. Once with a few young friends he camped for the night on a tiny island in Lake Quinsigamond to see the pond-lilies open at sunrise. There they sailed among "acres" of white lilies and hung wreaths of them on bow and mast. The boat he had owned at Newburyport went with him to Worcester, and he wrote to his mother: "This afternoon, under those wonderful clouds, I have been floating on Lake Quinsigamond, in the painted and rejuvenated Annie [Laurie]."

Another diversion was found in long walks, in which Mr. Higginson was sometimes accompanied by H. G. O. Blake, Thoreau's friend and biographer, and occasionally by Thoreau himself. On some of these expeditions he collected birds' eggs: "If you only take one or two," he wrote, "the birds are not troubled. There is no form of re-creation so wonderful to me as this of eggs. That all the flashing splendor of the oriole, all the magnificent melody of the red thrush, should be coiled within these tiny and fragile walls."

He officiated as president of an athletic club, exercising regularly in the gymnasium, himself; and was also president of skating and cricket clubs. One of his outdoor days is thus described in a letter: —

"Day before yesterday I went over to play a cricket match at Clinton, a thing I have been dreaming about ever since I was a child and found it as pleasant as I expected. We were all day in the open air, in the pleasantest green meadow near a river with high wood banks. We played from 9 till 3 with short intermissions and then all took a swim in the river and went to dinner. Every one in Worcester supposed we should be beaten, but we beat them so tremendously, 3 to 1, that our return was a perfect ovation and it was quite exciting."

To a young friend he wrote: —

"I have felt so much strength and scope to come to me from even glimpses of an outdoor life that I understand your occasional longings to be a gipsy.

I think it almost impossible to *waste* time spent out-
doors. . . .

> ' The hours the idle school boy squandered
> The man would die ere he 'd forget.' "

Mr. Higginson's interest in botany here found
scope; he continued the microscopic work begun in
student days; and was the prime mover in forming
the Worcester Natural History Society. He succeeded in securing only one woman member, and
this lady asserts that the meetings were most entertaining. The reluctance of other women to become
members is explained by the fact that in those days
most women shrank from the least publicity. Mr.
Higginson was also instrumental in organizing and
managing the free public library, being one of its
early trustees. In all these enterprises he enlisted a
band of enthusiastic Worcester youth. His unusual
gift for interesting young men is described by a
former Harvard instructor who testifies that he saw
"scores of instances of the perfectly extraordinary
way in which his character inspired a desire in the
hearts of young men to be like him."

Mr. Higginson early concerned himself with prison
reform and the problem of the future of discharged
convicts. In spite of his multiplicity of cares, it
was with a struggle that he decided on account of
fatigue to forego the duties of an overseer of the

poor. Although most responsive to appeals for help, the weary pastor sometimes rebelled a little, as in the following complaint: "Mrs. Dall writes to me about Woman's Rights petitions. Always there is the same difficulty; if I touch a thing with my little finger, I am always compelled, by the failure of co-laborers, to grasp it with my whole hand. . . . I have spent a large part of my life in trying to set men upon their legs who were constitutionally disqualified for standing there."

Many years later, in 1882, Mr. Higginson received a most unexpected tribute to his public work in Worcester. This was a bequest of five hundred dollars from a former resident of that town. The donor in his will left this sum to "Thos. Wentworth Higginson as a mark of my abiding appreciation of his noble labors in the city of Worcester."

VIII

ANTHONY BURNS AND THE UNDERGROUND RAILWAY

In the mean time the fugitive slave question was seething, and Mr. Higginson wrote to a friend, George William Curtis, whom he considered lukewarm, "Remember that to us, Anti-Slavery is a matter of deadly earnest, which costs us our reputations to-day, and may cost us our lives to-morrow."

In May, 1854, three years after the return of Sims to slavery, the Anthony Burns affair occurred. Colonel Higginson was often called upon in his later years to tell the details of this exciting episode. After the escape of Burns, a fugitive slave from Virginia, he had been, according to an old record, in the employ of a clothing dealer on Brattle Street, Boston. He wrote a letter to his brother in Virginia by the way of Canada, but as all letters to slaves were opened by their masters, his retreat was discovered. He was then arrested and imprisoned in an upper room of the court-house. A letter from Wendell Phillips notified Mr. Higginson of "another kidnapping case," saying, "you'll *come* of course," and signed, "in no hope." A placard was issued

headed, "A Man Kidnapped," calling a meeting in
Faneuil Hall and asking, "Shall he be plunged into
the hell of Virginia slavery by a Massachusetts judge
of probate?" Of this great meeting Mr. Higginson
was one of the vice-presidents, and one of the few
daring men who made the attack on the court-house
with the hope of rescuing Burns.

The scheme for the rescue was known to only a
few of those present at the meeting. It was decided
that in the midst of the proceedings an alarm should
be raised by announcing that a mob of Negroes was
attacking the court-house, followed by a sudden
dismissal of the audience. Meantime Mr. Higginson
went with a few others to Court Square to await
their allies. He had bought axes with which to
break in the doors, and the hardware dealer had
made out the bill to "Mr. Higgins," perhaps never
knowing who his customer was. Unfortunately for
the success of the plan only a crowd of curious spec-
tators reached the court-house, the handful of men
who were interested in the rescue arriving too late.
A stout beam was procured and with this implement
Mr. Higginson and one or two others proceeded to
force an entrance to the court-house. When the door
gave way, Mr. Higginson and a Negro sprang inside
and were instantly attacked by several policemen.
In this affray, the former received a cut on his chin

which left a permanent scar. While the policemen were hammering Mr. Higginson's head, a deputy marshal was killed. How and by whom was long a subject of controversy, for this was the first time a life had been sacrificed in an attempt to resist the Fugitive Slave Law.

Of the Faneuil Hall meeting, Mr. Higginson wrote to a Newburyport friend: "That meeting at Faneuil Hall was tremendous. I never saw such enthusiasm, and (though warned that it would be so) I could not possibly believe that it would exhale so idly as it did in Court Square. Still, twenty more men, in the right place, would have rescued the slave, that all acknowledge."

From Mr. W. F. Channing's house in Boston, where he had taken refuge, Mr. Higginson wrote to his wife: "There has been an attempt at rescue and failed. I am not hurt except a scratch on the face which will prevent me doing anything more about it, lest I be recognized." From the following letter, written two days later, May 28, to Rev. Samuel May, Jr., it appears that there was still hope of rescuing the slave: —

"The excitement in this city [Worcester] is tremendous; entirely beyond any imagination. . . . The wildest things are proposed, and by persons whom I have considered very 'hunkerish.' For instance,

they talk of arming 500 men to go to Boston. But
it would be *perfectly* practicable to arm and organize
100 if desirable. Shall we do it, and with what
immediate object?

"As it is, many will go to Boston to-morrow.
There is an intense indignation at the failure of the
Friday enterprise (though *I* call it a great success,
and so do they, so far as it goes) and I think
Worcester men, if they are at hand, may be relied on.
If they send the poor man through *Providence*, we
shall rescue him *to a certainty*. Any number could
be sent from this place by an extra train.

"But I have no idea that he will ever be taken
from Boston, for I think that either the Kidnappers
will be killed first; or else that Boston men will buy
him to save the peace of the city. This, though not
so good as a rescue, would come pretty near it, after
the event of Friday night. . . . Finally, should not
something be done by the Committee in the way of
assistance to the family of the man shot, supposing
it to be so arranged as to show no contrition on our
part, for a thing in which we had no responsibility,
but simply to show that we have no war with
women and children.

"I hear rumors of my arrest, but hardly expect it.
If true, I hope no U.S. Officer will be sent up, for I
cannot answer for his life in the streets of Worcester.
. . . Send for me if you want me again. I am
thankful for what has been done — it is the greatest step in Anti-Slavery which Massachusetts has
ever taken. And I am ready to do my share over
again."

Burns's master agreed to sell him for a certain sum, but after the money was raised, he changed his mind. The day on which Burns was returned to slavery, when he was marched through the streets of Boston guarded by United States troops, was known for many years after as "Bad Friday." The following Sunday Mr. Higginson preached a sermon called "Massachusetts in Mourning," in which he said, "The strokes on the door of that court-house that night . . . went echoing from town to town . . . and each reverberating throb was a blow upon the door of every slave prison of this guilty republic."

After the excitement had somewhat subsided, Mr. Higginson wrote: —

"I do not think they can prove much against the men arrested — I have been repeatedly told that I was to be one of that number myself, and have patiently waited for the officers; but they have not yet appeared (though there was a hit at me in the Post this morning) and I cannot stay at home for them much longer."

To his Aunt Nancy he wrote: —

"*You* will be especially glad to hear that it is considered quite doubtful *whether our cases are ever tried* — even in the United States Court.

"Don't be frightened if you see in the paper that *I* have fled to parts unknown with other people's money in my pocket — for the Rev. Mr. Higgins of this city . . . has done so, and I don't doubt that distant newspapers will contrive to get the name wrong."

Later he reported: —

"I *was* arrested on Saturday June 10, 1854, and 'bound over' to appear before the Municipal Court in Boston in April — on charge of 'riot' committed on *that* Friday evening. But I had been expecting it for a week — and even if I should be convicted of anything and imprisoned a month or two (which is improbable) it would do so much good to the community, that I could bear it very patiently."

It was claimed that the early hour of this arrest at 6.30 A.M., a few minutes before the Boston train started, was chosen lest the "Freedom Club" of Worcester should interfere and prevent the arrest. When Mr. Higginson was arraigned before the Boston Police Court, he was accused of assembling with five hundred others to disturb the peace of the Commonwealth and "did unlawfully and riotously attack the Court-House . . . did throw stones, bricks . . . did break the glass in the windows and did force in and break open one of the doors . . . [did] fire and discharge sundry firearms . . . did utter loud cries and huzzas . . . to the great terror and disturbance of divers citizens."

A Boston newspaper, reporting this incident, said of the accused clergyman: —

"He is a man of talent, a great enthusiast, and though he stands within the pale of Unitarianism, he is regarded as a suspicious character, theoretically speaking. His appearance in Court excited no little sensation."

Some months later, in December, he wrote to his mother: —

"I am to be tried before the U.S. Court with Theodore Parker and others. . . . I rather think therefore that the other process (before the State court) will be withdrawn. I don't think they will expect anything, on either charge — but of the two I prefer to be tried on charge of violating the Fugitive Slave Law than for 'riotous and routous behavior.'"

As the time drew near, his mother dreaded the "horrid trial," and fearing that her son would be shut up for a year, came herself to the rescue. "My impulsive young mother," he wrote, "came down for an unexpected night last week." This devoted visitor found her son somewhat the worse for his encounter, but she rejoiced that instead of joining in the "inflammatory" speeches at Faneuil Hall, he was engaged in battering down the door of the court-house. "The indictment," to quote "Cheerful Yesterdays," "was ultimately quashed as imperfect, and we all got out of the affair, as it were, by the side door." Rev. Cyrus A. Bartol, in an article on "Boston

Tea Parties," written in 1874, said in reference to this event, "To-day, we honor the man that last let go his hold — I believe it was Thomas Wentworth Higginson — of the battering-ram against the courthouse door."

Somewhat later, a Boston policeman named Butman, who had been instrumental in Burns's arrest, went to Worcester to find evidence against those concerned in the riot. The Worcester people were so enraged by this uncalled-for visit that Butman's life was in danger, and the pastor of the Free Church risked his own by helping him escape. The event was thus described in a letter to a friend:

"I was not seriously damaged in the Butman trouble. . . . It *was* a time of peril however, though it ended in nothing worse than frightening a bully into a coward. I wish the poor creature's face could have been daguerreotyped as he crouched into the bottom of the carriage when the stones came crashing in; I never saw such an image of abject fear. Our City Marshal had to drive him the whole way to Boston, too frightened to get into the cars; when they changed horses half way, he hid himself in the woods and could hardly be found again; he would not enter Boston till after dark, nor go to his house even then, but spent the night at a hotel. They have arrested a few persons for riot, chiefly those who were most instrumental in saving him! — so that not much will come of it.

". . . There comes over me at times a strange wonder whether greater and better persons in times past have taken their life as quietly while it was contemporary, and forgotten all the hubbubs in the little events of every day. . . . No affairs in which I was ever engaged have excited me so much as it would have excited me to hear the thing well told in story or history. I can understand the client who cried when his lawyer told the tale of his wrongs — 'he never knew how much he had suffered before.'"

A newspaper of the time says: —

"He [Mr. Butman] awards praise to those who defended him after the storm had been roused, especially Mr. Higginson. . . . Some of the crowd did not distinguish in their attacks between Mr. Butman and Mr. Higginson. The latter gentleman received a considerable share of the missiles, and one large stone was thrown into the carriage, narrowly missing his head."

Miss Higginson wrote an anxious letter of inquiry to her brother, expressing his mother's disapproval of the whole affair, but concluding, "It is evident you are going to be a real knight-errant, always on hand."

Several years later, Mr. Higginson wrote to a friend, "Did you ever see an extravaganza of a novel, 'Harrington,' of which I was said to be the highly melodramatic hero — though I never knew the author — and which certainly worked up some scenes of my life, as the Butman riot in Worcester, with some power?"

It was a time when fugitive slaves frequently needed assistance, and the Underground Railroad was in full operation. Mr. Higginson was always eager to lend a hand to these escaping wretches. In the Boston "Liberator" and Worcester newspapers of the period, communications over his signature frequently appeared, asking for financial aid, sometimes for a distressed family which was trying to buy its own freedom. "Now this sum must be raised speedily," he declared. "Let every man choose once for all, between his love for freedom, and for a full pocket; for, as far as I have observed, in this land of liberty it is difficult to combine both."

In other cases he attempted to find work or hiding-places for the refugees. In one instance a home was sought for two boys who had been emancipated by their Kentucky master on condition that they should be cared for in a free State.

This note of introduction, written by Mr. Higginson to "Mr. F. B. Sanborn or Mr. R. W. Emerson," is given as a sample of the correspondence between the active abolitionists of that day: —

"WORCESTER, Sept. 14, 1860.

"The bearer, Capt. Stewart — sometimes known as Preacher Stewart — of Kansas, is leaving here to-day and I have advised him to pass through Concord and call on you. He is the head of the Underground Railway Enterprise in Kansas and has just made a highly successful trip. Mr. Stearns and others are raising funds to assist him in his operations.

"He brought on this trip a young slave girl of 15, nearly white, for whom some provision must be made."

There are many letters to Mr. Higginson from Rev. Samuel May, Jr., in reference to fugitives needing aid. One of these describes a young woman with babies whose master had threatened to move "earth and hell" to get her back. Mr. May thought the fugitives would be searched for in Boston, and that Worcester would afford her "as much safety as this accursed Union can give to a class which has no rights that white men are bound to respect." Of this woman, Mr. Higginson wrote: —

"We are expecting here an interesting person, young and beautiful, white and a slave. She escaped 4 months ago from North Carolina, disguised in deep mourning, bringing her child 3 years old, also white. She has also a baby born since her arrival; they are her master's children, poor creature; and she is coming here for safety. She has always been petted and waited on, and can do nothing except sew; but we shall probably get her into some family where she can do housework: and perhaps the elder child will be adopted, if she is willing."

It happened during these anxious days that Sumner bought a Negro family and gave them their freedom. One of the children was white, and Mr. Higginson conceived the plan of adopting her and thus filling the vacancy in his own family. He wrote:

"I have made a new acquaintance, most fascinating to me — the dear little white slave girl whom Mr. Sumner purchased — 'Ida May' they call her — but her real name is Mary Mildred something. Fancy a slender little girl of seven . . . with reddish hair, brown eyes, delicate features and skin so delicate as to be a good deal freckled. She came up to be shown at a public meeting here, and it was love at first sight between us, she was like an own child to me, and when in Boston this morning I restored her to her tall mulatto father and her handsome little *dark* brother and sister, it gave me a strange bewildered feeling. They were owned in Alexandria; the mother and grandmother are described as almost white. I am going to see them. There is a photograph of the little girl, but not nearly so good as a daguerreotype which was taken here, of her sitting in my lap — her face is lovely in the picture, but mine (my wife declares) is *spoiled by happiness*."

Later he added:—

"When I was in Boston I went to see my darling little Mildred Williams Ida May: they, you know, are free. She is as gentle and refined as ever, with her delicate skin and golden hair. She may be adopted by a member of Congress."

In reference to this curious episode, Mr. Higginson's old Newburyport friend, Caroline Andrews (Leighton) writes: —

"Mr. Higginson was much moved at the situation of this lovely child. He wished me to take her home with me and keep her for a while in my vacation, at Newburyport. While I was there he wrote me the most explicit directions in regard to her care and enjoyment. I thought he hoped at one time to adopt her, as after I had returned to my school, and given her back to her parents, he wrote sorrowfully to me, 'My dream of Mildred is ended. I was not worthy of it.'"

A saving sense of humor was needed in those grim days; and in the midst of tragedies Mr. Higginson wrote to his mother: —

"One funny thing we have heard — a small child, endeavoring to describe a black man in the street, at last succeeded in stammering out, 'It's a Tom-Cabin!' and was quite satisfied that he had said the right thing."

IX

THE ATLANTIC ESSAYS

IN the midst of these public interests, Mr. Higginson did some of the best literary work of his life. In the winter of 1852, he dined with A. Bronson Alcott at James T. Fields', and Mr. Alcott amused himself by guessing, with astonishing success, Mr. Higginson's literary methods. Some of the features he had divined were the young author's habit of bridge-building, of composing much in the open air, and in separate sentences. This analysis the latter declared admirable, and reflected: "I might have said to him — in summer I bring home from the woods in my pockets flowers, lichens, chrysalids, nests, brown lizards, baby turtles . . . spiders' eggs . . . and scraps of written paper."

In November, 1853, Mr. F. H. Underwood wrote to Mr. Higginson, asking for aid from his pen for a new "literary and anti-slavery magazine" [the "Atlantic Monthly"], adding, "The articles will all be anonymous." In answer, he wrote: "I gladly contribute my name to the list of writers. . . . I am very much absorbed by necessary writing, speaking, and studies, and it is hard to do collateral work."

The essays which Mr. Higginson contributed to the early numbers of the "Atlantic" attracted a great deal of attention. "A Charge with Prince Rupert" was considered one of the most brilliant of these early papers; while the first one, "Saints and their Bodies," so impressed Dr. D. A. Sargent, afterward director of the Harvard Gymnasium, that he was led to adopt physical training as a profession.

In reference to one of the essays, "Woman and the Alphabet," [1] Rev. O. B. Frothingham wrote to ask the author if it was abstinence from soups — and salt — and pastry that enabled him to write such papers. "Tell me how much liquid," he asked, "I must exchange for such a flow of thoughts — how much pepper must be forsaken to leave such spice of wit? How much pie crust must be sacrificed for such a crispness of style?" This striking essay was at first considered by James Russell Lowell, then editor of the "Atlantic Monthly," as too radical for that magazine, but he afterwards decided to insert it.

In the diary of 1890, Mr. Higginson wrote, "Much gratified at letter from Miss Eastman telling me from Dr. —— that my 'Ought Women' was really

[1] This article was also published as a tract under the title "Ought Women to Learn the Alphabet?"

the seed of Smith College." A further tribute to the value of this essay came to the author in a letter from a thoughtful friend, who said, "I think it was one of the influences that opened Michigan University to women, and has now invited a woman professor on the same terms as men."

The anonymousness of the "Atlantic" essays caused some amusing mistakes, as when Mrs. C. H. Dall was many times congratulated on having written "Mademoiselle and her Campaigns." Finally she discovered the author, and wrote to him that no one except Macaulay could have written a better magazine article, "and his would have been half lies."

Mr. Higginson himself wrote to Harriet Prescott:

". . . I had more [letters] about 'April Days' than about anything I have written — sick women, young farmers, etc. One odd anonymous person, signing *Su Su*, sent me a root of double bloodroot postmarked "Snow's Store, Vt." It seemed pretty that bloodroot should come out of Snow's Store — though I suppose the donor never thought of it.

"I have a piece almost ready called 'My Outdoor Study,' based on a description of the lake where we go for boating. . . . These essays on Nature delight me so infinitely that all other themes seem tiresome beside them; I am sure that I have never come so near to Nature as during the last year, and therefore never so truly and deeply lived; and sometimes I feel so Exalted in this nearness that it seems as if I never could sorrow any more.

". . . I wrote from pure enjoyment, spending days and weeks on single sentences."

In the correspondence between Mr. Higginson and Mr. Underwood occurred this protest from the former: —

"I wish to be understood as giving a suppressed but audible *growl* at the chopping knife which made minced meat of my sentences. . . . It is something new. . . . I don't think I tend to such very long sentences; and it is n't pleasant to think that they belong to such a low order of organization that they can be chopped in the middle and each half wriggle away independently."

At thirty-six, in summing up his life, the author of these essays writes: —

"I do not expect any visible sphere or position except in literature — perhaps not there because I do not find that my facility grows so fast as my fastidiousness. . . . Certainly nothing short of severe starvation shall make me write and print what does not in some degree satisfy my own conception of literary execution."

And the joy he found in literature is thus expressed: —

"Nothing but Haydon's jubilees over his great 'canvas up' can describe my delight when I get a new budget of notes and materials into a fresh portfolio, and begin upon a new picture."

In regard to the publication of the book of sea poems, profanely called the "Marine Sam-Book" in distinction from the hymn-book compiled by Messrs. Longfellow and Johnson, and popularly known as the "Sam-Book," Mr. Higginson wrote to a friend: —

"The best result of S. L.'s [Samuel Longfellow] visit [to Europe] was to transform Thalatta from a past vision to a future reality. . . . We planned it six years ago and now Europe has revived it all in Sam and he has proposed it once more to James T. Fields (Ticknor & Co.) and that bold youth (also fresh from Europe, these two having visited the Brownings together) *consented*. So the book is to begin to be printed in February and between now and then what copying and debating and selecting!"

In 1859, the famous "Atlantic" dinner was given to Mrs. Stowe, which Colonel Higginson has described in "Cheerful Yesterdays." To his mother he thus reported a conversation on this occasion with Dr. Holmes: —

"He [Holmes] was very pleasant and cordial to me, but turned upon me when I refused a cigar. 'What,' said he, 'you don't smoke?' 'No,' said I. 'Then,' said he, 'you unquestionably chew the betel-nut.' I told him I was fond of nuts and also of beetles, but preferred my botany and entomology separate. 'Ah,' said he, 'but everybody must have *some* narcotic, if you don't chew the betel-nut, you take opium pills or laudanum in some form.' I assured him I took no pills but homœopathic and those rarely."

The incessant activity of these years wore even on Mr. Higginson's wonderful physique and he wrote: —

"I suppose that even I myself can hardly realize how much overworked I have been this winter — so much writing and speaking and visiting have I had to do (studying has been almost suspended) — to say nothing of travelling for various objects and the constant care of my wife who has scarcely ever needed more attention. . . .

"We suspended housekeeping awhile, for my wife's health, and have been boarding since New Year's at the queerest old rambling Hotel, one of the few old things in Worcester. . . .

"We are so very nicely placed here at the Lincoln House, M. is quite delighted. We have a pleasant parlor on Elm St. with a little bedroom and a large closet; it fronts South and the house is brick, so it is perfectly warm and M. has stood a snowstorm without a shudder. . . . There is a girl with a violent piano below, a man with a violent nose beside us, and two youths over our heads who apparently sleep in boots."

Winter lecturing with all its drawbacks afforded a change of scene. One of his journeys took Mr. Higginson to Maine, and he wrote from Orono: —

"Last night I drove from Bangor with a buffalo coat on, over wonderful sleighing and felt quite like a backwoodsman. Bangor streets are crowded with uncouth sledges and teams, and at the doors of the shops hang abundant moccasins and long red leggins and even snowshoes. To-day I am to have a lesson in these from Mr. L. and ride to where I can see Indians and Katahdin."

This glimpse of "the great lonely Katahdin," as he describes that mountain, led the next year to a nearer acquaintance; for in 1855 the Worcester parson, accompanied by a few of his friends, made the ascent of Mount Katahdin. This letter to Mrs. Higginson was written from Bangor: —

"I am writing behind the bar; many men here — they come up and read our names in the book and wonder what brings so many here from Worcester. One says, 'Higginson. He's the great abolitionist from Worcester, he who had the fuss in the U.S. Court — is that Theo. Brown beneath? *It ought to be Theodore Parker.*'"

And in the delight which this excursion gave him, he exclaimed: — "I am very happy and feel ready to mount up with wings as eagles."

Mr. Higginson wrote an account of this expedition

for "Putnam's Magazine," the article purporting to be written by a woman. The author amused himself by sending a copy to each member of the party, that they might guess its origin.

"We did have a charming time on the trip to Mount Katahdin," he wrote. "The 30 miles by water on our return, shooting the rapids, were the most exciting experiences I ever yet had."

A later visit to Maine was of a different nature, for he spoke at Bangor on "'Kansas and the Union,' the former being the bait and the latter the hook. I had a superb audience . . . and preached Disunion to 1500 people for $50 — and no hisses."

The Higginsons spent several vacations at Pigeon Cove, a wild, rocky sea-place on the North Shore. When they summered one season at the town of Princeton, they found quarters at the Post-Office. This seemed to Mr. Higginson a "funny" place to stay, as he fancied the mattresses would be made of "exhausted mail-bags." From Pigeon Cove, he wrote to a young author: —

"I enjoy the freedom of my life very much, and after having my thoughts poured regularly into one channel every week for so long, it is perfectly delightful to let them wander in other directions. . . .

"The bathing is a regeneration of existence every day. . . . If you could put on a boy's jacket and go to sea, before the mast, for a year, it would put a vitality into your inkstand that would last your life time. . . . Every month makes me think less, relatively, of books, and more of life. Indeed one gets but little out of books till we have taught them to know their places.

". . . I spent this morning wading after them [water-lilies] in a pond with two young ladies aged 10."

Involved again in the daily routine of parish work, Mr. Higginson felt the need of more leisure for thought and study and told his mother: —

"I yesterday propounded an arrangement to the Free Church people, by which I am to have — don't laugh — nothing less than a colleague. I cannot always go on at the rate I have been lately working. . . . The plan is that Wasson should so come and do the greater part of the preaching, taking of course a good part of the salary; this will leave me time for preaching, lecturing and writing, and by this I can make up a sufficient income, for the present at least. . . . In fact, my natural activity is so great, that I have to contrive means to keep myself out of work."

An unexpected break in this too laborious life came in the autumn of 1855, when the Higginsons sailed for Fayal for Mrs. Higginson's health. They spent the winter there, and Mr. Wasson took charge of the Free Church during this absence. Fayal proved to be more wonderful to the travellers than any dream, every inch of surface and each individual person being entirely different from anything they had seen before. In Mr. Higginson's "Atlantic" paper, "Fayal and the Portuguese" (1860), these strange experiences were described. And it was in Fayal that Mr. Higginson wrote his essay called the "Sympathy of Religions." This paper was afterwards read by the author before the Free Religious Association in Boston, and later before the Parliament of Religions at Chicago in 1893. It was reprinted in England and also translated into French.

While in Fayal, he was delighted to receive "a charming letter from Agassiz, begging me to collect corals, starfishes, etc., of which I already have a store." And after his return, he reported: —

"I spent part of yesterday with Prof. Agassiz and enjoyed it very much, and he was delighted with my collection from the Azores especially the sea-urchins, of which he found eight species, some of them new. Some of the things he is to return to me, labelled, for the [Worcester] Natural History Society."

The home-coming from Fayal Mr. Higginson described in this letter to his mother: —

"We arrived last night at $9\frac{1}{2}$ [June, 1856] after a three weeks' passage. . . .

"The world looks very odd, people talking English,

lighted shops last night, and *horses*. To-day everybody with bonnets and *shoes!!* People so well dressed, so intelligent, and so *sick* — so unlike the robust baseness of Fayal and Pico. And the foliage is so inexpressibly beautiful. Houses agonizingly *warm*, after the fireless rooms of Fayal, and the chilly ocean."

X

A RIDE THROUGH KANSAS

THE returned pastor was at once launched into exciting scenes. The assault on Charles Sumner in the Senate Chamber had but just occurred, and the contest between the free and slave States for the possession of the Territory of Kansas was at its height. There was then a reign of terror along the Kansas border, the advocates of slavery victimizing the Free-State settlers. An enthusiastic meeting was held in Worcester to welcome Mr. Higginson home and promote emigration to Kansas, and an earnest appeal was made for volunteers, rifles, and blankets in aid of the Free-State emigrants against whom the Missouri River was blockaded. "It is amazing," wrote the impatient clergyman, "how sluggish people have been in acting for Kansas. Nobody seems to feel the need of promptness or of a better organization."

A committee, of which Mr. Higginson was a member, was appointed to arrange for the passage and equipment of emigrants to Kansas. In June, 1856, he was sent to Chicago and St. Louis to give aid and advice to a party from Massachusetts who, to quote a newspaper account, "had fallen among thieves." From Alton, Illinois, he wrote to his wife, "To-morrow I expect to meet our disarmed troops in St. Louis — poor things. I shall send them on through Iowa, where Stowell has gone before them." At St. Louis, Mr. Higginson chartered a steamboat to take the party up the Mississippi to Davenport, Iowa. This party, led by a certain Dr. Cutter, had been charged by a Missouri paper with cowardice. To this charge Mr. Higginson responded in the Boston "Journal": "I have seen frightened men, in Massachusetts and elsewhere, and I never saw men look less like them than did Dr. Cutter's party. I went out to St. Louis partly to see how they had stood fire, and partly to give them instructions for the future. My instructions were, if they met a party of Missourians not larger than five to one, to fight to the last rather than surrender." This party of forty men had surrendered to three thousand of the enemy by whom they were disarmed and turned back.

"I almost hoped to hear," he wrote to the "Tribune," "that some of their lives had been sacrificed, for it seems as if nothing but that would arouse the Eastern States to act. This seems a terrible thing to say, but these are terrible times." Of the party led by Stowell, a Worcester man who was conspicuous in the Anthony Burns affair, Mr. Higginson said in the same letter: —

"Do you know that they came and absolutely begged of me to let them go up the Missouri River . . . pledging themselves to die, if need be, but to redeem the honor of Massachusetts. From the bottom of my heart I felt with them; one word from me would have done it, but I did not feel authorized to speak that word, and therefore sent them on by the other route. Had they gone by the river I should have gone with them, for I never found anything harder than it would be to quit this river, believing, as I do, that there are plans practicable by which the passage might yet be opened to free emigrants."

In these frequent articles for the newspapers, Mr. Higginson not only reported the progress of the different groups of emigrants, but called for funds. Soon after his return to Worcester, the city hall was crowded with eager listeners to hear the report of his trip and an account of the exciting events which were transpiring on the Missouri River. He wrote to his mother: —

"Our parties are getting safely on beyond Iowa City — there is stage connection now to the Missouri River below Council Bluffs — thence about 100 miles on foot to Topeka. . . .

"Beneath the stir of civil war we keep up a more perfectly placid domestic existence than ever before.

. . . We make little walks and visits in the cool of the evening, water our seeds, dig round the fruit trees, train our vines and plan for improving rose-bushes. The sunsets never were so lovely here; and copious dishes of currants (succeeding cherries) par-tially console us for the disasters of the times. . . .

"I am particularly popular in private just now, for what I am doing about Kansas, and it is rather pathetic to have them thank me for doing what they ought to have taken hold of, themselves, but have not. . . .

"I am probably to be Agent for Kansas parties from New England *officially*, which I have hitherto been unofficially — this will save me trouble by putting funds in my hands. . . .

"A party left Boston for Kansas on Tuesday — 20 were from Maine and the strongest looking men I ever saw — mostly in red shirts."

In September Mr. Higginson was made an agent of the Kansas National Committee, and in this capacity went to Kansas to superintend the move-ments of these very Maine lumbermen. In his let-ters to the New York "Tribune" describing this trip, and later printed in a little pamphlet called "A Ride Through Kansas," he says: —

"Coming from a land where millionaires think themselves generous in giving fifty dollars to Kansas, I converse daily with men who have sacrificed all their property in its service, and are ready at any hour to add their lives."

From Nebraska City, he wrote (September, 1856): —

"I have myself bought up for the emigrants all the cowhide boots to be found in town (except extra sizes) and nearly all the flannel shirts and blankets. . . .

"At present no person, without actually travelling across Iowa, can appreciate the injury done by the closing of the Missouri River. Emigrants must toil, week after week, beneath a burning sun, over the parched and endless 'rolling prairie,' sometimes seeing no house for a day or two together, camping often without wood, and sometimes without water, and obliged to carry with them every eatable they use. It is no wonder that they often fall sick on the way; and when I consider how infinitely weary were even my four days and nights of staging (after as many more of railroad travel), I can only wonder at the patience and fortitude which the present emigrants have shown.

"As soon as one approaches the Missouri River, even in Iowa and Nebraska, he begins to feel as if he were in France or Austria. Men are very cautious in defining their position, and wait to hear what others will say. Then, perhaps, their tongues are slightly loosed, if they think there are no spies about them. But it is no slight risk when a man may have to pay with his life, further down the river, for a free word, spoken at Council Bluffs or Sidney, both Pro-Slavery towns.

"The first night I spent in this place, it seemed as

if a symbolical pageant had been got up to remind me where I was. I sat writing by an open window in the beautiful moonlight. A party of boys in the street were shouting and screeching, playing 'Border Ruffian,' and 'storming a fort.' In a building beyond, two very inexperienced performers played martial tunes with a drum and fife. Within, the small tavern rocked with the music and dancing of a border ball. Thus I sat between tragedy and comedy."

To his mother the faithful son wrote from the same town: —

"This is a queer little cluster of houses, and a very crowded little tavern — nothing very abundant but watermelons which every body eats all day. . . . We hear often from Kansas, they are not in distress actually, nor besieged, and the invaders seem just now rather discouraged. We shall have a strong mounted escort to lead us in, a week hence, and probably not danger enough to make it exciting. There is also perfectly safe exit this way, so my spirit of adventure is a little checked. But along the lower river towns the Missourians have it all their own way and we are constantly seeing men who have been plundered of all they possess."

The traveller reported to his wife: —

"I have been for a week in a forlorn little town, arranging a train of emigrants to go into Kansas, armed and equipped as the law forbids.

". . . I am very busy, but lead a crowded, dusty,

dirty life — and though death for freedom is all very fine, when it comes to dirt for freedom, the sacrifice becomes unexpectedly hard."

Here he encountered General "Jim" Lane, commanding the "Free-State Forces of Kansas," but then retreating by order of Governor Geary. From the supplies sent from the East, Mr. Higginson helped to re-clothe the General's band, and was amused at receiving from the guerrilla leader a position on his staff with the title of Brigadier-General, an honor liberally conferred by Lane on sympathizers with the Free-State cause.

To his mother he wrote: —

"A new and important town in Kansas is threatened with the name of Quindaro, which means a Bundle of Sticks, after the Indian wife of the projector. This I deprecate and suggest Quincy — after old Josiah, as a substitute. Also I have urged your name of Sumner. The trouble of these family names is that by and by there must be Christian names to distinguish them, there will be so many. Fancy a town of South-Wendell Phillips or Wm. Lloyd-Garrison-4-corners, or Rev. Gen. Thos. Wentworth Higginson Centre!"

On September 24, Mr. Higginson wrote home from Topeka: —

"I got here yesterday afternoon after six days' ride and walk (chiefly the former) across the prairies of Kansas. A few of the fort teams came with me, — the rest of the train will be in to-day and to-morrow. . . . We camped out five nights which I enjoyed on the whole, though only in the last night did we have wood enough for the Maine style of tent, open toward the fire. Imagine me also patrolling as one of the guard for an hour every night, in high boots amid the dewy grass, rifle in hand and revolver in belt. But nobody ever came and we never had any danger. Only once, in the day time, the whole company charged upon a band of extremely nude Indians, taking them for Missourians. . . .

"We had in our camps some twenty tents and thirty wagons; including parties from Maine, Mass., Vt., Illinois, etc., and six large families from Indiana. On the other hand, we met quite as many going out of Kansas, some to avoid arrest, others from poverty. . . . At this moment, moreover, there are nineteen wagons on the two sides of the river here, moving away in despair.

". . . The people are braver than anything I ever dreamed of, and when they once adopt the policy of resistance to the United States will do it. But they will wait till after election first.

"This winter there will be much suffering, but not from the absence of food, only the money to buy it. All employment has been suspended and still is so."

The story is continued from "A Ride Through Kansas": —

"It was like entering Hungary just after the

treachery of Görgey. Each had his story to tell of arrests and tyrannies; how a Pro-Slavery witness had only to point at a man as identified with any measure of public defence, and he was seized at once. Several whom we met had been arrested in person, herded with a hundred others, like cattle, on the bare prairie, been scantily fed once a day, and escaped by rolling half a mile through the grass while the sentinels' backs were turned. The bravest young men of Lawrence were put under arrest, charged with treason, murder, arson, robbery, and what not; while not a Pro-Slavery man was seized. This was the penalty they had to pay for defending themselves vigorously at last, and clearing their own soil from the invading Missourians. 'The worst enemy Kansas had ever had,' they pronounced Governor Geary to be; and they were going into Iowa to wait for better times. 'Will you give up Kansas?' I asked. 'Never!' was the reply from bronzed and bearded lips, stern and terrible as the weapons that hung to the saddle-bow. 'We are scattered, starved, hunted, half-naked, but we are not conquered *yet.*'

"Some of these were young men, whom I had seen go from prosperous homes, well clothed and cared for. I had since heard of them performing acts of heroic courage in this summer's battles. Lane had praised them to me, and declared that there never was such courage in the world as that of the Free-State men of Kansas. 'I saw one of them,' said he, 'ride up alone within thirty yards of a body of a hundred and fifty men, during an engagement, take deliberate aim, and bring one down.' I now saw that very man — that boy rather, a Worcester boy — retreating from his adopted country, hungry, ragged, and almost barefooted, walking wearily on, with others hunted like himself, while some, who had been less scrupulous, rode by on horses which they had plundered from the Missourians, who had first plundered them."

Mrs. Higginson wrote to Brattleboro that the news from Kansas grew worse every day, and after describing various household economies she said, "Money is very scarce, and everything goes to Kansas, I believe." Then she told of a "Kansas Sewing Circle which is to meet *every* P.M. . . . Mrs. Le B. has begun the first pair of pants! . . . Martha Le B. says she shall sew all day for Kansas and the evenings for Anti-Slavery fair!"

Meantime, the traveller wrote from Lawrence, September 28, to his friend, Dr. Seth Rogers (afterward surgeon of his regiment) : —

"Yesterday morning I waked at Topeka and found the house surrounded by dragoons. To my amazement, on going out, the Captain addressed me by name. . . . He was very cordial, but their office was to arrest the leaders of the party just arrived if they proved to be a military company. They were happily already satisfied that we were not, and this was merely a matter of form; and they also wanted Redpath, the reported leader of the

party, and not me. Finally Col. Preston, the young
Virginia Marshal, decided to arrest no one, and he,
Redpath, Gov. Robinson, and I rode down in one
carriage to Gov. Geary at Lecompton, and after
some talk with the pompous, foolish, conceited,
obstinate Governor were honorably discharged. If
they had had wit to discover the Sharp's rifles and
cannon we brought in with us, we should all have
been arrested. . . .

"Lawrence is a beautiful place and this Kansas
People is glorious — so brave and patient and perfectly buoyant, no one depressed, even after 3 weeks
of green corn and squash. There has been and is
suffering here, and the greatest need is now of money
in *Kansas*, to keep people from moving out. Half of
those who come in as emigrants go out again, but
these old settlers *must* be kept here.

"Money can now buy flour here cheaper than it
can be sent in — say at $5 per 100 lbs. Clothing
should be forwarded instantly before the river is
closed again, but money is the great need.

"I shall stay till over election because there may
be trouble then. That is Monday Oct. 6. Next day
I shall leave and try to get home (by the river) on
the following Sunday. At any rate by the Convention of Oct. 14, which I see advertised to-day. I
am perfectly well and would not have missed this
visit for hundreds of dollars. . . .

"Two of the best Worcester Emigrants are among
the prisoners confined at Lecompton. They were
at first very badly treated, but are said to be better
off now. Gov. Geary promised us yesterday that he

would see that they had blankets. To-morrow I shall see them myself if possible."

The following day, Mr. Higginson visited the prisoners at Lecompton and found that most of them were young men, "the flower of the youth of Lawrence." One of the guards he described as "an evil-looking scoundrel with fixed bayonet," and said: "It is singular how much alike all Slavery's officials look. I saw half a dozen times repeated the familiar features of my Boston friend, Mr. Asa O. Butman." Relating the suffering of the new settlers, Mr. Higginson quoted a man whom he had known at the East, who had a wife and nine children, but who said, "I have in my house no meat, no flour, no meal, no potatoes, no money to buy them, no prospect of a dollar; but *I'll live or die in Kansas!*" And he added, "Such is the spirit of multitudes, many of whom are as badly off as this man."

In a letter to the "Tribune," dated Lawrence, October 4, Mr. Higginson said: —

"Last Sunday I preached in this place (though I must say that I am commonly known here by a title which is elsewhere considered incompatible with even the Church Militant). It was quite an occasion; and I took for my text the one employed by Rev. John Martin the Sunday after he fought at Bunker Hill — Neh. iv, 14; 'Be not ye afraid of them; remember the Lord, which is great and terrible, and fight for your brethren, your sons and your daughters, your wives and your houses.'"

A Kansas correspondent of the "Christian Register" of September 26, 1857, heard Mr. Higginson preach on that occasion and thus described the event: —

"The place where we congregated was a low chamber over a store, built up of rough boards and lined with cloth tacked to the walls in lieu of plastering. The sacred desk was an impromptu affair made of a packing box covered with buffalo robes, while the Bible rested on a smaller box covered with a coarse blanket. I shall never forget how solemn and appropriate the 4th chapter of Nehemiah seemed as Mr. H. read it so impressively in his opening service. . . . Every word of the excellent sermon which followed was full of magnetic power to me. It revived my drooping spirits, quickened my energies, and imparted some of the faith, hope and strength I had so long needed."

Mr. Higginson spoke again at Lawrence October 4, and the next day went to Leavenworth to witness a "Border Ruffian election." On McCarty's doorsteps (the principal tavern in the town) he overheard some interesting remarks which he thus related: —

"Said one man, just from Lecompton, 'Tell you what, we've found out one thing, there's a preacher

going about here preaching politics.' 'Fact?' and
'Is that so?' was echoed with virtuous indignation
on all sides. 'That's so,' continued he, 'and he fixes
it this way; first, he has his text and preaches religion; then he drops that and pitches into politics;
and then he drops that, too, and begins about the
sufferin' niggers' (with ineffable contempt); 'and
what's more, he's here in Leavenworth now.'
'What's his name?' exclaimed several eagerly. 'Just
what I don't know,' was the sorrowful reply; 'and
I should n't know him if I saw him; but he's here,
boys, and in a day or two there'll be some gentlemen
here that know him.' (N.B. At my last speech
in Lawrence, I was warned that three Missouri spies
were present.) 'It's well we've got him here, to
take care of him,' said one. 'Won't our boys enjoy
running him out of town?' added another, affectionately; while I listened with pleased attention,
thinking that I might, perhaps, afford useful information. But the 'gentlemen' have not yet appeared,
or else are in search of higher game."

Disunion still seemed to the more radical thinkers
the only cure for the prevailing troubles. On his
return trip from the afflicted territory Mr. Higginson
wrote:—

"STEAMBOAT 'CATARACT,'
aground on a bank in the Missouri River,
Oct. 9th, 1856.

"My best hope is that the contest may be at once
transferred to more favorable soil, Nebraska or
Iowa, and result in a disruption of the Union; for I

am sure that the disease is too deep for cure without amputation.

"I left here on Sept. 9th for six weeks; reached Nebraska City through Iowa in ten days, a weary stage journey. Staid nine days in and near Nebraska City, organizing and directing for a train of 150 emigrants, and then travelled with them to Topeka in six days, camping at night; since then I have been in Topeka, Lecompton, Lenora and Leavenworth. . . . Tell Sam I had an Allen's Rifle with me which is an improvement on Sharp's, but had no occasion to shoot anything with it except a superb hawk, whose wings I carry home as a Kansas trophy. Never have I been in any special danger, except that they talked of lynching me in Leavenworth, whither I went to witness an election; I was the only person in town who knew my name or person; but I was a minister that had been 'preaching politics'; . . . as however I gave no information, two of them shot each other instead, just as our boat left the wharf."

It is not strange that a sarcastic Buffalo paper, commenting on this errand of the Reverend Mr. Higginson's, said, "We do not know what denomination of the gospel of peace claims him."

At the twenty-fifth anniversary festival of the formation of the Massachusetts Anti-Slavery Society, Mr. Higginson thus spoke of his western visit: —

"I found a great deal in Kansas. . . . But I did not go there even to see an underground railroad,

THOMAS WENTWORTH HIGGINSON, 1857

for I had seen that in Massachusetts. I wanted to
see something above the ground. All my life I had
been a citizen of a Republic where I had seen
my fellow-citizens retreating, and retreating, and
retreating, before the Slave Power, and I heard
that away off, a thousand miles west, there was one
town where men had made their stand, and said to
Slavery, 'Thus far, but no farther.' I went the
thousand miles to see it, and saw it. I saw there the
American Revolution, and every great Revolution
of bygone days in still living progress. I was tired of
reading of Leonidas; I wanted to see him. I was
tired of reading of Lafayette; I wanted to see him.
I saw in Kansas the history of the past, clothed in
living flesh before me."

In January, 1857, a call was issued for a "State
Disunion Convention" to consider the expediency
of a separation between free and slave States, and
Mr. Higginson's name led the signatures. This meet-
ing was followed the next July by a call for a National
Convention which was signed by Wendell Phillips,
William Lloyd Garrison, Higginson, and 6400 others.
This proposed convention, however, was never held.

Some of his reasons for belief in disunion, Mr.
Higginson expressed in a letter to Harriet Prescott,
January, 1861: —

"I cannot agree with you and Mr. Seward about
the Union, because I think that the Free States
without the Slave will instantly command an influ-

ence, moral and material, which is denied us now. You know that even now the credit of Massachusetts Stocks is far higher in Europe than [that] of United States Stocks, and this symbolizes everything. A rough swearing mate of a vessel once told me he never dared own himself an American abroad, because he was so reproached in every port with slavery."

While in St. Louis in 1856, Mr. Higginson attended the slave market, and wrote the following description of the scene under the title "Assorted Lots of 'Young Negroes." This was printed in the "Tribune" at the time and widely copied, both in America and in England.

"I have before been in other slave States, but never in Missouri. The first thing that struck me on arriving in this city was the apparent absence of the Negro race. In a crowd of a thousand persons on the levee this morning, assembled to witness the burning of six steamboats, I could not count ten black faces. I was told, in explanation, that the colored people were all 'uptown,' not in the business part of the city.

"So, too, I searched the newspapers for slave advertisements, though I knew this city not to be a great mart for those commodities like Richmond; but in vain. At last, in a corner of the 'Republican,' I discovered the following: —

"'Negroes Wanted. — I wish to purchase a large lot of Negroes, expressly for the Louisiana 'and

Mississippi market, for which I will pay the highest cash prices. All those who have Negroes for sale would do well to give me a call. I can always be seen at the City Hotel, or at Mr. Thompson's Negro-yard, No. 67, Locust St., St. Louis, Mo.

"'JOHN MATTINGLY.'

. . . .

"'Negroes wanted and for sale. — Wanted and for sale Negroes of all kinds, at my office, No. 67, Locust St., between 2d and 3d Sts., St. Louis, Mo. Having a good and safe yard to board and keep Negroes, I will buy and sell on commission as low as any other house in this city. Please to give me a call.

"'CORBIN THOMPSON.'

"I took an early opportunity to call on Mr. Corbin Thompson. I found him in the doorway of a little wooden office, like a livery-stable office in one of our cities; he being a large, lounging, good-natured looking man, not unlike a reputable stable-keeper in appearance and manner. Inside his stable, alas! I saw his dusky 'stock,' and he readily acceded to my desire to take a nearer look at them.

"Behind the little office there was a little dark room, behind that a little kitchen, opening into a dirty little yard. This yard was surrounded by high brick walls, varied by other walls made of old iron plates, reaching twenty feet high. These various places were all swarming with Negroes, dirty and clean, from six years old to forty — perhaps two dozen in all, the majority being children under fourteen.

"'Fat and sleek as Harry Clay's,' said my conductor, patting one on the head patriarchally.

"Most of them had small paper fans, which they used violently. This little article of comfort looked very odd, amid such squalid raggedness as most of them showed. One was cooking, two or three washing, and two playing euchre with a filthy pack of cards. The sun shone down intensely hot (it was noon) in the little brick yard, and they sat, lounged, or lay about, only the children seeming lively.

"I talked a little with them, and they answered, some quietly, some with that mixture of obsequiousness and impudence so common among slaves. Mr. Thompson answered all questions very readily. The 'Negroes' or 'Niggers,' he said (seldom employing the Virginia phrases 'servants' or 'people'), came mostly from Missouri or Virginia, and were with him but a little while. 'Buy when I can and sell when I can, that's my way; and never ask no questions, only in the way of trade. At this season, get a good many from travellers.'

"On inquiry, he explained this mystery by adding that it was not uncommon for families visiting Northern watering-places to bring with them a likely boy or girl, and sell them to pay the expenses of the jaunt! This is a feature of the patriarchal institution which I think has escaped Mrs. Stowe. Hereafter I shall never see a Southern heiress at Newport without fancying I read on her ball-dress the names of the 'likely boy or girl' who was sold for it. 'As for yonder Sambo and Dinah' (I meditated), 'no doubt, young Bulford Dashaway, Esq., is at this moment driving them out to Saratoga Lake, as a pair of blood-horses. O Miss Caroline Pettitoes, of Fifth Avenue, how odd it would be if, as you sit superb by his side, those four-legged cattle suddenly resumed the squalid two-legged condition in which I now behold them, in Thompson's Negro-yard, No. 67, Locust Street.'

"I strolled back into the front office and sat down to see if anything turned up. The thing that turned up was a rather handsome, suburban-looking two-horse carriage, out of which stepped lazily a small, spare, gentlemanly man, evidently a favored patron of my host. After a moment's private talk Thompson went out, while the gentleman said abruptly to me, 'Well, it is all bad enough, housekeeping, marketing, and all, but I'm — if servants ain't the worst of all.' We then talked a little, and I found him the pleasantest type of a Southerner — courteous, kind, simple, a little imperious — finally, a man of property, member of the city Government, and living a little out of town.

"Thompson came in and shook his head. 'Can't let Negroes to anybody, Mr. ——. Glad to sell, anyhow.'

"'Got a good article of a small girl?' said the gentleman suddenly.

"'Martha!' shouted the slave-dealer, and presently three good articles, aged eleven, nine, and seven, came trotting in. I had not seen them before. Nice little pink frocks, not very dirty — barefooted, of course, but apparently well taken care of, and evidently sisters. With some manœuvring, they were arranged in a line before my new acquaintance, the purchaser.

"He fixed his eyes on Sue, a black marble statue, aged seven. Nothing could have been kinder than Mr. ——'s manner in addressing the little thing. 'Will you like to come and live with me, and have some little girls to play with?'

"(It is a little patriarchal, I said. That kind voice would win any child.)

"I looked to see the merry African smile on the child's face. But no smile came. There was a moment's pause.

"'Speak up, child,' said the merchant roughly. But she did n't speak up, nor look up, either. Down went the black marble face, drooping down, down, till the chin rested on the breast of the little pink frock. Down, down came one big tear, and then another over the black marble cheeks; and then the poor little wretch turned away to the wall, and burst into as hearty an agony of tears as your little idol Susy, or yours (my good New-England mother), might give way to, at such an offer from the very kindest man who ever chewed tobacco in the streets of Missouri!

"Human nature is a rather unconquerable thing, after all, is n't it?

"My kind purchaser looked annoyed, and turned away. The slave-trader gave an ominous look to the poor child, such as I had not seen on his face before. 'Beg pardon, sir' (said he gruffly); 'they only came from Virginia yesterday, and have n't learnt how to treat gentlemen yet' (with an emphasis).

"Poor little Sue!

"The purchaser next turned to Martha, the elder sister, a bright Topsy-looking thing.

"'What's that on her cheek,' he asked, pointing to a sort of scar or streak of paleness. Martha grinned.

"'Somebody's whacked her chops, most likely,' said the slave-trader, coolly (in whose face I saw nothing good-natured after that). Nothing more was said about it.

"The gentleman drew the child to him, felt the muscles of her arm, and questioned her a little. Her price was 700 dollars, and little Sue's 450 dollars.

"'Well, Martha,' said he at last, 'would n't you like to go with me and have a pleasant home?'

"Strange to say, the African smile left Martha's merry face, too. 'Please, sir,' said she, 'I wish I could stay with my mother.'

"'Confound the girls,' said the good-natured purchaser, turning to me in despair; 'they must be sold to somebody, you know. Of course, I can't buy the whole of them, and the mother, too.' Of course not; and there was the whole story in a nutshell.

"'Nonsense, gals,' said Thompson; 'your mother'll be up here, maybe, some day.' (Pleasant prospect, in the lottery of life, for three 'articles' under twelve years.)

"On inquiry it appeared that the mother was in Virginia, and might or might not be sent to St. Louis for sale. The intention was, however, to sell the children in a day or two, together or separately, or else to send them south with Mr. Mattingly.

"To avert this, I hoped earnestly that my good-
natured friend would buy one or more of the poor
things. 'For,' said he to me, 'I mean to bring her up
well. She'll be a pet for the children — black or
white it will make no difference — and while I live
I shan't sell her — that is while it is possible to help
it.' (A formidable reservation, considering the condition of most Southern estates.)

"The little pink frocks were ordered to stand off,
and a bargain was finally struck for Martha, quite
to Mr. Thompson's chagrin, who evidently hoped to
sell Sue, and would, no doubt, have done so, but for
her ignorance 'how to treat gentlemen.'

"'Girl is sound, I suppose?' carelessly inquired
the purchaser.

"'Wind and limb,' responded the trader. 'But
strip her naked and examine every inch of her, if you
wish,' he quickly added; 'I never have any disguises
with my customers.'

"So ended the bargain, and I presently took my
leave. I had one last glance at little Sue. It is not
long since I set foot on the floating wreck of an
unknown vessel at sea, and then left it drifting
away in the darkness alone. But it was sadder to
me to think of that little wreck of babyhood drifting off alone into the ocean of Southern crime and
despair.

"St. Louis must unquestionably be a very religious
place, however, for in returning to my hotel I passed
a church with inscriptions in four different languages.
There was Jehovah in Hebrew, 'Deo Uno et Trino,'
'In honorem S. Ludovici.' Finally in English and

French, 'My house shall be called the house of prayer,' with the rest of the sentence, in both cases, omitted. Singular accident, is n't it?

"I forgot to mention that I asked Mr. Thompson, out of the dozen children in his 'yard,' how many had their parents or mothers with them. 'Not one,' he answered, as if rather surprised at the question; 'I take 'em as they come, in lots. Hardly ever have a family.'

"'I suppose you would rather keep a family together?' I put in, suggestively.

"'Yes,' he answered carelessly. 'Can't think much about that, though. Have to shut up shop pretty quick, if I did. Have to take 'em as they come.'

"This was evident enough, and I only insert it in the faint hope of enlightening the minds of those verdant innocents who still believe that the separation of families is a rare occurrence, when every New Orleans newspaper contains a dozen advertisements of 'Assorted lots of young Negroes.'"

XI

JOHN BROWN AND THE CALL TO ARMS

ALTHOUGH John Brown's name was familiar to all
who were interested in the Kansas struggle, Mr.
Higginson's first interview with him was in the
winter of 1858. At this time Brown wrote to him
saying, "I have been told that you are both a true
man and a true Abolitionist, and I partly believe the
whole story." In this letter, he asked aid for what
he called "secret service," stating that he should
need from five to eight hundred dollars within sixty
days, "for the *perfecting* of BY FAR the most *important* undertaking of my whole life." Mr. Higginson
asked if this project was connected with the underground railway and received this reply: "Rail-Road
business on a somewhat extended scale is the iden-
tical object for which I am trying to get means."
This letter, dated February 12, contained an urgent
invitation to meet John Brown with Sanborn and
others at Peterborough, New Hampshire. Not being
able to do this, Mr. Higginson met Brown in Boston
in March. The impression made on him as described
in "Cheerful Yesterdays" was that of simply "a
high-minded, unselfish, belated Covenanter."

The plan which Brown proposed was to get together bands of fugitive slaves in Virginia and either colonize them in the mountain fastnesses or guide them to Canada. In this project Mr. Higginson and his friends were willing to coöperate and to help raise the needed money. "I am always ready," Higginson wrote to John Brown, "to invest money in treason, but at present have none to invest."

At this juncture a certain Hugh Forbes, who had drilled John Brown and his men in guerrilla warfare, threatened to expose his plans unless unreasonable demands for money could be met. Thereupon, the majority of Brown's Boston advisers advocated postponing the whole affair until the next winter or spring. This proposed delay made Mr. Higginson very impatient, and he wrote to Brown, May 7, "I utterly protest against any postponement." He also wrote in the same vein to Theodore Parker, saying, "If I had the wherewithal, I would buy out the other stockholders and tell our veteran to go on." To Brown again, May 18, he wrote, "I, for one, am willing to leave the whole matter to you. . . . The sum raised by me was all I can possibly provide, but I have written to the others, strongly urging them not to give up the ship." When Mr. Higginson talked this matter over with Brown, meeting him in Boston again about June 1, the latter sympathized with this opposition to delay, and said, to quote a letter of Higginson's describing the interview, "If he [Brown] had the means he would not lose a day. At my wondering that the others did not agree with us, he said the reason was *they were not men of action*. But the sly old veteran added he had not said this to them." A scrap of paper pasted on the letter adds: "I went to see Dr. Howe and found that things had ended far better than I supposed. The Kansas committee had put some $500 in gold into his [Brown] hands and all the arms with only the understanding that he should go to Kansas and then be left to his own discretion. He went off in good spirits."

In October, 1858, Sanborn wrote to the Worcester clergyman that Brown was anxious about future operations, and asked if Higginson could do anything for him before the following spring. In March, 1859, and again in April, Sanborn appealed to Higginson for more funds; and May 1, the latter wrote to Brown that he had drawn so largely for similar purposes in the past few years he could raise no more money. "My own loss of confidence," he added, "is also in the way — loss of confidence not in you, but in the others who are concerned in the measure. Those who were so easily disheartened last spring may be deterred now. . . . Did I follow only my own inclination, without thinking of other ties, I should join you in person, if I could not in purse." And he declared that he longed to see Brown "set free from timid advisers." In June, Sanborn wrote to Higginson that John Brown had set out on his expedition, having secured some eight hundred dollars; and September 4, he again wrote, beseeching him to raise fifty dollars if possible.

After the sudden defeat of Brown's enterprise, followed by his arrest and imprisonment, most of the friends who had been active in assisting his project went temporarily to Canada or to Europe to avoid threatened prosecution, but Mr. Higginson stood his ground, declaring it a duty " to at least give him [Brown] their moral support on the witness stand."

The next step was the attempt to provide able counsel for Brown and his fellow-prisoners. A circular was printed, November 2, 1859, asking for contributions to this end and signed by S. E. Sewall, Dr. Howe, R. W. Emerson, and T. W. Higginson. Appended to the circular, which is preserved in the Boston Public Library, is this note in Mr. Higginson's handwriting and signed by him: "An expense of about $1000 is already incurred for counsel. Mrs. Brown must also be aided to join her husband, and her two widowed daughters-in-law, aged 20 and 16, need help greatly." Meetings were held in Boston and Worcester, in which Mr. Higginson took part, to plead for help for Brown's family. An anonymous letter from Alabama to the militant pastor is included in the John Brown Collection, condemning him for trying to procure counsel for the prisoner, and warning him that should he and his friends attempt "any such work a little farther South, we will burn every mother's son of you."

Mr. Higginson's wish now was to rescue Brown from prison, but the latter absolutely prohibited any such attempt. Thinking that perhaps Mrs. Brown could shake her husband's determination and ultimately help in his rescue, Mr. Higginson travelled to the mountains of North Elba, New York, to take her to visit him in prison. This visit to Brown's home the author has described in a paper called "John Brown's Household" included in his "Contemporaries." In this article he says: —

"It had been my privilege to live in the best society all my life — namely, that of Abolitionists and fugitive slaves. . . . But I had not known the Browns. . . . Here was a family out of which four young men had within a fortnight been killed. I say nothing of a father under sentence of death and a brother fleeing for his life, but only speak of those killed. . . . Yet there was not one of that family who could not pronounce that awful word with perfect quietness.

. . . To the Browns killing means simply dying —
nothing more; one gate into heaven, and that one a
good deal frequented by their family. . . .

"I was the first person who had penetrated their
solitude from the outer world since the thunderbolt
had fallen. . . . They asked but one question after
I had told them how little hope there was of acquit-
tal or rescue — 'Does it seem as if freedom were to
gain or lose by this?' That was all."

After this visit, Brown's daughter Ruth wrote to
thank Mr. Higginson for his "soul-cheering letters,"
and to say, "How much sunshine you brought into
our desolate homes is left only for us to tell." In his
own account of the visit, Mr. Higginson records that
he spoke to Salmon Brown about the sacrifices of
their family. "He looked up in a quiet, manly way,
which I shall never forget, and said briefly, 'I sometimes think that is what we came into the world for
— to make sacrifices.' . . . And it seemed to me
that any one must be very unworthy the society I
had been permitted to enter who did not come forth
from it a wiser and a better man."

The next scheme to enlist Mr. Higginson's interest, after Brown's sentence had been pronounced,
was a plan of revenge formed by a Boston abolitionist, Lysander Spooner, to kidnap the governor
of Virginia and keep him as "hostage for the safety
of Brown." A scrap of paper exists on which Mr.

Higginson had written, November 14, 1859, "Would it not be practicable for a party of men to go in a steamboat to kidnap in the night —— and hold him as a hostage for the safety of ——." Spooner wrote Higginson, November 20, that the men, a pilot, and a boat could be furnished, and adjured the latter to come at once and persuade men in Boston to furnish the money. November 22, Le Barnes, another sympathizer in this wild project, wrote to give the price of tugs, and November 27, he wrote from New York, "The men are ready and determined. . . . They are confident, strange as it may seem to us, of success, but they want money. . . . It is for you in Boston to say 'go' or 'stay.'" But owing to the impossibility of raising funds the plan was abandoned.

John Brown wrote a letter of farewell to Mr. Higginson, November 22, 1859, expressing deep gratitude for his visit to North Elba, thanking him for sending his family money and newspapers, especially the latter, and adding, "Truly you have proved yourself to be a friend in need."

After Brown's execution a project was formed by the most daring of his friends to rescue the two members of his party — Stevens and Hazlett — who still awaited trial. While this scheme was maturing, the journalist, James Redpath, wrote to Higginson that he had reason to believe the clergyman was watched by spies, and warning him that letters must be written and received with great caution. Funds were raised for the proposed rescue, and Mr. Higginson sent a messenger to Kansas to enlist Captain James Montgomery as leader of the enterprise, the rallying-point being Harrisburg, Pennsylvania. In February, 1860, Mr. Higginson arrived there under the name of Charles P. Carter. When Montgomery came with a few valuable recruits, — called in letters and telegrams "machines," — Mr. Higginson jotted down on paper, which can still be seen, a list of the lions in the way. The Kansas leader was not dismayed by this array of difficulties, which included a week's journey through a mountainous country by night, carrying arms, blankets, and provisions; attacking a building — the Charlestown jail — protected by a wall fourteen feet high and defended by sentinels without and within; and followed by a retreat with prisoners and wounded by daylight. Montgomery, however, insisted on first exploring, with but one companion, the region to be traversed.

In the midst of these plottings, Mr. Higginson wrote to his wife: —

"I was so amused this morning. When Mr. Winkle has been in the mud [in 'Pickwick'] the hostler brushes him down, shooing him and soothing him with a gentle noise all the time as if currying a horse. My pantaloons were deluged with mud from Broadway [New York] and the Irish waiter did precisely that to me."

And a little later, he wrote: —

" I shall be back from Yellow Springs a week from to-morrow night. If he [Montgomery] is not back then, and if the ground is still covered with snow, I shall probably not wait for him, but go home and be on call. . . . Give me credit for wisdom in not throwing up the whole Western trip and going with him."

While Montgomery was absent on this secret errand Mr. Higginson went as far west as Ohio to lecture, returning in time to hear the disappointing verdict. On reaching Charlestown, Montgomery's associate, Soulé, feigned intoxication, and being confined in the same jail, obtained an interview with Brown's confederates.[1] The prisoners considered all attempts at rescue as hopeless; and heavy snow-falls, combined with the fact that both authorities and the community were on the alert, converted Montgomery to the same opinion. Thus the bold scheme of rescuing the two doomed men was reluctantly abandoned.

After returning home Mr. Higginson wrote to one of them — Stevens — the following letter, March 12, 1860: —

[1] Villard's *John Brown*.

"DEAR FRIEND, —

"As I cannot see you in the body I feel a strong wish to stretch out my hand to you once and say *God bless you.*

"You may not remember me, but I saw you in September, 1856, at Nebraska City when you were coming out of the Territory with Gen. Lane. . . .

"Death is only a step in life and there is no more reason why we should fear to go from one world into another than from one room into another. . . . The world where John Brown is cannot be a bad one to live in. . . . My wife would have been willing that I should risk my life to save yours had that been possible."

Recalling these events in October, 1860, Mr. Higginson wrote in his journal: —

"Last year at this time I was worn and restless with inability to do anything for John Brown. Not that I grudged him his happy death — but it seemed terrible to yield him to Virginia. The effort to rescue Stevens and Hazlett — undertaken on my sole responsibility — restored my self-respect. It did not fail like the Burns rescue through the timidity of others — but simply through the impracticability of the thing. I would not have accepted any one's assurance of that impracticability except Montgomery's.

"I think it was a disappointment to me not to be summoned to testify before the [Senate] Committee, nor do I know why I was passed over, after Wilson's assurance. Certainly I should have told them all I knew — and whether that would have done good or harm, I cannot now say.

"So far as John Brown is concerned, I should like this for an epitaph, 'The only one of John Brown's friends and advisers who was not frightened by the silly threats of Hugh Forbes into desiring that year's delay which ruined the enterprise.' I had the old man's own assurance that in his secret soul he regarded this delay as an act of timidity — and acted on it only because those who held the purse insisted."

Afterwards, in 1862, Mr. Higginson wrote a friend about these stirring events: —

"I remember in a letter which I thought might be the last I should ever write to you, when I had sent for Montgomery and seven men from Kansas, because I could find nobody in New England, and we lay in wait a fortnight in Harrisburg hoping vainly to penetrate Virginia and rescue Stevens and Hazlett — I remember then telling you how I had always held to a Mohammedan proverb that no prophet is called of God till he has reached the age of 40 — and *to-day* I am only 39, so I don't think my time has come yet to do the thing I was born for — but certainly I never enjoyed anything more."

Many years later, in 1879, Colonel Higginson went to Charlestown, Virginia, to see this very prison. When he looked at the high and apparently impregnable wall he felt fully convinced that Montgomery's judgment was sound.

After the tragic death of Brown, there came a renewal of the old conflict in Boston between the Pro-Slavery men and the "Antis." Wendell Phillips spoke once a month on Sunday at Music Hall and it was necessary to guard the building to prevent the meetings from being broken up by riotous young men. Mr. Higginson described this new duty in a letter, dated January, 1861, referring to the annual meeting of the Massachusetts Anti-Slavery Society: —

"This week has been given over to mobs; I have been one of the captains of the fifties spoken of in Scripture; that is we had sixty men armed and organized, under my direction, to protect the platform and Wendell Phillips. Part were Germans and part English; this was done prior to the Sunday meeting at Music Hall, but there was no danger then; before the end of the convention it grew rather formidable. It was worth it all to see Mr. Emerson addressing the meeting and interrupted with all kinds of insults and he so utterly undisturbed, — not stooping even to control and put it down, which might perhaps just then have been done — but rising above it by sheer dignity. Wendell Phillips never was so buoyant and charming as through it all. Many have always had the impression that he was not personally courageous because he had not the sort of boyish courage that I and many others get credit for: but his is far higher, not a Puritan courage like John Brown's either, but a sort of highborn chivalrous courage, careless of danger, despising it too utterly to give it a thought — such as one fancies Montrose for instance might have had. We who were with him in the midst of great danger, possible and even actual, were all equally struck with this. We had to control him, he was reckless of danger not from adventurousness nor from ignorance but because he really could not stoop to keep it in mind."

In an estimate of the radical leaders of the day, found in his journal for 1857, Mr. Higginson said of William Lloyd Garrison: —

"Of all the heroes of ancient or modern days, that man stands most firmly on his feet. If he knew that at his next word of truth, the whole solar system would be annihilated, his voice, in saying it, would not tremble."

Apropos of the duty of guarding Phillips, the Worcester clergyman again wrote to his mother, January, 1861: —

"I spent yesterday in Boston for a wonder, not having been away on Sunday for a long time. They sent for me to come down because it was feared that there would be trouble at the Music Hall as Wendell Phillips was to speak . . . and the Mayor refused to have any Police. The previous time when he spoke there were 200 police and trouble at that. So we had a meeting at the German 'Turners' Hall on Saturday evening, and they appointed me Commander in chief and organized into small companies of 6 each with a leader, and Sunday morning we posted them in different parts of the Hall and carried the meeting quietly through, though there were a few symptoms of trouble at first — and took W. P. home afterward, with quite a crowd around, — so that all went well. Gov. Andrew brought a good deal of pressure to bear on the Mayor and he sent police after all — but not in uniform so that it was not generally known till afterwards. As there is to be an Anti-Slavery Convention next Thursday and Friday it was thought important to have a good organization and make sure of carrying the meetings all through — but I think everything will go well now."

In February, Mr. Higginson spent another Sunday in Boston, to help protect Wendell Phillips, and wrote that "a thousand people or so waited on Winter Street to see him — friends, foes and idlers — while we quietly walked him out by the Bumstead Place entrance."

When the war-cloud burst in April, 1861, and there was alarm about the safety of Washington, Mr. Higginson conceived the daring scheme of recalling Montgomery and his men from Kansas and going with them into the mountains of Virginia to divert the attention of the Confederacy from the national capital. In reference to this plan he wrote to his mother: —

"I vibrate between rumors of wars — and high school examinations. Since our troops went, things are quieter, though many are drilling. Think how honorable to Massachusetts that her first troops marched through New York before the famous 7th Regiment had started. . . .

"If you see I have enlisted don't believe it yet, but I am trying to get means for equipping a picked Company for John Brown, Jr. — to be used on the Pennsylvania border. How much I may have to do with the undertaking if it ever comes to anything — the future course of events must determine. I want at least to get the *name* of John Brown rumored on the border and then the whole party may come back and go to bed — they will frighten Virginia into fits all the same."

With Dr. S. G. Howe's help, he raised money for this purpose and consulted Governor Andrew, who gave him a letter of introduction to Governor Curtin of Pennsylvania. This letter Mr. Higginson took in person to Harrisburg. Some doubts arose in Governor Andrew's mind after sending the letter and he wrote another to the Pennsylvania governor advising caution. In this second letter the Massachusetts governor said of Mr. Higginson: "He is a man capable of facing great perils, of gallant and ardent spirit, and one whose plans I would not endorse in blank or in advance. You may find on enquiry that he proposes some scheme not only courageous, but wise." Governor Curtin, after talking with his eager visitor and reflecting upon his plans, wrote to

Governor Andrew that such a move would precipitate a border war, and that the time for such warfare had not yet arrived. He also said that if Mr. Higginson should enter western Virginia "with the kind of troops he purposes to enlist it would not only destroy the loyal sentiment of that part of the State, but would influence the people of Kentucky, Tennessee, and Missouri." This project was therefore abandoned.

On Mr. Higginson's return to Worcester, he was offered a position as major of the fourth battalion of infantry. This he declined, partly from a feeling of unfitness, and partly on account of his wife's invalid condition. He also felt doubtful about the Government's attitude on slavery, and feared he might be ordered to return fugitive slaves to their owners. However, he continued to study military tactics; took fencing lessons; and before going into active service, had belonged to five "drill clubs." In his journal of January, 1862, he gives a list of these clubs, he having been president of two of them, and records practising with rifle and bayonet, as well as studying the manual of arms. One of these clubs, "The Old City Guard," was formed, he wrote, of "a clique of very small men with whom good sense had one long tussle till it broke up. . . . Disbanded with regret and thought I should join the militia." But after a few months of this work he wearied of it and recorded that he felt "a certain satisfaction in having escaped a monotonous winter's drill at the seat of *peace* — the Potomac."

In the midst of these exciting public duties, the youthful delight which Mr. Higginson had found in nature revived. From his journal or " Field Book," kept at the time, these extracts are taken: —

"I need ask for nothing else when I find myself coming round again into all that old happiness in Nature, which my years of hard labor seemed to have dulled. I verily believe that I am to have it all again. A thousand delicate tendrils seem to be tremulously thrusting forth within me, to bind me to the blissful world once more. What an exchange for the life of a minister—St. Lawrence bound to a gridiron, with every seventh bar redhot. . . . If I could obtain but a slight addition to my certain income, so as to keep a saddle horse, I should have nothing more to ask of the world. . . . I see nothing but war which is now likely to change my life and it may be that war is the last of these public schools which I am destined to go through. But that I shall certainly enter, if I can.

"Much of my enjoyment of Nature seems to come from the fact that all animals and even plants are more *human* to me than they appear to most people. When I come suddenly on a beautiful flower in a lonely place it is like meeting with a rare person there, and I never forget that association. So, birds are kindred and children to me. . . . There are outdoor moments so rich, it seems as if a single walk

would furnish an essay. But I do not wish my essays
to be milk but cream. They must skim the wealth of
many days and nights, besides 36 silent years behind. . . . How inexpressibly weak it would be in me
to wish for money or more fame, when by modera-
tion and patience I have secured not merely a certain amount of usefulness, but the rare and unspeakable luxury of living precisely as I would wish to
live. Had I unlimited wealth or fame I do not see
that it could add anything important to my summer life, while it would certainly bring many new
and great drawbacks. . . . I enjoy it [literature] so
much more than any other form of work that I am
sure it must be the best thing for me. With our
moderate aims and desires it will not be necessary
for me to become a drudge, or of so over-doing as to
produce distaste for it. But for M.'s ill-health and
the disturbed condition of the country (and in both
cases I see some indications of hope beyond) — my
sky would be unusually cloudless, so far as I can
compare it with that of others."

The uncontrollable desire to have a share in the
war was at times manfully quelled and dismissed as
the diary under date of August 15, 1861, shows: —

"I have thoroughly made up my mind that my
present duty lies at home — that this war, for which
I long and for which I have been training for years,
is just as absolutely unobtainable for me as a share
in the wars of Napoleon. This being the case, let me
swallow down all rebellious desires and philosophi-

cally use the opportunities and enjoyments I have. Perhaps good may yet come from this enforced abstinence."

The same purpose is more fully expressed in this letter written to a friend: —

"I have been much taken up, of course, with the exciting and exhausting affairs of this summer. . . . At one time I saw prospects of coming nearer to the scene of action, but my plans of irregular service failed, and it would be very wrong for me to enlist for three years or even one, so that I am just turning it all into a school for patience. There is a certain experience of action and danger which is very fascinating to me and to which I should take perhaps as readily as most men, — but I always turn very easily to the thought of immortality and cannot doubt that all experiences which are really needed will be forthcoming first or last. It seems funny, to be sure, to wait for heaven to supply the place of secessionists, but I have n't a doubt of some good and exciting training being afforded, beyond this limited chance we have here."

It was hard to always exercise this philosophy in the face of such experiences as the following: —

"WORCESTER, Aug. 1861.

"We had Col. Leonard's regiment on their way to the war also, and the 'John Brown War song' was sounding through the streets all the evening. . . . I never heard anything more impressive and it seemed a wonderful piece of popular justice to make his name the War song."

The sense of duty to his country, in distinction from the claims of home, was also aroused by such reflections as these: —

"It seems to me of the greatest importance that men of Anti-Slavery principle should take their full share in this war. . . .

"A great many Anti-Slavery men, all over the state, are holding aloof, and can only be brought in by *leaders* in whom they have confidence.

" . . . Some of our most influential young men here have been telling me, for some time, that they would enlist under me and nobody else, and they stand ready to raise one company or more, here. And from letters I have had, at different times, I know that there are many who would prefer to serve under some man of anti-slavery sympathies."

In the autumn of the same year, feeling the need of more time for literary work, Mr. Higginson severed his connection with the Free Church. A unique tribute to his popularity was the gift of a basket of artificial fruit, the contents having been made from the hair of members of his congregation!

On Thanksgiving Day, he expressed his satisfaction with the new leisure: —

"Years I have wasted in efforts to do people good — preaching, speaking, lecturing, conventioning, organizing, politics, newspaper writing, private philanthropies, etc. — in all of which I have succeeded as well as the average, perhaps better — but never with that hearty zest a man feels when he knows he is leading his true life. Now I have wrenched myself away from all these things, feeling that I have served my time at them and got my Experience — and I have come back to the one thing which I always thoroughly enjoyed, a quiet life with literature and nature. It has cost me all these years to *dare* to do this."

These dreams of peace were suddenly dispelled in the autumn of 1861. He wrote to his mother: —

"I have authority from Governor Andrew to take preliminary steps toward raising a regiment, which when formed will be placed under charge of an U.S. officer — probably Captain Saxton of the naval expedition, who is an anti-slavery man. At any rate the Colonel is to be satisfactory to me and I to be under him."

But by the time several companies for the new regiment had been recruited in different parts of the State, an order was given to stop all recruiting. Mr. Higginson had been hard at work for three months, and his disappointment at this turn in affairs is shown by this entry in his journal, January, 1862: —

"Went through all the interest and hope of my regimental prospects, and came out of it all again. . . . Whatever sorrows or regrets there were I dis-

posed of in [writing] my Letter to a Young Contributor and have passed it all by."

However, in the following spring, hope was re-
awakened, for a new nine-months' regiment was
called out and the irrepressible ex-clergyman opened
a recruiting office in Worcester. He wrote, March 3,
1862: —

"The day after the call for 9 months troops I
called on the Mayor and told him I did not wish to
be exempted on the score of profession, not being
properly a clergyman and it is settled with M——
that if drafted I shall go.

"Yesterday it grew obvious that the number of 9
months men might be raised without a draft and it
suddenly became clear to me . . . that I ought to go
for that time, even without a draft. I have not mentioned it to M—— and may not have strength to
carry it through, but it seems to me that if I do not
I shall forfeit my self respect and be a broken man
for the remainder of my days. I have sacrificed the
public duty to this domestic one as long as I can
bear."

In August he wrote to his mother: —

"I have something to say which may surprise you.
. . . I have obtained authority to enlist a military
company for 9 months, I go as Captain. . . .

"I do not think I should ever have made up my
mind to go for 3 years — but those recruits were
raised slowly here, and I decided that I never could

hold up my head again, in Worcester or even else-where, if I did not vindicate my past words by actions though tardy. It seemed to me also, which is more important, that beyond a certain point one has no right to concentrate his whole life on one private duty."

Two weeks later he told her: —

"I am going to Boston to-day with my company roll full, to get authority to choose officers; and next week we expect to go into barracks in a large building a little way out of town. . . . Everybody praises the material of my company and their appearance on the street."

The inner conflict was over, as his journal shows, under date of August 31: —

"Since I have decided on my duty, my whole path has been perfectly clear; I have been like a ship in [the] bay, all other paths obstructed, but this one perfectly clear. . . .

"I see at every moment that all the currents of my life converge in this direction and that my time is absolutely come. . . . What I could write I have written and should I never write anything more, no matter. So far as any personal plans of my own are concerned, I am absolutely free and could I leave M—— out of view could die to-morrow with no feeling but of a happy confidence in the Eternal Laws, not unmingled with a sweet curiosity."

To his mother, he wrote: —

"Lincoln House,
"Worcester, Sept. 7, 1862.

"I have my commission and we go into barracks when they are ready. . . . I drill my company every afternoon two hours out doors and enjoy it much."

And later in the same month he added: —

"I feel just like a father of a family when I go up to the quarters at meal times and see my sage first sergeant taking tea . . . sitting . . . behind a pine board, eating baked apples, illumined by a stearine dip stuck in a potato. Or later when four beautiful voices sing quartettes. My sergeants hold evening prayers, to which many of the company go, sometimes half; and at nine there is a roll-call, after which all go to bed and nine hundred men snore in concert in one vast hall, with scarce a partition between.

"At five A.M. comes a rolling of drums, like churning and boiling in one, which is the reveillé . . . to which all the men bundle up and one commissioned officer at least to each Company — then drill from 6 to 7 and then breakfast and four hours more, drilling through the day."

A month later the new captain reported: —

"We are sailing smoothly now at the camp. . . . They cannot be said to love me, and I heard yesterday of an inebriated Irish private singing along Main St., 'Old Higgie is so strict, so strict,' etc., while another in a similar condition came to the company quarters yesterday and asked for me, saying he was drunk and wished to go to the guard-house."

In November, he wrote that they had everything but guns and might be ordered off at any time, and on the following day he telegraphed his mother, "We have orders to leave this week." But he was still in the Worcester barracks a fortnight later, when he received a thrilling letter from Brigadier-General Saxton, of the Department of the South, offering him the command of a regiment of freed slaves.

XII

THE BLACK REGIMENT

BEFORE resigning his commission in the 51st Massachusetts, Mr. Higginson went to South Carolina to make sure that the new regiment of freed slaves was really more than a scheme. Satisfied with his survey of the ground, he eagerly accepted General Saxton's offer. When he returned home and announced his decision, a lively niece exclaimed, "Will not Uncle Wentworth be in bliss! A thousand men, every one as black as a coal."

On his way to take command, when the steamer was nearing Charleston, he wrote, November 23, 1862: —

"As I approach the mysterious land I am more and more impressed with my good fortune in having this novel and uncertain career open before me. . . . Here is . . . a position of great importance; as many persons have said, the first man who organizes and commands a successful black regiment will perform the most important Service in the history of the war. . . . To say that I would rather do it than anything else in the world is to say little; it is such a masterpiece of felicitous opportunity that all casualties of life or death appear trivial in connexion with it."

A few days later the new colonel recorded that his only discomfort came from the cold nights, and that he was perfectly satisfied he was doing his duty. He was most warmly received by the other officers, and wrote to his mother, "Fancy 500 black faces at dress parade, and 2 red legs to each face."

For two months the regiment remained quietly in camp near Beaufort, South Carolina, and this proved a fortunate opportunity for Colonel Higginson, as it gave time to get his soldiers into fighting trim. He succeeded in securing his friend Dr. Rogers as surgeon, and entered into his new life with an enthusiasm which was contagious. He wrote to his mother that his whole faculties had been switched off in a new direction, and that if he did not come home "jet black" she ought to be very grateful. "Do not regret," he added, "that I am here. I should have missed the best fortune of my life had I not come and this I should say were I recalled to-morrow."

One of the officers of this regiment, the late Reverend A. W. Jackson, wrote an account of his life as captain under Colonel Higginson, and from his unpublished manuscript these facts are taken. The men were undisciplined and undrilled and the officers despondent and sceptical about the possibility of making soldiers out of plantation slaves. The low esteem in which the black regiment was held by

COLONEL THOMAS WENTWORTH HIGGINSON, 1862

white regiments also made the officers discontented.
The new Colonel's arrival at once infused fresh courage into these faint hearts. "He was a born commander," wrote Captain Jackson. When General
Saxton, somewhat later, witnessed the dress parade
of this regiment, he said of its Colonel that he knew
of no other man who could have magically brought
the blacks under a military discipline that made the
camp "one of the most enviable." Colonel Higginson's service for his men was summed up in one
sentence by Jackson: "He met a Slave; he made
him a Man."

This officer relates his surprise when he discovered
that the Colonel was a writer, and his delight in a copy
of "Outdoor Papers" that was loaned him by the
author. The unusual combination of gifts — physical vigor, dashing courage, and literary ability —
whimsically suggested to the younger man "a union
of Jim Lane and Addison." Colonel Higginson cultivated friendly relations with his officers but permitted no undue familiarity, and they never ventured
upon coarse remarks in his presence. Once he heard
an officer swearing at one of the men, simply hurling
oaths at his luckless charge. The Colonel asked
gently if so much profanity was necessary and requested the officer to come to his tent. After the
interview, the offending captain with tears in his eyes

swore a big oath that he would never swear again!
The officers were not allowed to inflict "degrading
punishments" on the men, or to indulge in "insulting
epithets"; the word "nigger," for instance, was
tabooed even in conversation. The soldiers were
held to strict obedience, but also treated like men.
The result Captain Jackson says was a miracle, and
that "the affection and reverence of his soldiers for
their Colonel were beyond words." Captain Jackson once expressed a wish to transfer to canvas
a picture of his "stately Colonel" bending with un-
covered head to listen to the complaints of a ragged
and ignorant Negress. "No grand lady," he added,
"could win a more responsive interest or a more
royal courtesy."

As for the officers, it was a new experience to be
associated with a man of refinement and culture and
they received with delight the books and magazines
which he sent to their tents. The Colonel wrote
home: —

"I wish you could see how pretty our encamp-
ment looks, with its 250 tents glimmering white in
the moonlight. . . . The white curlews hover and wail
all night invisibly around us in the air, like vexed
ghosts of departed slave-lords of the soil. . . . This
was considered an especially severe plantation and
there is a tree which was used as a whipping post, so
that the marks of the lashes are still to be seen. . . .

"As I sit in my tent door and adjudicate contested cases where the lingo is almost inexplicable, and the dusky faces grow radiant and sometimes majestic with eager expression, I seem like Rajah Brooke in Borneo; or like Whittier's lost Southern playmate:

> 'The dusky children of the sun
> Before me come and go.' . . .

"Who should drive out to see me to-day but Harriet Tubman [the escaped slave, who rescued many of her race and conducted them to freedom] who is living in Beaufort as a sort of nurse and general care taker. . . . All sorts of unexpected people turn up here. . . .

"My regiment has now 630 and they come in tolerably fast. They are easy to discipline and drill, and do as well as any regiment of equal date, — as well as the 51st. I enjoy it all very much and have never for a moment regretted my promotion: though, without my two months in that regiment, it would have been almost impossible."

In his War Journal, Colonel Higginson noted: —

"Just now a soldier was here, defending himself against a Captain's complaint and said indignantly, 'I ain't got colored-man principles, I's got white-gentleman principles.' . . . I am not sure if it was one of our men who when asked insultingly, 'What are you, anyhow?' answered 'When God made me, I was n't much, but I's a man now.' . . . Their buoyant spirits are proof against everything. . . . Their little sorrows are usually like those of children —

once make them laugh, and the cloud is dispelled. — Meanwhile on board the transports with white troops, there is generally grumbling and dissatisfaction. — Every captain of a transport who has once taken my regiment wishes to take it again in preference to whites. . . .

"The very listening to these people is like adjusting the ear to some foreign tongue. Imagine one of the camp washerwomen saying dramatically to-day, 'I took she when she am dat high, and now if him wants to leave we, let he go'; the person thus chaotically portrayed being a little adopted girl who had deserted her."

In January, the Colonel reports that he has presented a sheep to a fellow-officer's wife, and says: —

"You don't know how pastoral I feel, when I contemplate my little flock of sheep straying round to find something to nibble; as soon as they succeed they will grow fat and we shall nibble them. They are pro-slavery sheep, as Kansas used to say."

It was necessary to exercise some ingenuity in order to keep up military guise, for Colonel Higginson wrote to his wife: —

"When any occasion requires the Doctor to be magnificent, I am to whip off my shoulderstraps and put on his. So we shall both have a dress coat. No longer will the sentinels in Beaufort shoulder arms remotely to my buttons (salute for a captain) and then hastily present arms when my colonel's straps come within ken. I feel like Hosea Biglow's militia officer, who had brass enough outside 'let alone what nature had sot in his featers, to make a 6-pounder out on.'"

As to the difficulty of getting money to pay his men, Colonel Higginson wrote home: —

"CAMP SAXTON, Jan. 19, 1863.

"About money . . . I don't know when I can get any and there is nothing to be done. . . . If Uncle Sam keeps afloat, I shall have enough for everything, though it seems rather mean to be drawing pay for such pleasant things as power, philanthropy, drilling, outdoor life, and unlimited horseback. . . . The one [horse] which Gen. Saxton 'turned over' to me, has sowed his wild oats and become sensible and I ride him at battalion drill."

On January 21, General Hunter made this regiment a visit, promising pay, muskets, and blue trousers, also authorizing the regiment to go on an expedition along the coast to pick up cotton, lumber, and above all recruits. A similar expedition had been declined by the Colonel shortly after his arrival, on account of lack of drill and discipline among both men and officers. In his journal he wrote: —

"Jan. 21, 1863, Camp Saxton. . . . Our danger in such expeditions is not nearly so great as one would think, as we have cannon and the rebels have not, and they would run away from them. But I think they would run away from our men, even without the cannon — I should think they would — I should. They are perfectly formidable."

The first expedition led the happy Colonel with his dusky troop up the St. Mary's River, which divides Florida from Georgia. He reported to his wife early in 1863: —

"We are five days out on a rambling expedition, I with 3 steamers and 400 men, having a very pleasant semi-piratical time. We have had one midnight fight in a wood, with a cavalry company, 1 killed, 7 wounded of ours, mostly near me, but I had not a scratch. The men are splendidly courageous. . . .

"We have iron, lumber, rice, recruits, 67 prisoners, a cannon and a flag."

Three days later he wrote to his mother: —

"We have made one of the most daring expeditions of the war, forty miles up the St. Mary's river, fought a cavalry company in open field, and defeated it overwhelmingly, and many other things which you will see in my Report to Gen. Saxton. The men have behaved splendidly and I have enjoyed it inexpressibly. When the whole is known, it will establish past question the reputation of the regiment."

To assure his friends, who were anxious about his exposing himself in times of danger, Colonel Higginson wrote February 23: —

"I am kept under a tight rein in that respect already; never was a man so teased and badgered as

I was on this last trip — I do not need it, because though naturally enjoying danger as much as most men perhaps, I am not such a fool as not to see the value of my life to this regiment."

And again: —

"I never shall have a chance to risk myself much. . . . I wore my iron plated vest too, which is very light and comfortable."

Captain Jackson once told the writer of this memoir that his Colonel was always fearless, riding with notebook and pencil in hand amid flying bullets. The fact that the officers of colored regiments were, to use Colonel Higginson's own words, "fighting with ropes around their necks," did not detract from the charm of that strange life. The ordinary courtesies of war had been denied to officers of Negro regiments, the Southern Confederacy having issued an order to the effect that such officers, if captured, should be hanged.

"Nothing can ever exaggerate the fascination of war," wrote the Colonel. "I hardly hear the crack of a gun without recalling instantly the sharp shots that spilled down from the bluffs at us, along the St. Mary's, or hear a sudden trampling of horsemen without remembering the moonlight and midnight when we were suddenly stopped by hearing it before us, at Township Landing. I never can write about those wakeful yet dreamlike nights of moonlight, it was all too good. . . . As for the courage required

and all that, it is infinitely exaggerated—to stop
furious runaway horses, to enter a burning house,
to plunge in a boiling ocean, requires far more personal pluck than to have 'dem dar bullets let loose
after we' as my men describe it; the danger is so invisible, it is not nearly so hard to disregard it; I
know what I say. Bomb shells are far worse, but
we have only fired, not received them.

"It amuses me . . . to hear Colonels and Majors
of freshwater regiments say guardedly 'Your regiment does much better than I expected' when they
know and I know and they know that I know that
their regiments could n't form square forward on the
centre even if there were to be an adjutant's wedding
in the middle."

For the delights of skirmishes with the enemy
were varied by a wedding in camp, and of this event
Colonel Higginson wrote in his journal: —

"Well, the Adjutant is fairly and thoroughly married. . . . The band of the 8th Maine Regiment appeared at Dress Parade; the men looked neat and
soldierly in their blue uniforms (having got rid of the
wretched red trousers, which they hated) and all
was well. . . . The Army Regulations do not provide
for regimental weddings; as Colonel I was first to
congratulate the bride, but omitted embraces as not
being specified in the Tactics."

Of two of his officers, he wrote: —

"Poor weak fellows, they would have been splendid officers without their wives — [who were] two

Irish friends; one [of them] swore worse than all my officers put together and the other never opened her lips and was the most formidable tyrant of the two — Those two brave men whom I had seen stand to their guns in the hottest fire on the St. Mary's were like whipped spaniels before those women."

In March, 1863, Colonel Higginson was sent in command of two regiments (1st and 2nd South Carolina Volunteers) to Florida, the objects of this expedition being to occupy Jacksonville, and to carry Lincoln's "proclamation of freedom to the enslaved." He wrote to his wife on the 12th that he was quartered in a palatial abode, embowered in tea roses, and that the town had capitulated "without a gun." Here more or less light skirmishing went on, but the Colonel reported that his regiment lived in clover and brought in " contrabands," horses, and provisions every day. To hold this post with only a garrison of nine hundred men, it having been evacuated twice before by Union troops, made the officers uneasy, but reinforcements relieved this anxiety. Shells were thrown into the town, with the only result of disposing of a mosquito net; and on March 27, the Colonel in command noted that danger was about over and they were eagerly expecting further orders from General Hunter.

Then came an order for the third evacuation of

Jacksonville, and Colonel Higginson with his regiment sorrowfully returned to Beaufort. But in a few days relief came in the form of an order to go "out on picket at Port Royal Ferry." This new field, the devoted son thus described in a letter to his mother.

"ADVANCED PICQUET STATION,
"PORT ROYAL ISLAND,
"April 8, 1863.

"We have happened into the most fascinating regions and life, riding all day through lanes over-arched with roses and woods dense with young emerald leaves and looking across blue streams to the wooded and sunny mainland of South Carolina. A life that is as good as anything we have had, were only the zest of immediate danger added!"

A few days later he wrote: —

"This charming life among Cherokee roses and peach blossoms will last awhile. . . . How funny some of the rumors were about the capture of our expedition — one Democratic paper writing my obituary!"

Meantime the delay of payment caused more or less anxiety, though promises kept up hope. "The paymaster writes," recorded the Colonel, "that he is really making up our payrolls and we shall probably be paid in a week or ten days."

The infinite pains Colonel Higginson took to keep

his men in good training is revealed in such notes as
these: —

"White soldiers [are seen] with coats unbuttoned
and black with them buttoned; for this is a cardinal
point with me, you know, and my test of the condition of a regiment; if a man begins with swearing
and stealing, bad practices grow and you always
find him at last with his coat unbuttoned."

In "Army Life," Colonel Higginson tells of his
delight in studying the characteristics of his men and
of listening to their "spirituals," but occasionally
in his journal or letters are bits of description not
heretofore printed. For instance: —

"One of the men [said] to the Quartermaster who
had tried long to explain something to him — 'You
know, Quartermaster, no use for nigger to try to
comb he wool straight, he always short and kinky
— He brains short, too, sa.'"

At Port Royal, Colonel Higginson encountered, in
the Brigadier-General commanding opposing troops,
a former Brattleboro acquaintance. He wrote,
April 19, 1863: —

"The best thing is that this Brigadier-General
Walker . . . is an old friend! He is that Lieutenant
Walker, U.S.A., who was sick at the Water Cure and
liked me because of my physique and my abolitionism, he being a desperately pro-slavery invalid; who
afterwards met me in Kansas as Captain Walker,

with a cavalry company to arrest Redpath and me, and would n't do it for old acquaintance sake — and here he is across the river, face to face with me again!"

In July, the absent son wrote of the delight with which a box of goodies from the North was received: —

"I am sitting at my tent door and there is a great moon rising: the tents look like the Pyramids against it. I have a box from mother with eatables — real boarding-school and I give them to the boys."

And describing the contents of a later box from home, he says, "All the pauses of life filled in with crackers and new books."

To his mother's anxious inquiry as to food, he wrote: —

"I do not know why you think we do not live well, for we certainly do. . . . We have also *napkins*.

"To-day I dined on roast opossum — Done to perfection, done brown with such crackling as Charles Lamb in his vision of roast pig only dreamed of. I found it a dish of barbaric fascination."

And he added that the menu was also varied by alligator steak.

Meantime reports of Northern victories in Virginia arrived, and were duly exciting to Colonel Higginson and his officers. Although the former kept ample notes in his journal, he did not attempt much literary work while in camp. He wrote to his wife: —

"Perhaps Hooker's victories will give that cheerfulness to the public mind which J. T. Fields thinks favorable to book publishing; and thus do great events link on to small ones and affect literary Colonels."

It was a great satisfaction to Colonel Higginson, as time went on, to know that the peculiar responsibility which he had felt as commander of the first regiment of freedmen was diminishing, owing to the rapid multiplication of Negro regiments.

"Any disaster," he wrote to his mother on May 18, 1863, "or failure on our part would now do little harm. . . . There is no doubt that for many months the fate of the whole movement for colored soldiers rested on the behavior of this one regiment. A mutiny, an extensive desertion, an act of severe discipline, a Bull Run panic, a simple defeat, might have blasted the whole movement for arming the blacks.

". . . Col. Littlefield (30 regiment S.C.V. in future) says that Secretary Chase told him the Cabinet at Washington kept their whole action in regard to enlisting colored troops waiting to hear from us in Florida, and when the capture of Jacksonville was known, the whole question was regarded as settled, the policy avowed, and Adjutant General Thomas sent out on his mission. This is, I think, the best expression of the importance of our action that has yet occurred.

"The other is the saying of one of our men who was asked if he belonged to Col. Montgomery's regiment. 'No,' said he proudly, 'I'se belong to Colonel Higginson's regulars.' This is the triumph of self-respect, with a witness! . . .

"This war seems to me glorious, however slow, when I think of these freedmen and women here. These are days of the Lord, each a thousand years."

It was while at Port Royal doing picket duty that Colonel Higginson passed a rash night in the water which he described in an "Atlantic" paper and afterwards included in "Army Life." In July, the regiment made another expedition up the South Edisto River, being gone thirty-six hours. After the capture of Port Royal, the plantations along the coast were abandoned and the slaves withdrawn into the interior. In order to reach the black population, it was necessary to navigate shallow, winding, and muddy rivers for miles. This proved a disastrous adventure for the Colonel. He wrote to his mother from Beaufort: —

"July 12, 1863.

"Only time to say that we have had another expedition up the South Edisto River . . . 30 miles and brought away 200 contrabands — such a scene — 'like notin' but de Judgment Day' they said. I had a knock on the side, not breaking the skin, I don't know from what, which still lames me somewhat but it does n't amount to the dignity of a wound, though the papers may spread it. I submit to be quiet for a few days and be taken care of, but I am in camp and have a nice time. You need not fear any bad result."

The curious wound of which the disabled Colonel made light, proved in the end to have jarred his whole system, making the victim a semi-invalid for several years. The surgeons agreed that his life would probably have been sacrificed, had he not always been a total abstainer from whiskey. He wrote to his mother: —

"We are now satisfied that nothing touched me, but the shell passed within about six inches of my side just above the hip, making by the concussion a black and blue spot as big as my two hands. . . .

"Of all the humbugs of war, commend me to being 'wounded.' . . . No pain, no dressings or doses, a pleasant languor, nothing to do and no wish to do anything, a beautifully kept house and nobody but Dr. R. and myself in it, the hostess herself absent . . . to lie all day on a breezy balcony with green leaves and floating clouds, — why it is Arcadia, Syrian peace, immortal leisure. I blush to have bought it so cheaply as by a mere black and blue spot on the side, to show where a bombshell did *not* touch me."

Not recovering from his injury, Colonel Higginson procured a month's furlough and went North to recuperate. When he had been at home a week or two, he assured his surgeon that although he was in a haven of peace he wanted to be with the regiment and sometimes felt quite homesick for black faces. This eagerness to return to active duty led the impatient Colonel to go back to´ the regiment too soon, and finding on his return an accumulation of work, and a visible loosening of discipline, he exerted himself beyond his strength. He wrote to Dr. Rogers who had been obliged to resign on account of ill health: —

"Headquarters, 1st S.C.V.
"Aug. 22, 1863.

" My dear Doctor:

"You may thank your stars if you have any love for this regiment that I *did* come back before I felt fit to do it — for if ever a family of grown up babies needed a papa, this was the one. To be sure if I had come back here *sick* I should probably have died in a day — for anything so forlorn, dismal, despairing as these dozen officers who were *not* on the sick list, you can scarcely imagine. Such lachrymose bugbears of diseases, discords, delinquencies, Captains under arrest, officers suspected of cheating their companies, companies of mutiny. . . . Lt. Col. Strong sick in hospital and going North, Major Trowbridge ditto. . . . The first Brigade review of the regiment to come off that afternoon — and no field officer! The Adjutant yellow as gold, and no Quartermaster! In the midst of which gloomy gallery, in popped I!

"You are the only person in the Universe who can conceive the picture.

"Now you are to observe that by some extra-wonderful stroke of my accustomed good luck, I come on shore from a comfortless voyage perfectly buoyant and hilarious — feeling better than for 6 months back and so invincibly cheerful that everybody began to melt before it — from that hour the Lt. Col. and Major began to mend (though still mere wrecks of themselves) all the wheels began to turn, all cards turned out aces and at this moment I don't see one *real* worry except that, no doubt, some of the officers are sick. Never was there a greater triumph of sheer health and an unalterable habit of looking on the bright side."

Although the Colonel was himself abstaining from action at this time, his men made occasional sallies into the enemy's territory. On one of these raids a colored sergeant, Henry Williams, engineered the escape of all the slaves from a plantation, and the adventure is thus described in a letter to Mrs. Higginson : —

"CAMP SHAW, NOV. 26.

"We have had quite an excitement in a fight of some of our men on the main land where they brought away 27 colored people and 2 rebel pickets and beat off a cavalry company headed by five blood hounds, all of whom were killed. We have the body of one which James Rogers has skinned and taken to N.Y. to be stuffed and shown. Two of my men were drowned and six wounded — One edifying result is that there was a flag of truce a few days after and the rebel officers readily held official communication with our officers which last summer they would n't do.

"One amusing thing was, just before the fight began, the pickets across the river farther down were taunting our pickets — 'Why don't you come over,' to which our men answered — '*Coming soon enough for you*' and even as they spoke the fire up river began and the rebels forthwith mounted their horses and went off in a hurry!"

Health and strength did not return to the wounded Colonel, and after getting affairs straightened out there came a collapse. Perfect inaction was enjoined, but with his usual hopefulness the invalid wrote to his wife, "With milk and eggs and soup and Scotch ale I think I shall soon come round. . . . No new symptoms develop, only the same 'General Debility.'"

Colonel Higginson then adopted the resource of spending his nights at a neighboring plantation, returning to camp by day. He reported to his wife that the doctor said he had been "thrust through and through by malaria without knowing anything about it, because of temperament."

There were still hard days to live through, official inspections, brigade reviews, and court-martials.

HENRY WILLIAMS,
FIRST SERGEANT, 1ST SOUTH CAROLINA VOLUNTEERS

Four regiments took part in the brigade drills and the Colonel of the 1st South Carolina wrote: —

"I think mine does best, but perhaps each little Col. thinks the same. . . .

"I am sitting in Court Martial waiting for the court; this is the 3rd day we have tried to meet ineffectually — we are to try several men for their lives who have tried to desert to the enemy and [we] ought to get at work. Several of the conscripts have tried to bribe negroes to take them to the other side, and have actually started."

Meantime, Mrs. Higginson had decided to remove to Newport, Rhode Island, for her health. Her husband wrote from Camp Shaw, November, 1863: —

"I can now see you at Newport, cat and two kittens. . . . I agree with you that at the end of my military pilgrimage, we might try Cambridge — indeed as people grow older they gravitate toward their birthplace."

As Christmas Day approached, the Colonel wrote to his mother that the colored people were planning a great fair in Beaufort "which enlisted all hands"; and that on New Year's Day there was to be a barbecue and dance in the evening at the principal restaurant. He added: —

"This saloon was to have been called Higginson Hall but the painter objected telling the proprietors that the other Colonels might take offence, so that immortal honor was lost. Instead, the proprietor is one of six (all black) who have made up $60 to buy a sword to be presented me on New Year's Day."

December 28, he wrote: —

"We are busy with preparations for New Year's Day. My sword has come, but I have not seen it — it was selected by Frank Shaw and cost $75. This with my captured one and the one given at Worcester will be a memorial, when the war is over, of my share in it."

After the presentation of this sword he reported:—

"Jan. 8, 1864.

"Did I tell you that after the New Year's Festivals, the little Tribune correspondent came to me for my 'wemarks' (he is English, 3 feet high; and a goosey) and the inscription on my sword. I could not give him the former but the latter was easily made visible. It ran thus

'Tiffany & Co.
'New York.'"

These three swords entwined with a faded sash are still where Colonel Higginson hung them in the Cambridge house.

The trouble about securing the soldiers' back pay continued, and the anxious Colonel was kept busy writing to various people in Washington and stating the case in Northern newspapers. He said to his former surgeon, "I suffer much from anxiety about the arrears of pay, especially since Fessenden's unexpected opposition." At length the men were paid in part, but the majority preferred to have nothing if they could not have all. Some of the remarks made by the indignant soldiers are quoted in the War Journal: "'We's willing to serve for notin', but the Guvment ought not for insult we too, by offering seven dollars' [instead of thirteen]. Several said, 'It's the principle we look at.' Another said, 'If we take it, it's because our chilen need it, but it *takes de sojer all out of we*, to be treated so unjustly.'"

Through the remaining months of service, impaired health was a constant drawback. Camp life was brightened at this time by the arrival of the Quartermaster's baby, and later Colonel Higginson wrote a paper called "The Baby of the Regiment" which was printed in "Our Young Folks," afterwards in "Army Life," and included in Whittier's "Child Life in Prose." The author wrote to his wife in February, 1864: —

"Our ladies are quite alarmed at a Department order inquiring as to the number of officers' wives in the regiment — it is feared they are to be sent North, which heaven forbid. If you could see our evening parlor you would think it very pleasant — the brightest fire and walls decked with holly and vines. They play whist a good deal, but the baby eats up the cards so fast, it is hard to keep a pack full. Pretty little thing — she lies in the hammock on the piazza with her little scarlet hood and cloak and little fat arms coming out through the meshes. . . . A little hen roosts there at night. . . . The baby cements everybody and goes from one pair of arms to another all day; she is a darling."

A proposition that Colonel Higginson should write Senator Sumner and present his claims to be appointed Brigadier-General in command of colored troops — this appeal to be fortified by an urgent letter from General Saxton, himself, — was thus noted in the War Journal: —

"I told him [General Saxton] with some indignation that if I could be made a Major General by writing a note ten words long to a Congressman I certainly would not do it; that I never yet had asked for any position in life and never expected to; that a large part of the pleasure I had had in commanding my regiment grew out of the perfect unexpectedness of the promotion. . . . Emerson says no man can do anything well who does not feel that what he is doing is for the time the centre of the universe — I thank heaven that I never yet have supposed for a moment that any brigade or division in the army was so important a trust as my one regiment — at least until the problem of Negro soldiers was conclusively solved before all men's eyes."

In February the regiment was ordered to Florida, and all was excited anticipation. The Colonel wrote home: —

"The expedition is a very powerful one—where I went with 1000 men Gen. Seymour goes with 10,000 including 3 brigades of infantry, eight batteries and 2 mounted regiments. It is not therefore expected that it will take much fighting to repossess Florida, though there may be some marching. Nobody knows what the plans are."

A few days later, he added: —

"The steamer is come at last and we go on board the Delaware to-morrow morning. So that matter is settled. The officers and men were all very desirous to go and I should have been sorry had we not done so."

To Dr. Rogers, Colonel Higginson wrote an account of this plan and its outcome:—

"HEADQUARTERS, 1ST S.C.V., CAMP SHAW,
"BEAUFORT, S.C., Feb. 20, /64.

. . . .

"Such a time as we have had this last fortnight. Sent out on picquet Monday—sitting in great hilarity on Wednesday eve, with a blazing fire, and suddenly summoned back by telegraph that we might be ready to move at a moment's notice—then moving in next day, full of hopes of Florida — hopes checked by Gen. S.'s remonstrance — then a definite order to go when the 4th N.H. came and to report to Gen. Seymour at Jacksonville — then arrived the 4th N.H. but no transportation for us — then came the 'Delaware' and we were ordered on board — then Gen. S. played his last card in 13 cases of Small Pox and failed. Up early in the morning (you can judge *how* early our men might be —), everybody in the highest spirits, taking all our earthly goods in vast wagons and bequeathing all lumber to the 4th N.H. or to the men's wives — working furiously on the wharf till noon and then just as the last board but one was disappearing into the capacious jaws of the 'Delaware' — down rode Gen. S. with an order countermanding our going because of small pox!

"Such a set of forlorn creatures as I marched back to camp that day were never yet seen — they were all so doleful, I rose at last into the highest spirits . . . and now after four cold days, the Camp is in some degree itself again — But there was not one who did not feel the disappointment most keenly, even I who was unfit to go. The S.C. men felt almost as bad as the Florida. Serg't McIntyre sat crying like a child, handkerchief to eyes, several hours after our return.

"At first we expected to go when the Small pox had diminished . . . but it is now evident that not much more is to be done in Florida. . . . It was a great delight to Gen. S. to keep us, as you may imagine, and the men with their wonderful elasticity seem to have got over it. One thing pleased me, though they knew for a week they were to leave the post forever, there was not a single desertion. . . .

But the excitement and work of our abortive departure set me back enough to show how poorly I am fitted, at present, for a campaign."

The Colonel wrote to a Worcester friend, "Do you know how near we came to being in that infinitely disastrous and useless defeat of Seymour's in Florida? . . . As senior colored regiment, we should have had a prominent place in the fight and suffered as badly as any." He mourned that they had missed "both glory and danger," and added: —

"The night the first load of wounded came in [from the Battle of Olustee] we were having a ball for Washington's birthday — really a fine affair and the description in Childe Harold is not finer than the chill and hush which came over all as in the middle of the Lancers, General Saxton came in, pale and stern, and with a word stopped every foot and every chord — and said that it was wicked to be dancing amidst such suffering and disaster—Lt. Col. Reed, actually dying, had just been carried past the house. There had been a shadow over us all the evening from the mere rumors."

The regiment was now, in the spring of 1864, on "advanced picket" duty, and Colonel Higginson described the life in his letters home: —

"Our life here seems like a pleasant country seat with everything very free and easy. Part of the household are just setting off for a little church in the woods about 4 miles off — some on horseback — others in a four wheeled farm wagon called by the people on the plantation reverentially 'the buggy' — shutters are taken down and laid across for seats, then restored to their legitimate office on returning. Harness chiefly rope of various dates.

" . . . A great dilapidated parlor with hardly a whole pane; and a vast blazing fireplace o' evenings, with arms and accoutrements hung all about, and people reading, working or playing perennial Euchre, with which Dr. Rogers, bless him, demoralized the regiment forever.

"By day or night there are interminable rides through woodpaths over the whole island to the different picquet stations . . . your favorite yellow jasmine high and nodding and fragrant and abundant everywhere."

One day Colonel Higginson mentioned in his journal that a few mysterious guns had been fired by the Confederate picket.

"Next day there was a Flag of Truce and a courteous young Captain from the other side was asked for information, as it is usually the understanding that the picquets will not fire or be fired on. He only answered, smiling, 'You gentlemen are training your Buckinghams (which, it seems, is now their cant phrase for colored soldiers) to shell us from the gunboats, and this little bombardment was our only way to retaliate.'"

The following letter, written in March, reminds one of scenes described by Hawthorne: —

"CAMP SHAW, BEAUFORT.

"I saw in town a sight singular and painful — In front of the Provost Marshal's office in the busiest part of the main street of the town, stood upon a box a well dressed man, large and commanding in appearance, and with gaping gazers all around. He was sentenced by Court Martial to stand there two hours daily for a week, with the inscription on his breast 'I sold liquor to soldiers' and with a 24 lb. ball and chain attached to his leg; after which he was to be fined $500 or be imprisoned 6 months, and then sent from the Department forever. But Gen. Saxton in pity for his wife, who is here, took off the inscription and the ball and chain and let the rest take its course. I felt it the more from the fact that I was on the Military commission which tried him, though I happened to be unable to attend the trial. Popular indignation sustains the verdict, partly because of the enormous price at which the man sold the surreptitious whiskey ($12 per gallon) and partly because he came down here as a preacher and like most of that class, exhorted and cheated on alternate days; it is most remarkable how badly all the clerical envoys have turned out. I literally have not known an exception; the only preacher who is respected here is a young lawyer from N.Y. the acting Post Chaplain who can only be 'acting' because he has never been ordained. . . .

"The man excited my sympathy and showed some

character by the way which he took to shun the ig-
nominy of this standing pillory. He stood bending
over a little blank book or diary in which he was
writing busily all the time. He looked as far removed from the world as St. Symon Stylites on his
pillar. Indeed there was something inconceivably
remote and foreign in the whole scene — the man
wore a broad brimmed hat, long straight overcoat
and high riding boots and seemed to have stepped
out of Puritan days."

Picket duty, which Colonel Higginson regarded as
a sort of vacation, was interrupted one April morning, by an order to relieve a departing colored regiment. He wrote: —

"The men, always ready for change, enjoyed the
suddenness of the order and the march out was as
jolly as usual . . . my chief fun came this time from
the Drum corps among whom there is wit and frolic
and deviltry enough to set up a legion of Topsies. . . .
"The 9th is a very fine looking regiment and the
officers appear well. The men have different songs
and ways from our men, and their type of religious
enthusiasm seems different. Our men are chiefly
Baptists and those Methodists; the former is certainly better for the body, as involving at least one
complete ablution in each life. The 9th U.S. men
are farther divided into two subdivisions, in this regard — the Holy Jumpers and the Holy Rollers.
The difference between them is that when under conviction, the Holy Jumpers jump and the Holy Roll-

ers roll: a division decidedly more palpable than
most sectarian barriers."

In the journal, at about this time, there appears
this abstract from acting chaplain Private Thomas
Long's sermon: —

"We can remember, when we fust enlisted, it was
hardly safe for we to pass by de camps to Beaufort
and back, lest [unless] we went in a mob and carried
our side arms. But we whipped down all dat — Not
by going into de white camps for whip um; we
did n't tote our bayonets for whip um; but we lived
it down by our naturally manhood; and now de
white sojers take us by de hand and say Broder
Sojer. Dat's what dis regiment did for de Epiopian
[Ethiopian] race.

"If we had n't become sojers, all might have gone
back as it was before; our freedom might have
slipped through de two houses of Congress and
President Linkum's four years might have passed by
and notin' been done for we. But now tings can
neber go back, because we have showed our energy
and our courage and our naturally manhood.

"Anoder ting is, suppose you had kept your freedom widout enlisting in dis army; your chilen
might have grown up free and been well cultivated
so as to be equal to any business, but it would
have been always flung in dere faces — 'Your fader
never fought for he own freedom' — and what could
dey answer? Neber can say that to dis African race
any more. . . ."

"He also said 'Notin' makes you more trouble dan dat red flag you keep wagging out of your mouf' [the tongue]."

Colonel Higginson's enjoyment of the racy qualities of his men never failed, and he hoped that they would not become so civilized as to lose their piquant use of the personal pronoun. As an example, he gives an imaginary General Order improvised by one of the men: —

"Headquarters No. 1. General Order No. 162; Heretofore no man must fry he meat, must always boil he."

Perpetual pleasure was also found by the Colonel in the Negro songs.

"When I am tired and jaded in the evening," he wrote, "nothing refreshes me more immediately than to go and hear the men singing in the company streets. There is such a world of trustful peace in it, I feel as if they were a lot of babies in their cradles cooing themselves to sleep, the dear, blundering, dusky darlings!"

And he illustrates by the following anecdote their curious mingling of military and scholastic training: —

"Dear old Uncle York leans in the doorway of Dr. Minot's tent, with his broad brimmed hat on, like a retired Seraph in easy circumstances. Along

comes little Ben, Mrs. Dewhurst's page, $2\frac{1}{2}$ feet
high, and swaggeringly says, 'Uncle York, gwine to
school?' and the blessed veteran gets down his
primer, dog-eared now as far as four syllables and
away they go to the moss house where Mrs. D. holds
sway over drummers and divines. . . .

"Pete says Uncle York told them that he once
walked from a certain point to Darien, twenty miles
'discoursing' all the way to himself and that he had
finally to stop outside of Darien 'to end de discourse' — In this and many other points he constantly reminds me of Socrates, only that Socrates,
as it would appear, never did end. . . .

"Pete, the Major's boy-servant, who had picked
up Gallop dances from native Africans, leads the
boys in 'shouts' and decorates the school tent very
prettily on his own plan. He is rather hard to wake
in the morning and when the Major's boot is thrown
at him with or without the owner's foot, he pleads
apologetically that it is bad luck to wake de fus time
you are called. 'Sometimes ghosts do call um,' he
adds in explanation, which implies the necessity of
a wholesome caution."

Colonel Higginson compared Uncle York to the
hero of "Uncle Tom's Cabin." His son, named John
Brown, had been killed in the first armed encounter
between the Negroes and their former masters, and
Uncle York always firmly believed that the celebrated John Brown song related to his son. Another
anecdote in the diary about the same old Uncle, who

became Colonel Higginson's servant when discharged from the regiment for old age, ran thus: —

"Uncle York was telling, the other day, about a master with whom he had deposited his odd earnings and who died without refunding them, so that they were lost altogether. Uncle York finally officiated in driving to the grave, and as the vehicle jolted over the roots in the woods he says, 'I did n't care how much I jolt he — *I pure tink of my money all de time.*' This use of the word pure is genuine old English."

Meantime the chaplain of the regiment, who had been in the habit of varying his spiritual duties by daring forays into the enemy's country, was captured. The Colonel wrote, March 26, 1864: —

"We have just heard from our dear old Chaplain, Feb. 12, at Columbia Jail, as cheerily as usual — he says 'I find this a good place for study and have concluded to stay two years. I am doing excellent well and am satisfied.' Think of that for a prisoner!"

In April, Colonel Higginson felt that he must leave the army. The bursting shell which caused his wound had shattered his digestion. He was obliged to live on rice and hominy and confided to his mother, "I feel very weak in these days." General Saxton was unwilling to consider his resignation and wished to substitute a six months' furlough. But the disabled officer was unconvinced, and wrote home: —

"My surgeon's certificate is sent in to the Surgical
Board in Beaufort, who have to approve it, and as it
contains the word Toxicohaemia, it certainly ought
to pull me or any one through. . . . I expect to
leave in about 10 days . . . I feel that I have
done my work here and am perfectly willing to close
it up. . . .

"Sometimes I think the greater activity in the
book-world makes me feel more as if I had been here
long enough — you know when I first came away
there was a great stagnation there, and now it seems
as if all the wheels were busy again and I must not
stay too long away. . . .

"People whom I left young come down here old
men; last night Carter brought into my tent a handsome man with hair and beard almost silver, and it
was Underwood formerly of the Atlantic whom I left
a handsome brown-haired youth not long ago."

To his mother, he reported, May 9, 1864:—

"All goes well enough in the regiment and I have
got all the special jobs done about which I was
anxious and have now nothing particular to do and
am leading a sort of *posthumous* life in my military
relations, though still in command. I have thoroughly made up my mind to resign, but it takes some
three months to get one's Ordnance accounts settled and that must be done first. It seems very wonderful to be recommencing life again and I alternately feel very old and very young when I think of
it, usually the latter. . . . I think I shall feel my
conscience entirely clear as to my share in the great

drama, and quite willing to renounce farther participation."

The following note, received after Colonel Higginson's return to the North, is without date and came from the Office of the United States Tax Commissioners, at Beaufort: —

"COLONEL: —

"We take pleasure in informing you that we have given the small village for freedmen, situate just Northwest of this town, the name of Higginson, in honor of yourself, and the valuable services which you have rendered the cause of Constitutional Government."

The recipient of this honor derived much amusement from the ultimate fate of his namesake; as the town of Higginsonville, some years later, was blown away in a hurricane.

The retired Colonel retained an active interest in his regiment, and kept himself informed of all its movements. Reporting its departure from Beaufort to his old surgeon, Dr. Rogers, he adds: —

"The men enjoy the way 'de shell dey do pop' over their heads: and are quite cheerful — though the parting was hard as they had no money for their families. About this time they are being paid I trust, though I have almost abandoned hope — but not effort — about their arrears.

" . . . I am mending at the rate of an inch a week or so."

From Pigeon Cove, he wrote in August: —

"It is strange to come back from the war; one feels like Rip Van Winkle and instinctively grasps round to see if all one's friends are still alive; it is not that one feels old, but only strange, and as if one had been in a trance, during which almost anything might have happened."

It was a relief to Colonel Higginson to receive, in October, his order of discharge, having feared that he might be retained in some recruiting or other minor service. After the regiment was disbanded, the Negro soldiers often wrote affectionate letters to their former Colonel, and he was able to help them in various ways. This extract from one of the men's letters gives a fair sample of their loyalty and orthography, "I meet manny of the old Soldiers I Spoke of you — all hailed your name with that Emotion (that become you) of the Sould when hearing of one who when in darkness burst light on their part way."

The following winter, the returned author reported to Dr. Rogers from Newport that he was writing about the St. Mary's expedition:[1] —

"I never did anything so distasteful to me. It is a kind of posthumous life, now that that book of my existence is closed. My instinct is always to live in the present and it is hard for me to reproduce my

[1] "Up the St. Mary's," *Atlantic Monthly*, April, 1865.

own Past. I do it mainly from a sense of duty and because, until it is done, the way will not seem clear for other things. . . .

"I am just opening fire on Congress again about the pay. Wilson presented my petition in the Senate and Boutwell was to do so to-day in the House. I have written a letter to the 'Tribune,' which is strangely delayed."

This weary and humiliating struggle for justice finally succeeded, and the promised payment to his soldiers was made in full.

Forty years after this wonderful experience as leader of the first regiment of freed slaves, its officers met in Boston. Their old commander was unable to be present at this reunion, and a memorial signed by his former associates and containing these words was sent to him: —

"In those brave days you were not alone our commander; you were our standard also of what is noble in character. We were young and untutored; we saw in you a model of what, deep in our hearts, we aspired to be. Your example was a rebuke to our shortcomings, and from your contact our feebler virtues took healthier tone. Though you parted from us your influence remained with us, a constraint from what is unworthy, and an incentive to what is high. We cannot say that through these many years we have been faithful to the standard; but we may say that in its presence it has been easier to be noble and harder to be mean."

XIII

THE removal of his home to Newport, Rhode Island, was not altogether acceptable to Colonel Higginson, as he disliked leaving his native State. Soon after his arrival there he related in a letter to his sisters this curious incident: —

"Nov. 30, 1864.

"I have been received very cordially here but have encountered one delicious rebuff. Judge —— wished to get off the [School] Committee, and proposed to another member of the committee that he himself should resign and I be appointed in his place. Upon this the man flew into a passion, began to swear and asked Judge —— what he meant by the proposition. 'Why,' said the Judge, 'he would be a very useful man on the Board.' 'Don't know anything about that,' said the astute individual, 'but I am not going to sit on the same Committee with a *black man*.'"

However, Newport virtually adopted the stranger, making him chairman of the school committee and inviting him to give the Fourth of July oration. After some hard work the new chairman succeeded in abolishing separate colored schools, and in consequence was dropped from the committee. Six years later his course was justified, for he was reinstated upon the school committee, and, moreover, in this later service one of his fellow-members was a colored man. He also became instrumental in organizing a Library Corporation and was one of the directors.

The beloved mother, with whom Colonel Higginson had so faithfully kept in touch, died in 1864, aged seventy-eight. In an article called "The Future Life," written in 1909 for "Harper's Bazar," the loyal son wrote: "Of my own mother, I can say that I never saw her beautiful face so calm and so full of deferred utterance as when I sat alone beside it after death; it was of itself a lesson in immortality."

A less frequent chronicle of daily events was henceforth sent to his sisters; for instance: —

"I read a chapter in 'Alice in the Looking Glass' after breakfast to the boarders to begin the day well. It is very rich. . . .

"Spring opens and business drives. We have alder blossoms and snowdrops and six manuscript stories from 3 different young ladies with affectionate requests to read and criticize. . . .

"Mothers now heap their babies on me more than ever, but I can stand it if they can. . . . I have a new admirer, partially insane, like most of mine."

The Higginsons made their home in a boarding-house kept by a gentle Quaker lady, and of their hostess Colonel Higginson wrote: —

"Dear Mrs. Dame is as lovely as ever, and when she has young kittens to drown, warms the water to save their feelings."

And of the Newport Quakers in general: —

"They seem like a kind of mild and virtuous machines from oldest to youngest, without passions or imaginations. Their stormiest impulses seem but mild predilections, extending at certain times toward the tea table, or a shade more forcibly towards dinner, or among those most emancipated towards a domestic game of croquet."

In order to give his now helpless wife an airing, Colonel Higginson procured a sort of cab and had one side removed so that Mrs. Higginson's chair could be wheeled directly into the vehicle, and in this curious equipage they drove up and down Newport's fashionable avenue with characteristic independence.

How the author spent each hour of the day is recorded in his journal. After his own breakfast, he sawed wood for half an hour; then sat with his wife during her breakfast. He then worked from ten until two at his desk which was in the room where Mrs. Higginson sat all day in her wheeled chair, with an open book before her on a rest. Here she received her friends, and her husband's writing was often done in the midst of lively conversation. Over his desk hung a photograph of the equestrian statue of the Venetian Coleone, and from this picture of the invincible warrior Colonel Higginson felt that he derived strength. The remaining time was given to miscellaneous duties and pleasures.

His old interest in athletics revived, and led him to start a gymnasium which he daily frequented, and where he led a large class. He joyfully recorded that he could do all he ever did "despite lingering traces of my army ailment"; and added: —

"I have felt that perhaps I should gradually recur to that blissful mood of life in Nature in which I lived at Worcester just before the War. In the army I was constantly in the presence of nature, but the weight of responsibility submerged it altogether and I can now only look back on Nature as the *setting* or frame of my life. . . . Sat by Fort Greene after breakfast and thought how much lovelier autumn than summer and what a relief when one gets to it. It gives a sense of permanent enjoyment — no more hurry in the thought that each day is going."

Newport afforded great opportunities for the old recreations, and sailing, rowing, and swimming became once more daily delights. On a friend's boat Colonel Higginson rigged a red Venetian sail "to

light up the harbor," and children were often found
to share his excursions. These sometimes took the
form of fishing for mackerel. On one occasion he
wrote: —

"I got 5 children back with no injury or loss beyond a hat, a sack and a pair of india-rubbers. This
I think was doing well."

Exercise was his panacea for all ills, and if he felt
under a cloud "a longish walk" was the remedy.
After a walk of nine miles, he reported, "On leaving
I was rather depressed, but came back satisfied with
everything in the world." To vary these walks riding
on horseback was again attempted, without much
success. He wrote in May: —

"First ride for season. . . . I have ridden only
once or twice since the war — partly from surfeit (at
first) partly economy, partly some uneasiness about
my side where I was wounded."

But he learned to ride the old-fashioned velocipede,
and found that his work at the gymnasium helped
him, in body and mind. "It stops off all other
thoughts for an hour — a day — which walking does
not, besides the delightful glow in chest and arms."

For evening amusement there was a chess club,
and the dramatic talent which was so effective in
Colonel Higginson's story-telling and conversation

was often called into play. He wrote to his sisters, February 20, 1866: —

"I performed Mrs. Jarley and her waxwork show with immense éclat and ten people came to tell M. about it next day."

The famous watering-place attracted many celebrities and a current newspaper reported that nearly "the whole 'Atlantic' force" were permanent or summer residents of that place. The "Town and Country Club," with Mrs. Julia Ward Howe for president and Colonel Higginson for vice-president, drew together these congenial spirits, and Mrs. Howe's home was always an attractive resort. Describing a visit to this spot, he exclaimed, — "delicious there in valley! The sight and smell of wild flowers refreshed my soul — they are so rare here."

To Newport and to Mrs. Dame's table drifted in those days sundry bright women, whose sparkling conversation and witty repartees made meal-time a brilliant occasion. One of these gifted women was Helen Hunt, who became an intimate friend of the Higginsons. The Colonel was glad to be her literary adviser, reading in manuscript all the Saxe Holm stories, whose authorship Mrs. Hunt struggled to keep a profound secret. After she became Mrs. Jackson she wrote to him in 1877, "He [her husband] knows how much I owe to you — all my success as a writer."

One of the Newport residents whom Colonel Higginson especially enjoyed was La Farge, of whom he wrote: —

"I ought not to complain of living in a place which has La Farge. . . . He is one of the few men to whom it is delightful to talk — almost the only one with whom I can imagine talking all night for instance as that is not my way. He is so original and cultivated at the same time, and so free from unworthy things. He seems like a foreigner too — it is getting the best part of France to talk with him. How unimportant is physical ugliness in a man! If I were a woman I should fall in love with him, delicate and feeble as he is physically."

Of a farewell dinner given for Wilkie Collins in 1874, Colonel Higginson wrote: —

"There were only eight literary men there and I remember noticing how much brighter were Mr. Whittier's eyes than those of anybody else, though he looks old and thin and sick."

On this occasion he first saw Mark Twain who impressed him as "something of a buffoon, though with earnestness underneath; and when afterwards at his own house in Hartford, I heard him say grace at table, it was like asking a blessing over Ethiopian minstrels. But he had no wine at his table and that seemed to make the grace a genuine thing." This hasty estimate of the popular humorist was a passing one, and the acquaintance developed into a cordial friendship.

Public men as well as authors and artists were drawn to Newport, and when President Hayes visited Rhode Island in 1877, the Colonel wrote to his sisters: —

"He looks just like his pictures, and gives a great impression of manly equilibrium and quiet strength. I was pleased with the quiet way he said to me when the people were calling and I told him he would have to make a speech: 'No: — there is nothing easier than to keep silence.' I shall never forget it; it was a key to the whole man. His nieces afterwards told me, 'He never brings business to the dinner table' — the 'business' being the government of the nation! . . . On Friday they all came here and I saw Mrs. Hayes and liked her quite as much . . . . She has nature's good manners, making society manners quite superfluous — just such manners as a Republican presidentess should have. She clapped her hands like a girl when she saw the ocean (for the first time in her life) and repined a good deal in being carried off to tea in a fine house, saying that she could take tea at any time but might never see the ocean again."

He also records May 30: —

"Talked with Admirals Farragut, Porter and Capt. Worden. . . . He [Farragut] is a good looking

well-knit man — P. less showy with black beard —
W. coarser looking, with auburn beard and still
burnt with powder."

Colonel Higginson had been more or less associ-
ated in Worcester with Dr. E. E. Hale, who was for
a time the only clergyman in that city who was willing to exchange with the pastor of the Free Church.

"I had such an amusing glimpse," he wrote, "of
Edward Hale and his numerous offspring. I was at
the Redwood library [Newport] and heard the tramp
of many feet and supposed it an excursion party;
then his cheery voice. . . . They had stopped on
their way from Block Island to the Narragansett
region where they live. I showed them a few things
and presently they streamed out again, I bidding
them farewell. Going toward the door I met the
elder girl returning, and looking for something as if
she had dropped a glove or a handkerchief. I said,
'Are you looking for anything?' and she said, smiling shyly, 'For a pair of twins!' It was even so.
Hale, counting up his party on the sidewalk, missed
nothing but a pair of twins and sent her back to find
them in some corner; which being done, they proceeded to the steamboat."

Various foreign notabilities often found their way
to Newport.

"To-day," wrote Colonel Higginson on June 18,
1876, "I have been to lunch with Dom Pedro of
Brazil and the Empress at Bancroft's — the most

bourgeois and good natured of sovereigns, especially the latter, though she is . . . a Bourbon. He looks like a heavy professor of a country college and she like any little stout middle aged lady. . . .

"It is pleasant to think," he mused, "that summer visitors are always a source of pleasure, if not by their coming, then by their going."

In the midst of this pleasant social life Colonel Higginson was still sending monthly articles to the "Atlantic," besides doing much miscellaneous writing. Some of these papers describing Newport life were later published in a volume entitled "Oldport Days." Meantime he kept himself informed of the whereabouts and welfare of the men of his old regiment, and in June after attending a military funeral, he reflected: —

"How great the charm of military life; it makes me almost unhappy to see men form in line and think of the happy time when that was the daily occupation of my life. . . .

"How like a dream it all seems. . . . That I was in it myself seems the dreamiest thing of all; I cannot put my hand upon it in the least, and if some one convinced me, in five minutes some morning, that I never was there at all, it seems as if it would all drop quietly out of my life, and I should read my own letters and think they were some one's else. This is one thing that makes it hard for me to . . . write anything about those days, though sooner or later I shall do it all. . . .

THOMAS WENTWORTH HIGGINSON, 1865

"It seemed like a dream to go to Worcester and see how three years had restored my young recruits to their old places in shops &c., and swept away all traces of those stirring days. Yet the Old Guard of those elderly gentlemen were still parading the streets, and that made all the real soldiering seem more a dream than ever."

"To keep up my interest in slavery," wrote Colonel Higginson to his old army surgeon, — "I am translating Epictetus who is far superior to your dear Antoninus." Somewhat later another most congenial literary task was accomplished by the retired Colonel and he told Dr. Rogers: —

"I have undertaken a job — to edit the memorial volumes containing lives of those Harvard boys who have died in the war — it will take me a year almost. I write editorially for the Independent too, as well as the Commonwealth and Atlantic — so you see I have enough on hand. . . .
"I have been invited to be agent for New England of the Freedmen's Union with a salary of $2500."

This proposal Colonel Higginson was obliged to decline.

Public speaking had been promptly resumed when his military life ended, and was never again entirely given up. He spoke easily without notes until age made memory treacherous, and his enunciation was so clear that even when his voice grew weak in later years he could still be easily heard. As a presiding officer he was always in demand, having a gift of lighting up a dull occasion by ready wit or anecdote, of tactfully suppressing long-winded speakers, and of gracefully preserving harmony between conflicting opinions. Invitations to lecture which involved a night's absence were usually declined while in Newport, on account of his wife's failing health, but this rule was sometimes broken; and on one of these occasions, he wrote from Washington, D.C.: —

"Last night my lecture was a real success, they say, and I repeat it because I am prone to humility about speaking and put all my conceit into my writing. It seemed rather an ordeal to speak before Congressmen and Washington people, they have such a surfeit of it; and Gen. Grant had taken a special interest in the lecture and made his friends buy tickets."

Again from Ann Arbor, Michigan, he wrote: —

"To-day I have been in some of the classes — one most tumultuous class of 350 law students who were in ecstasies over a little speech I made — I thought they would carry me on their shoulders. Then I had to make a little speech to Prof. Tyler's class in English literature also (35 young men 6 young women) to whom he introduced me as the best living writer of the English language! Thus much for western zeal; but I am very glad to have been here, it is so well to get beyond one's accustomed circle."

In the winter of 1867 the lecturer arranged to break away from his moorings for a fortnight and thus describes some of his experiences: —

"I have a great renewal of interest in the 'Atlantic,' [Monthly] from my trip out West where it preceded me everywhere and I have realized what a clientèle it gave. In two places people came 12 miles to hear me, because they had subscribed from the beginning. I heard of a little town in northern Iowa (Caspar) where there were 50 houses and (before the war) 25 copies. . . .

"The remotest places I liked best; it was so strange to dip down on these little western towns and find an audience all ready and always readers of the 'Atlantic' so glad to see me. One man, an original subscriber to the 'Atlantic Monthly,' brought his family 20 miles to hear me. This was at Decorah near the Minnesota border and 10 miles from a railway."

He also met a young farmer who said: —

"He and his father always looked for my articles in the 'Atlantic' and cut those leaves first — the best compliment I ever had. . . .

" My lecture is on 'American Society' a modification of one on American Aristocracy which I gave at Brattleboro before the war. It goes very well and I get $100 a night and make about $450 by the trip — beside the interest and satisfaction of it, which pays for itself."

His lectures nearer home often gave him pleasant glimpses of the life of old friends.

"At Amesbury," he wrote to his sisters, "I staid with Whittier who . . . seems brighter than I expected in his loneliness. . . . He has a singular companion — a wonderful parrot, 30 years old, an African parrot *Quaker colored* with a scarlet tail. The only sensible and intelligible parrot I ever saw, and we had much conversation."

And when he lectured in Concord he wrote: —

"I staid at Mr. Emerson's and it was very sweet to see him with his grandchildren . . . tending the baby of 7 months on his knee and calling him 'a little philosopher.'"

The Sons of Temperance claimed Colonel Higginson's aid, anti-slavery conventions were still in vogue, and he went several times to Washington and Cleveland to preside at Woman Suffrage Conventions. Mrs. Higginson's letters to the Brattleboro family always contained characteristic comments on her husband's doings.

"Wentworth has been away two days this week," she wrote, "and going to-night to Washington to fight for women. I wish they had been fixed before we were born. . . . Lately he has been trying to find a father and *Grandfather* for some stray girl — I don't know who — but he has n't found them yet, but I suppose he will persevere — I should think *one*

would be enough — but he is naturally thorough you
know."

The Colonel explained in a postscript: —

"The case of this girl is that she wants a pension
because her father was a soldier and died in the
rebel prison. . . . I have come upon only two ob-
stacles to her wish:
"1st that she is *not* the man's daughter.
"2d that he is still alive."

Occasionally Colonel Higginson attended meetings
of the Boston Radical Club, a society of advanced
thinkers which met once a month at the hospitable
house of Rev. and Mrs. J. T. Sargent. Here an essay
on some philosophic or theological subject was read
and discussed, often with great animation. A bomb
was thrown into the camp one day in the shape of a
clever anonymous poem, a parody on Poe's "Raven,"
taking off the members of the club. One verse introduced Higginson thus: —

> "Then a colonel, cold and smiling,
> With a stately air beguiling,
> Who punctuates his paragraphs
> On Newport's shining shore."

At one of these meetings where Rev. Mr. Weiss re-
pudiated a "peace-basis" for either earth or heaven,
Colonel Higginson labelled his theories "The Gospel of the Shindy." In spite of his own independent views, the latter always took the part of the

"under dog." On one of these occasions he answered certain caustic strictures on the Bible with such earnestness that a listener exclaimed, "How rich to hear Higginson standing up for the Orthodox ministers!"

In 1867 he was instrumental in forming the Free Religious Association of Boston, and according to the records of the society he "has been present at more of its councils, has presided over more of its festivals, and has delivered more addresses from its platform than any other person." He was one of the officers of the association from its beginning, serving either as president, vice-president, or on the board of directors. Of the convention in 1868, he wrote in his diary, — "Very successful and Potter and I are well repaid for our hard work. Still my insatiate industry of temperament seems to give me no time to enjoy."

He was sometimes asked to state his religious belief, and among his unpublished manuscripts was found this paper entitled "My Creed": —

"In the life of every thoughtful man, no matter how sunny his temperament, there are moments of care, sorrow, depression, perplexity when neither study nor action nor friends will clear the horizon. . . . It is at such times that the thought of an Unseen Power comes to help him; by no tradition of the churches, with no apparatus of mythology; but simply in the form that the mystics call 'the flight of the Alone, to the Alone.' . . . It may be in a church; it may equally well be in a solitary room or on a mountain height. . . . The test of such an experience, call it prayer or reverie or what you please — is as substantial as anything that can come to us. . . . I am not so sure of what I see with my eyes — not so sure that two and two make four — not so sure of any of the forms of the logical syllogism as I am of the genuineness and value of these occasional moments. . . . Far be it from me to claim that any such experience is essential to a moral life, or even to a self-devoted life; that would be a mistaken assumption, and indeed the very fact that one is without this source of refreshment and comfort may only make his self-abnegation more complete, his virtue more heroic, because accompanied with the renunciation of joy. But I am not one of those who believe that life should consist mainly of renunciation and self-abnegation, whether of the Roman Catholic or of the agnostic type; but that it should attain to peace and joy. We can all see that a great deal of brave work is done by heroic men in a spirit so grim and determined that if it does not fatigue the world for which it is applied, it wears out the man who applies it; and the experience of personal religion, in the old sense, but purified from all the repulsive associations of cant and hypocrisy — this surely supplies the oil that is needed, in order that there may be some relief to this terrible friction which wears out so many lives. All honor to the great scientific investigations which are to so many the only path out of crushing opposition; but let us recognize also that science is not all, and that help and strength may still come from a region unexplored by science. Grant that its experiences and lights are as yet unsystematic, unmeasured, occasional; and that few lives can be kept always at their high level, yet it is something to know what that level is."

He was fond of quoting Emerson's saying, "Better that the book should not be quite so good, and the bookmaker abler and better and not himself often a ludicrous contrast to all that he has written."

"Perhaps no sentence," he wrote, "ever influenced my life so much as this since about 1844. It has made me willing to vary my life and work for personal development, rather than to concentrate it and sacrifice myself to a specific result. . . . The trouble with me is too great a range of tastes and interests. I love to do everything, to study everything, to contemplate and to write. I never was happier than when in the army entirely absorbed in active duties; yet I love literature next — indeed almost better; and I need either two lives or 48 hours in the day to do all. How plain that there must be other spheres!"

It was with amused surprise that he read one day a proposal of the Springfield "Republican" that he should be made president of Harvard University. "It is a compliment," he told his sisters, "to be even talked about for this position. There is no possibility of my being appointed. . . . Heard from Stephen [his brother] that he had urged me for President of Harvard College! . . . I might add that I am to be President of Harvard University because one zealous relative is pushing me. But I think I had better wait fifty or a hundred years ere announcing so extreme an impracticability as that."

At one time he received an invitation to become chancellor of the State University of Nebraska. "Such things gratify me," he said, but "I should give up my literary life very unwillingly." He was also urged to apply for the collectorship of Newport, which he declined to do. Some of the attentions which he received caused the recipient much amusement. For instance, he wrote in 1877: —

"I had such an odd letter from a New York pilot who has just built a fine vessel and wished to name it after T. W. Higginson as a Christian, philanthropist and a whole string of epithets which were quite intoxicating till they ended with 'and one of the most eminent *bankers* in New England.' This not being my strong point I was convinced at last that he had jumbled George H. [the father of Henry Lee Higginson] and me hopelessly together, so I sent the letter to George H. — with the less reluctance as he [the pilot] delicately hinted at least that I should be expected to provide 'the maiden suit of colors' at $75 in return for the honor."

For the summer months the Higginsons were in the habit of moving to the "Point," which the Colonel once described as the most captivating place he ever lived in — "amid birds and elm boughs and the lovely walk along the Bay, close by." Here they occupied the house in which the scene of "Malbone" was laid, and where the winding secret staircase described in the novel actually existed.

"We have just removed to new summer quarters," he wrote, "namely a very old and stately house by the bay, with grand mahogany stairways, several rooms panelled to the ceiling and as much carving as any Newburyport house. . . . We are wholly apart from the fashionable region here, and it seems like a fishing hamlet in the suburbs."

A family of New York children who also summered at the "Point" gave great delight to Colonel Higginson. He taught them to swim, took them sailing, and thus described one of them: —

"My little Marie's charms are at present in a state of chaos, some other child having snipped off her hair, and nature having borrowed her two upper teeth; but her eyes are like great deep ocean caves, with such unconscious lashes!"

When in the autumn he was obliged to part from these little companions he complained, "It is a heart-breaking business this setting one's affections on other people's children." Yet he tried to comfort himself by thinking, "It never has been clear to me till lately that the great aim of this life is to show us what happiness might be — leaving it for other spheres to secure it."

In one of his Decoration Day addresses, when an allusion was made to the growing amity between the North and the South, Colonel Higginson said, "I never can forget that my black soldiers, when decorating graves for our own army, forty years ago, proposed for themselves to put flowers also on the graves of those who fought bravely on the other side." It was after one of these occasions that the poem "Decoration Day" was written. This has probably been more widely read and copied than any of Colonel Higginson's verses, except the poem called "The Things I Miss." In a letter to a friend he explained the origin of the latter verses: —

"Did I ever tell you the secret of that bit of confidence with Heaven? . . . I published the verses [in 1870] without initials and nobody knew who wrote them . . . but they have been twice as much praised by strangers as all I have written beside in verse."

This poem touched many hearts and, after the authorship was revealed, brought the writer so many letters of praise that he once said he thought it would be his "best bid for immortality."

In reading these verses, it is well to remember that, whatever privations were known to Colonel Higginson, he had a marvellous faculty of forgetting personal troubles: —

"There is one trait of mine which I almost regret, growing out of that elasticity of nature to which I owe so much. No matter what depression, anxiety or fear I may have had, the moment it is removed all trace of it vanishes. There is no 'recoil of bliss' to correspond to the discomfort; the latter simply drops off and is forgotten."

This period seemed to him to be the high tide of his intellectual activity, and he wrote: —

"This feeling of fertility is a happy thing, it enriches all life and enables me to do without many things."

In analyzing his own style, the author noted in his journal: —

"I have fineness and fire, but some want of copiousness and fertility which may give a tinge of thinness to what I write. . . . What an abundance, freshness and go there is about the Beechers, for instance. They are egotistic, crotchety and personally disagreeable, and they often 'make fritters of English' but I wish I could, without sacrificing polish, write with that exuberant and hearty zeal . . . Shakespeare may have written as the birds sing, though I doubt it — but minor writers at least have to labor for *form* as the painter labors — the mere inspiration

of thought is not enough. . . . There must be a
golden moment but also much labor within that moment. At least it is so with me, and I cannot help
suspecting that it is even so with the Shakespeares."

On New Year's Day, 1866, the thought first came
to Colonel Higginson, while reading Hawthorne's
"Marble Faun," that he might write a romance, a
project always before rejected. The thought rapidly
took shape in his mind, too rapidly, he wrote in his
diary, for his own comfort, being overworked as
editor of the "Harvard Memorial Biographies." In
March, he reports himself as still crushed under letters and memoirs, having himself written thirteen of
the biographies for these volumes. But on his long
solitary walks, he dreamed happily about the projected story. He wrote in his diary: —

"A wild afternoon and I imagined a scene for my
romance so vividly that it now seems real to me.
. . . Walked to cliffs late in afternoon — it is astonishing how much dearer is one spot to me since
I planned a scene there for my romance."

In 1866, he finished the "Memorial Biographies"
and wrote, "Liberty at last." A few days later his
diary chronicles, "Offer from Fields to write 10 articles for 'Atlantic' for $1000 — from Jan. 1." Of one
of these papers, "A Driftwood Fire," he wrote in his
diary: —

"Jan. 24, 1867. When I print a thing like the Driftwood Fire — which seems to me to have a finer touch in it than anything I ever wrote — I feel as if it were thrown into the sea and as if nobody living cared for it. How can a man write who does not enjoy intensely the writing itself as I do? When I first read anything of mine in print, it is with perfect delight — then comes depression and the doubt whether anybody cares for such things and then I let it go, and get interested in something else."

His birthday meditations that year ran thus: —

"Looking back . . . I feel renewed gratitude for that wonderful cheerfulness and healthiness of nature I inherited from my mother. This season always gives some feeling of loneliness to one of my temperament who is childless . . . and whose home is a hospital and who sees the only object of his care in tears of suffering daily. . . . And while literary sympathy or encouragement come slowly, I yet do surely feel an enriching of the mind this winter, more ideality, more constructive and creative faculty — such as I should think my Driftwood Fire would prove to all, if anybody cared for such things. For I am sometimes haunted with the feeling that it is too soon for any ideal treatment in America. Who reads 'Twice-Told Tales'?"

In 1867, Colonel Higginson translated various sonnets from Petrarch, wrote essays and short stories for the "Atlantic," continued his army papers, and compiled a little book by request of Ticknor and Fields, called "Child Pictures from Dickens," which was issued at the time of Dickens's second visit to this country.

The summary of a single day's occupation, jotted down in the diary, illustrates the truth of Mr. A. Bronson Alcott's description of Colonel Higginson as "a man of tasks." In one day he had revised a memoir for one of the numerous literary aspirants who continually sought his sympathetic aid, written a book notice and several letters, made the first draughts of two "Independent" articles, aided in a written examination of the high school for one and a half hours in the afternoon, and spent two and a half hours examining school papers in the evening, besides his usual exercise.

In the summer of this year (1867), he embodied some of his translations of Petrarch's sonnets in a paper which he thus described in a letter to J. T. Fields, whom he called his poet-publisher: —

"I am writing a species of rhapsody called Sunshine and Petrarch, supposed to be written out-of-doors; a kind of plum pudding, Nature furnishing the pudding — Petrarch the plums, translated sonnets being inserted at proper intervals. It is charming *to the writer* which is dangerous, as the ratio of fascination is generally inverted ere reaching the public. As puddings should be thoroughly boiled, I shall keep this the rest of the week, probably."

His diary records: —

"For the first time took my Petrarch writing out-doors . . . sat at different points, chiefly at Myers House — yard full of spiræa, lilac, clover, grass in blossom, daisies — robin's nest oddly placed in birch tree far out on bough. A delicious time!"

In 1903, a dainty volume of these sonnets was published and a copy sent through the American ambassador to Queen Marguerite of Italy who received it with gracious commendation. The book also received a flattering reception from an Italian society at Arezzo formed to honor Petrarch's memory.

The beginning of Colonel Higginson's work on "Malbone" is thus noted: —

"To-day I felt an intense longing to work on my imaginary novel. . . . The impulse was so strong I yielded to it and got a first chapter into shape that satisfied. This was enough and afterwards I could return to the essay."

January 1, 1868, he continued: —

"I know that this Romance (Malbone) is in me like the statue in the marble, for every little while I catch glimpses of parts of it here and there. I have rather held back from it, but a power within steadily forces me on; the characters are forming themselves more and more, . . . and it is so attractive to me that were it to be my ruin in fame and fortune I should still wish to keep on."

On March 11, he wrote four pages for the story, and says, "I enjoy this extremely and am much encouraged, but cannot afford to reject the offer to write Margaret Fuller's life." This was an article for a volume by different writers called "Eminent Women of the Age," and for the same publication Mr. Higginson wrote a memoir of Lydia Maria Child. His biography of Margaret Fuller Ossoli was published sixteen years later in the "American Men of Letters Series."

A few days later, he had accomplished —

"5 pages Malbone — and letter to N.Y. Standard. I have now 50 pages of this novel. For the first time perhaps I have something to write which so interests me it is very hard to leave it even for necessary exercise. I hate to leave it a moment — and yet I have to write about Margaret Fuller."

A week later, he added: —

"6 pages Ossoli. Like this very well, but grudge the time taken from Malbone, about which I was beginning to feel very happy.

"I do not think that anything except putting on uniform and going into camp has ever given me such a sense of new strange fascinating life, as the thought that I can actually construct a novel. It is as if I had learned to fly."

In April he decided not to interrupt "Malbone"

again, but to postpone "Army Life" if necessary, and adds: —

"Told Fields about Malbone — and he was very sympathetic and asked many questions and said must have it in 'Atlantic.'"

Before the book appeared, the author reflected: —

"It is impossible for me to tell what will be thought of this book, whether it will be found too shallow or too grave, too tragic or too tame; I only know that I have enjoyed it more than anything I ever wrote (though writing under great disadvantages) and that the characters are like real men and women to me, though not one of them was, strictly speaking, imitated from life, as a whole."

Yet two of the characters in "Malbone" were suggested by real persons. Many of Aunt Jane's witty sayings had originated with Mrs. Higginson, and Philip Malbone was drawn from memories of Hurlbut, the author's early friend. On September 25, he had ended the story and sent it to Fields, and quoted in his diary a passage from Browning's "Paracelsus": —

> "Are there not . . .
> Two points in the adventure of a diver,
> One — when, a beggar, he prepares to plunge,
> One — when, a prince, he rises with his pearl?
> Festus, I plunge!"

In November he had finished working over the manuscript and says: —

"There is, with all my fussy revising and altering, always a point where a work seems to take itself into its own hands . . . and I can no more control it than an apple-tree its fallen apples."

The advent of "Malbone" was announced to the writer's sisters with this comment: —

"I expect dismay on your part, my dear sisters, before you see it and perhaps after — but I had to write it. I enjoyed it so much, so we must acquiesce."

After the book was actually published (1869), he wrote: —

"As for my new literary venture, it is received with quiet approbation apparently though not with eagerness. . . . It seemed strange to me to hold my own novel in my hand, after all the thought and feeling I had put into it — and after thinking for so many years that I never could or would write one."

The announcement of an English reprint of "Malbone" pleased the author, and when in after years he revisited the scene of the story, he wrote in his diary: —

"Walked along the bay, beside the empty houses, and the dismantled house where I wrote Malbone. The fog bell tolled and the whole scene was full of ghosts; how long it seemed since those dreamy summers! That was the ideal epoch of my life: I have written nothing like that since and may not again."

In January, 1869, he continued: —

"I begin this year with a feeling of publicity and perhaps assured position such as never before. This is due to the reception of Malbone and my paper on the Greek Goddesses and also to lecturing more and to my participation in Woman's Suffrage Movement, Grand Army affairs and (prospectively) Free Religious Convention . . . I like it — and especially in view of the diminished society around me in Newport."

In April he felt "rather tired of writing," and held back from his "Army Life," adding, "Shall I compel myself to it?" However, he was soon hard at work on this collection of army papers, and on September 22, wrote: —

"'Army Life in a Black Regiment' published to-day. It is amazing how indifferent I feel as to the reception of this book, compared with 'Malbone,' which was so near my heart. It scarcely awakens the slightest emotion."

But a little later this feeling changed: —

"After reading a graphic military novel turned to my 'Army Life' and read it with surprise and interest; and with a sort of despair at the comparative emptiness of all other life after that."

Twenty years afterward, he wrote to Dr. Rogers: —

"Those times are ever fresh and were perhaps the flower of our lives."

After the publication of "Malbone" and "Army Life," Colonel Higginson was able to command a higher price for his writings.

"This is a substantial gain from my increased reputation," he reflected. "But after all no amount for mere writing yields a large income — only lecturing pays. . . . I have never in my life felt so easy as to money as in the 3 months past — nor sure of so large an audience — but I feel the intellectual solitude here more than formerly."

The year after "Malbone" appeared, its author began "to have a great craving after another story — even if nobody cares for it but myself. . . . Sometimes I fancy that I am wasting my life in trying to be an architect of Alhambra for a people who demand plain brick and mortar. I see a dozen themes for tragedy just around me — the want is not of material but of demand. . . . So slowly has my small portion of reputation been acquired that it always rather surprises me if any one cares for anything I write."

One of this busy author's amusements was planning for more literary work than he could possibly accomplish, making out lists of projected essays and stories. "Thinking of many books lately [to write]," says the journal. "A little money would help me wonderfully about these." On a page of his 1872 diary is a list of ten books which he had planned to write, the last of which was to be "The Intellectual History of Woman." Of this he wrote, "My *magnum opus*, if I can really ever get to it." For this contemplated work Colonel Higginson collected for many years all the books he could find bearing on the development of woman. The "magnum opus" was never really attempted, but the collection of books numbering several hundred volumes in a variety of languages was finally given to the Boston Public Library and entitled the "Galatea Collection," the name being suggested by the old fable of Pygmalion and Galatea. Higginson took great interest in adding to this unique collection from time to time, being assisted in this rare pastime of buying books by an annual donation for the purpose from Mr. Carnegie. But his attention was soon turned to a different sort of history.

At this time there was great need of an attractive juvenile history of the United States, and Mr. George B. Emerson, a popular Boston educator, suggested to Colonel Higginson that he should furnish such a book. To make this plan practicable, Mr. Emerson advanced one thousand dollars to supply the means of livelihood while the task was under way. "I am trying to write a History of the United States for young people," reported the new his-

torian after a year's labor, "but don't know whether
it will be readable after all." While collecting material for the book, he records writing one day ten
postal cards in "10 languages — English, French,
Spanish, Italian, Portuguese, German, Swedish,
Latin, Greek, Hebrew."

The first draught was considered by Mr. Emerson
too juvenile, and it was therefore necessary to re-
write it. The work was finally completed in 1874
and the author wrote: —

"It is a relief to me at last to have this work done,
as it pressed on me a good deal, and especially this
month. On the whole I have rather enjoyed it,
though so long continued a work. . . . I should not
have a doubt [as to its success] were it written by any
one else. My luck may turn but I don't think I was
born to be rich. I have had to economize unusually
these last two years, for Mr. Emerson's $1000 has
been far from compensating for the time I have
given. And unless I clear something beyond that
first $1000 which goes to him, I shall be out of
pocket.

"It will be pleasant to think, in any case, that I
have done something to make American history
clear and attractive."

This book inaugurated a new era in writing history
for children, and Mr. Emerson assured the author
that he had done the world a great service. After the
history was in print, Higginson wrote: —

"What puzzles me about the Young Folks' history is that work which so often (certainly) dragged in the writing should be found so universally attractive in the reading. . . .

"I was in Boston on Wednesday (a few weeks after the publication) and found the 9th thousand of the history then in press — about 6000 of these sold and ordered, and constant demand. They feel very confident of a continued sale, by all the signs. I am now making some farther alterations for a new edition. The publishers wish me to make a manual of Universal History now — pleasant offer!

"I think I have now for the first time accepted the fact that I have achieved a worldly success at last and may really have those additional few hundred dollars a year that would seem wealth to me. Perhaps even this year I may. . . . It does not excite me, but I confess to agreeable sensations."

A month later the diary records: —

"A memorable day. In the morning I had a note telling that Mr. Shepard expected to sell 40,000 of the Young Folks' History this year and 200,000 in all. . . . Then at evening came the kindest letter from Mr. Emerson saying that he was 'sufficiently repaid' for the money advanced on the book, and should not take it back. This munificence gives me $1000 additional in August — probably $2000 in all. For the first time, I think, I begin really to believe that I am to have some money to spend — after fifty years of care and economy. This economy I have never really disliked, indeed have found a cer-

tain amusement and satisfaction in. But I shall like
the other still better, though it will be hard to adapt
myself and even now I can hardly count on it."

These half-doubting anticipations received a
check three months later in the financial failure of
his publishers.

"It is curious," he meditated, "to study the currents of life. For 3 months I have felt as if I really
had some money — but now the great depression of
business prevents Lee and Shepard from collecting
or sending and I have been obliged to be more careful than ever, this month. . . . How suddenly my
supposed increase of income has been interrupted and
I have even less than before. Waldo said, 'It only
involves some waiting!' I said, 'I've been waiting
all my life.'

"Sept. 16. To Boston — Lee and Shepard —
meeting of creditors — about that convenient little
cup that has slipped from my lips. However I had
for two months the sensations of a comfortable
income. . . .

"Sept. 25. Tried in vain to write; I am so heavily
weighed down with anxiety and care between M.'s
wretched condition and Lee and Co.'s failure that it
is almost impossible for me to write. The walls seem
only to draw closer around me year by year."

But this depression was only temporary, and in
October the tables were turned.

"All my life I have had a sort of Bank of Faith in

money matters," wrote the relieved author, "when pretty low I always expect a windfall — so to-day came a letter from Lee & Shepard . . . with check for $247.9? for sales since their failure . . . a very reassuring letter at once removing that uncertainty for the future which was my chief solicitude."

This successful history was translated into French in 1875, and two editions were published. In 1876, a German version was printed, and it was translated into Italian in 1888. In May, 1879, the book was adopted by the Boston public schools. This seemed to the author "a real access of fortune — yet I always think how little money can give after all." One of the best endorsements of the book came from a boy of eight, the son of a Harvard professor, who declared, "I like your History of the United States about as well as the Odyssey." Another came from a teacher in North Carolina: "My class is intensely interested in it [Young Folks' History]. The book has in it more to arouse the child's patriotism than any book that I have ever seen. . . . The teaching profession is under many obligations to you." In 1905, an edition of this History was, by private generosity, printed in raised letters for the blind.

The Higginsons made an occasional attempt at housekeeping, and during the latter part of Mrs. Higginson's life they were able to keep up this mode of living, which gave both much pleasure. "We have now in the kitchen," wrote the Colonel,"as cook, the black minister's mother, very large and 70 — she . . . gets on well, makes pretty bad bread and is too old to come upstairs." Again: "Able to enjoy a quiet Thanksgiving at home. M. was very happy and the little house seemed very pleasant. I desire not to get used to it, but to keep freshly in mind what a pleasure it is to have a home."

The diary of 1870 recorded that the writer was reading and planning for Europe. On each birthday or New Year's Day, Colonel Higginson wrote in his journal a brief summary of his life, and under date of January 1, 1870, occurs the following: —

"I begin the year under some new spiritual influences, I hope, with some firmer purposes, more patience. I shall miss 'Malbone' and feel yearly the want of social interests here — but I have the prospect of Europe, which will be a great era."

This plan was sorrowfully relinquished, and in March he wrote: —

"I am suffering under unusual depression, for me, partly the disappointment about Europe . . . and partly the stagnation of this place and my monotonous life."

However, two years later the European project was revived and he actually went abroad for two months, his sister Anna taking his place during his absence. An account of this memorable visit to Europe will be found in a later chapter.

In 1876, Mr. Higginson began to write reviews of "recent poetry" for the "Nation," and this critical work was continued for more than a quarter of a century. Looking over his outdoor notebook he exclaimed, "How I should love to devote the greater part of the summer to insects — but I am now more committed to the study of men and women."

During his wife's long helplessness, Colonel Higginson's devotion was unceasing, and when the end came, September 2, 1877, he wrote to a friend: —

"My wife died . . . after a week's illness of 'intestinal fever.' She has been losing strength this summer and was perhaps unable to throw off an attack that she could else have resisted. She did not suffer much and closed her courageous life quietly. You are one of those whose personal experience has taught you what it is to lose an object of *care;* how little there seems left to be done, how strange and almost unwelcome the freedom."

The long continued weight of responsibility could not at once be thrown off, and for a time Colonel Higginson was haunted by the bewildering thought that he was neglecting his duty. This feeling was expressed in his touching unpublished verses, called

"Relieved from Guard," two of which are given below: —

"O! I shrink from this untried freedom
In a world I do not know.
Give me back the long, long watching
And the pacing to and fro!

"They will pass, these weak repinings;
And only one thought be hard,
That I know not which of God's angels
Is now at my post, on guard!"

XIV

In the spring of 1878, Colonel Higginson went abroad for several months. After his return in the autumn, he moved his goods and chattels to Cambridge. Here he took delight in planning a new home, and in February, 1879, was quietly married to the writer of this memoir. His old friend, Rev. Samuel Longfellow, performed the ceremony. The "being beauteous" of Longfellow's poem, "Footsteps of Angels," was my mother's sister, and the poet was present at the wedding.

A visit made soon afterward to my kindred in Harper's Ferry was described by Colonel Higginson in a letter to his sister: —

"You can imagine nothing more curious than our arrival at Harper's Ferry. It was in the evening. . . . The train stopped in a dismantled sort of station where stood an old man with soft white hair on his shoulders holding a lantern and attended by two blooming, fair-haired daughters; they seized us with joy. There seemed no houses anywhere and we set off to walk across ruined pavements feebly lighted by the one lantern. Presently they turned up a flight of

stone steps. . . . At the top we saw a lighted chapel
and throngs of people were descending from it. We
went up and up with the dim outlines of river and
mountains below us and the sound of the waters over
their shallow bed; then we turned into a narrow
street or lane paved with the natural rock and with
high narrow stone houses chiefly in ruins. . . . It was
all precisely like a Swiss or Italian mountain village
and I felt as if I had made one step from Zermatt.

"The church was the family church, they being
Roman Catholics. The old Doctor is of Irish birth
and has lived all his life in Virginia. His house is one
of a block of four, two in ruins and empty belonging
also to him. From another ruined house the cow
looks out all day. . . . Our arriving was an excitement to all Harper's Ferry. All knew that the bridal
party was coming. In the evening came Jacob [a
Negro factotum]. He brought the largest round of
beef I ever saw — with only us two to eat it until
Easter, this being Friday — also a basket of provisions, and himself most important of all. He cooked,
talked, waited at table in a Madras turban and glo-
rified himself through the village at other times. . . .
On opening an unexpected curtain in the morning,
the whole glorious valley view was before us. . . .
The poor town looked shabby and ruined by day";
[but there were Turkey rugs and the rustle of silk
gowns in the crumbling old house]. "During the war
they were here when only five families staid in the
town. After eight all windows had to be darkened,
otherwise the Union pickets fired on them from the
Maryland heights and the rebels from the other side.

There were bullet marks on the table. . . . We had a beautiful drive up the Shenandoah hills with Blue Ridge always in sight, amid large farms looking like Pennsylvania and very fertile. We went to Charlestown, eight miles, a flourishing village with nice houses and buildings. Here we saw the jail yard where John Brown was confined, the field where he was executed, the new court house on the site where he was tried, and most interesting of all, the very records of the trial of him and his men — the successive entries alternating with the commonest things. The road we came was that over which they were brought, wounded, from Harper's Ferry. The only memorial of him at the latter place is the little building close by the railroad — the engine house which he held — which has 'John Brown's Fort' painted on it."

After this trip, we began housekeeping, and then Colonel Higginson earnestly threw himself into the interests of his native town. In January, 1880, our first little daughter was born and called Louisa for her grandmother Higginson. On the day that his lifelong wish for a child was realized, Colonel Higginson wrote in his journal: —

"God! May I be worthy of the wonderful moment when I first looked round and saw the face of my child. . . . How trivial seem all personal aims and ambitions beside the fact that I am at last the father of a child. Should she die to-morrow she will still be my child somewhere. But she will not die."

RETURN TO CAMBRIDGE 295

When seven days old the baby received a visit
from the poet Longfellow, who saw beauty and intelligence in her face, and said she had the hands of a
musician. "These three," wrote her father, "beauty,
observation, and music, when coming from the lips
of a poet were quite equivalent to gifts from a fairy
godmother."

Although the child seemed very robust, when a
few weeks old she died of meningitis after one day's
illness. "Thus end our pride and our earthly hope,"
wrote the bereaved father. "Yet so unspeakable has
been the joy of her little life; so profound and wonderful the feeling of parentage; so perfect a sense of
individuality about this baby child that we shall
soon be able to thank God for all. . . . O but the
heart-break and the yearning! . . . O the hopes, the
dreams, the fancies all now done, or exchanged for
profounder thought belonging in the world unseen."
A niece of Colonel Higginson's recalls the burial and
writes: "I shall never forget Uncle Wentworth's
beautiful, transfigured look when he said in a broken
yet strong voice, 'The Lord gave, the Lord hath
taken away. Blessed be the name of the Lord.'"
After a few weeks' absence, the Colonel with his
usual elasticity wrote: "To-day we are back again in
our dear home and I feel a sense of new life and joy
and hope this lovely spring day."

The following summer was spent at Plymouth, New Hampshire, where we jogged about with an old horse named Dorcas, studied ferns, and ransacked farms for old furniture. Colonel Higginson once had an opportunity while there to indulge his boyish passion for responding to fire-alarms. He had established himself on a roof to help extinguish the flames of a burning house and was startled when he heard the order, "Hand the bucket to the old gentleman!" — this being the first time he had been thus designated. From Plymouth the same season he made the wild ascent of Mount Moosilauke described in his "Atlantic" article, "A Search for the Pleiades." This paper so pleased the proprietor of the mountain hotel that he offered the author rooms and board *gratis* for the next season. At the end of the summer, this note was made in the diary: —

"The old love of nature seems to have come back and the sorrow which threatened to overshadow us has been mercifully soothed. I have neither 'looked before nor after nor pined for what is not.'"

In the fall of 1880, he was chosen representative to the legislature, where he served for two years. The same year he accepted an invitation from Governor Long to serve as chief of his staff. While in the legislature, of course he championed the Woman's Suffrage Bill. It is stated on good authority that "certain Irish members, who hated Woman's Suffrage but loved the Colonel, sat outside growling while the vote was taken. They could not bring themselves to vote for the bill, but would not annoy Higginson by voting against it."

In December of the same year we moved into the little Queen Anne cottage on Buckingham Street which we had built and which was henceforth Colonel Higginson's home. A certain policeman's opinion of this new abode afforded much amusement to the owner. When asked where Colonel Higginson lived, this guardian of the peace replied, "Look till you see the ugliest house in Cambridge." Another, somewhat later, opinion was that of our daughter Margaret, who said, "O papa, I am glad you are not rich! You have such a dainty little clean house and not fancy either — no lace curtains at all."

The fifty-seventh birthday, December 22, 1880, was celebrated by skating on Fresh Pond, and he wrote to his sister: —

"I have not been on that black ice for more than thirty years and it seemed a very appropriate birthday celebration, the ice and hills and sky were so unchanged. It led me to the thought that this is certainly the happiest birthday since those days and probably of my life. It is such inexpressible happiness to have at last a permanent home and one so wholly to my mind and to look around and think that all in it is ours and we are not temporary occupants of the comforts of others only."

In July, 1881, a second little daughter arrived and was named Margaret Waldo. These were family names, and, contrary to popular belief, were not borrowed from Margaret Fuller and Emerson. "Rejoice with us!" her father wrote to a friend; "another little girl, as fine and beautiful as her elder sister!" After three months he declared, "A more blissful possession no one ever owned. . . . The darling baby seems to have brought a good omen in every way."

In reference to his legislative experience, Higginson wrote: —

"I went to the legislature (having both years had the nomination wholly unsought) because it was a thing I had thought I should always like to try. . . . I have never thought for an instant of 'going into politics' as people say, but simply took it as it came my way knowing it would not last long. . . . I also tried nearly a year ago to get off the staff thinking I had done the Governor all the services I could, but he was unwilling . . . going to Cowpens was a great privilege and opportunity and in a manner a piece of poetic justice. . . . Last summer the Governor wished me to be a trustee of a lunatic hospital which I declined. This year after resigning my place on staff he wished me to take either a similar trustee-

THE HOUSE ON BUCKINGHAM STREET, CAMBRIDGE

ship vacant — or to go on the Board of Education.
With some reluctance I did the latter."

The allusion to Cowpens referred to the address
which Colonel Higginson gave in May, 1881, at
Spartansburg, South Carolina, the occasion being
the celebration of the Battle of Cowpens during the
Revolution, which Bancroft called the "most extraordinary victory of the war." Governor Long had
requested his chief of staff to represent Massachusetts and incidentally the original New England
States at the one hundredth anniversary of this battle, although it was one in which the New England
colonies had no direct share. The letter quoted above
continues: —

"All these things have much interfered with literature and I was getting impatient with myself and
feeling that I had lost power of writing. Then on
waking very early one morning I suddenly decided
to make a book out of my 'Woman's Journal' articles and similar things. I jumped up, went downstairs for a volume of the 'Woman's Journal' and
began in bed the process of selection which went
rapidly on and now the book is finished. . . . And
this détour into public life has been an immense
benefit to me in the way of extempore speaking
which is now really no effort at all.

"The result of all is that I am a truly happy
man and can well wait and accept whatever comes —

only knowing that I cannot have that boundless horizon of years (at 57) that stretches before one at forty or almost at fifty. Margaret gives me a new love of life, and I should like, at 75, to go into company with her at 18!"

On Thanksgiving Day of the same year, he yet further moralized: —

"That I should at 57 have the happiness dreamed of (as impossible) for so many years — with a healthy and beautiful baby of my own . . . and a charming home . . . this is a boon beyond asking or thanking. I have had much of what the world calls success and yet feel profoundly what Howells suggests that perhaps success always looks like failure from inside. I have what would have seemed to me reputation and wealth from the standpoint of my early years; I have also a singular health of body and youthfulness of mind; even the fire of passion and adventure is I fear unabated in me; but in the anchorage of my own home I am guaranteed from danger. . . . My imagination is as active as ever, and my literary faculty; they are only checked by the multiplicity of cares and interests that come with advancing years."

On his sixty-third birthday, the author wrote, "Can work better than ever in my life." And again: —

"Had a striking instance to-day of that great wealth and activity of mind which seems to come to me in rushes for a short time together especially the first thing in the morning. In fifteen minutes . . . I entirely planned two addresses on distinct subjects — the birthday address at Concord on Emerson and the address for the blind. . . . For all this — but chiefly for my wife, child and home, let me give thanks. . . . Whenever I think of illness or death, then it seems beautiful to have one child on earth and one in heaven."

In 1882, he began the chapters of his "Larger History of the United States," which were published in "Harper's Magazine"; of these he told his sister, August 24, 1883, "I have written one of my Harper's papers regularly every month for the last eleven months; besides other things too much for anybody." It was a rare thing for him to admit that he worked beyond his strength, but such was often the case. In the autumn of this year, Colonel Higginson wrote to his sister: —

"I invited Matthew Arnold to spend a few days with us, but he is not coming, being engaged to Phillips Brooks."

And later: —

"This morning I spent in taking Matthew Arnold to schools in Boston. . . . He is very cordial and appreciative, not in the least cynical, or patronizing."

In the poem called "Sixty and Six," Colonel Higginson describes the joy he found in the "blithe lit-

tle, lithe little daughter of mine." The following extracts, referring to his new and absorbing possession,
are taken partly from his letters and partly from his
diaries: —

"To-day the crocuses are up and I have been taking off part of their covering of leaves. . . . But what
is all the promise of early spring beside the round
rosy cheeks of our darling, her great earnest brown
eyes and her happy little face. . . .

"Margaret rosy and sunburnt with dandelions and
sand-pies said this morning, 'Oh, won't it be beautiful in the autumn, when it is all red and ripe' . . .
then she added, 'I do like it awfully.' 'What?' She
looked down meditatively a moment and said, 'To
live.' . . . Baby is wheeling her little barrow of red
crab-apples under the trees. . . . Every morning she
wakes laughing. We hear this delicious little singing
sound from her crib. . . . You may well imagine that
I could not have a happier birthday celebration than
to take baby out for the first time on her new sled!
. . . Showed her little icicles which interested her like
a new flower and she picked them off eagerly. . . . It
is delicious thus to show her for the first time one
wonder after another in the beautiful world. We
threw snowballs too. . . . She inherits from me
amusingly a trait I remember very well and still occasionally manifest — a dislike to being watched
when doing anything difficult. 'Pe'se don't watz
me,' she often says. . . . Margaret had this morning
her first introduction to the masterpieces of English
literature. She brings a copy of 'Christobel.' Papa

objects: 'But that has no picture.' 'Papa read Baby 'at.' Papa dutifully reads —

> " ' 'T is the middle of the night by the castle clock
> And the owls have awakened the crowing cock.'

Baby points to the stuffed owl in the hall. 'Dere he are.' Then Papa reads on about the toothless mastiff bitch with illustrative 'bow-wows.' Baby runs to the window, looks out and says, 'Where bow-wow?' Then returning says, 'Papa, play ball,' having had enough of English literature for the first time.

"She has had a great access of lovingness lately. 'Papa, I love you so much it breaks my heart'; or 'Papa, I shall never leave you.' . . . Margaret said this morning, 'What church shall I go to when I am big enough? Why do people go to church?' After some reflection I said, 'To learn to be good.' After some reflection she said, 'But they're good already!' — a happy conviction.

"This morning she asked her favorite question, 'Where God?' and when her mother said, 'He is everywhere,' she answered with superior information, 'He in Heabby' (Heaven). . . . She is growing sternly speculative. 'Papa dear, do the little fishes at the Botanic Garden *like* to be caught?' 'No, dear.' 'Well, they've got to be caught or how can we have fish to eat?' I do think it would be much prettier to [follow a] vegetarian [diet] in rearing children; I hate to have her kill even a mosquito, it seems to be a profanation of her own life. I tell her to drive them away as papa does — but even then I kill clothes-moths — not in her presence, though. . . . She said one time when I was neglectful, 'Papa, why don't you amuse me? That is what you came into the world for, to amuse people.' . . . When we spoke of some one's being married — she slipping down to my side as usual, 'Papa, whisper! What is married?' (Papa, hesitating.) 'It is when two people live together in a house.' 'Well, then you and I are married.'"

To the above record of this close companionship Colonel Higginson added: —

"I have always hoped that if I might not live to see her grow up, I might at least fix myself so definitely in her memory that I should always be a vivid and tender recollection and of this I now for the first time feel sure."

Margaret's first intimation of the difference in age came one day when her little hands wandered over his face and she exclaimed in a surprised tone, "Why, your face is as twinkled as a little star. Anyhow, Papa, when did you get so many lines in your face?" The proud father's little letters to his daughter show his innate sympathy with childhood: —

"FRANKLIN SQUARE, NEW YORK.

"MY DEAR LITTLE GIRL: —

"This morning I went to see if I could find a fur coat for dolly, but you see they don't make fur coats for dollies. I think you had better catch a little mouse and say, 'Please! mousey, will you lend dolly

THOMAS WENTWORTH HIGGINSON AND HIS
DAUGHTER MARGARET, 1885

your little fur coat.' If he says *No*, what can we do?
But it will soon be spring and she will not need it.
"From your loving PAPA."

"NEW YORK.

"MY DEAR LITTLE GIRL: —
"This morning I went along a great big street
called Broadway and what do you think I saw?
Why, you and me riding on the tricycle; that is I saw
the picture in a window, where the same photo-
graphers who took us have a store here in New York!
Some people stopped to look and one of them said,
'I wonder who that man is with a little girl behind
him.' I could have told him, but I did n't. I might
have said, 'That's Margaret Higginson and I think
the man must be her papa.'
"Good-bye, darling.
"Your own PAPA."

Father and daughter rode on the tricycle together
until one day he looked around and discovered with
alarm that the child of four was fast asleep. After
that he decided to ride alone.

When Margaret was still a small child we spent
three successive summers on a farm in Holden,
Massachusetts, a village near Worcester. It was
Colonel Higginson's delight both there and in Cambridge to amuse Margaret's little friends by making
bonfires and roasting potatoes and apples in the em-
bers. He wrote to his sister: "We have now a cow,

calf, dog, two white fantail pigeons, two kittens and
expect a lamb to-morrow to complete the menagerie." Both father and child entered into the
farm labors, tossing pumpkins into the barn and
feeding the animals.

"This has been the after breakfast programme.
She and I go out of the back door taking with us stale
bread for the hens, soft bread for the doves; then in
the barn we get ears of corn for the rabbits and a pan
of 'shorts' for the calf and lamb. Then we open the
high gate of the great pleasant poultry yard, sloping
down the hill and crossed by rows of raspberries and
roses and sunflowers and apple trees. The creatures
all come to us except the rabbits which are in their
own enclosure within. The hens and ducks scramble
and flutter; and I always wish I could make a sketch
in oils of Margaret as she stands rosy and sunburnt
holding the pan of grain as best she can against the
vehement appetites of calf and lamb growing daily
stronger and larger, nudging each other away and
stretching over or under each other's heads till the
pan is empty. Then they trot along by us in hope of
more, the hens and ducks also following till we go
inside the rabbit hutch and tempt the timid things
with clover and green corn. Then Margaret looks for
eggs in the various boxes and we climb on the hay-
mow to see if the doves are laying. . . . Our two
white fantails are the most devoted little creatures
and seem like two immaculate ladies, always keeping the rooms in order. Yesterday we found some

eggs of the common pigeons just hatched; one little creature had got his head out before and his tail behind but the shell hung round its neck and almost choked it till I loosened it; I never helped a pigeon into the world before."

In the village of Holden, Colonel Higginson rendered signal service, as was his wont in all his abiding places, by advice as to the management of the library and selection of books, by willingness to give public addresses, and by his kindly interest in the people of the town, all of which was warmly appreciated. One of the Holden women said to him afterward, "It seemed so nice to see you there; you seemed like one of us"; and the diary commented, "This identifying with the simple village life is what I like best about it all."

To go back to Cambridge; it was in February, 1884, that the occupations of one week were thus enumerated: —

"During the last week I have had the laborious and careful closing days of my 'Life of Madame Ossoli'; have spoken four evenings (out of five successive evenings) on four different subjects, two of them new, and have had the great excitement and absorption of Phillips's death and funeral, with two papers to write on him — one ('Evening Post') very elaborate, besides one speech about him and revising the report. All this has made more work than I hope

ever to be entangled in again. I have had the immediate prospect too of two more chapters in 'Harper,'
and a revision of my 'Young Folks' History,' these
being demanded at once."

He adds: —

"I finished and sent the last of my 'Harper' papers and also corrected the last proof of my Ossoli
book. Thus ends the most anxious literary task I
ever undertook and one which I shall never try again
— virtually writing two difficult books at the same
time."

Of his weekly editorials he said: —

"Sometimes I have to write my editorials at a
gallop or not at all."

Later in the same year he discontinued his papers in
the "Woman's Journal" and wrote to his sister: —

"I have engaged to write a weekly article for
'Harper's Bazar,' under the general heading 'Women and Men' similar in tone to my 'Woman's
Journal' papers, but not entering on the suffrage
question. On the latter point I expect to write occasionally in the 'Independent.'"

And the following winter he noted: —

"I enjoy writing my 'Bazar' papers, having an
audience of 100,000 all over the world."

In 1884, Colonel Higginson also plunged with
ardor into the "Mugwump" movement, calling anti-

Blaine meetings and making campaign speeches for
Cleveland. His diary reports an anti-Blaine meeting in early June, — "Great success, which gratified
me, since it was I who proposed it and drew up call
which was signed by 1500." From the same record
it appears that in the autumn he gave political ha-
rangues on five successive evenings in as many
cities. This letter gives his impressions of Cleveland and Beecher, that of the latter being less
flattering than an earlier estimate, some thirty years
before.

"New York is fairly seething. . . . Business is practically suspended — nobody talks of anything but
politics. . . . Gov. Cleveland was at my hotel. . . .
I found him a large man, nearly as tall as I and heavily built . . . decidedly plain, but with a very good
clear eye and a frank and honest though not handsome mouth. He has not an air of polish —
rather what we should call a Western than Eastern
type, — but prepossessing through frankness and
strength. . . . On the whole my impression was favorable.

"Not so my impression of Beecher, who is the
only man I have spoken with in public of whom I felt
ashamed. The Jersey City audience was a regular
Bowery audience and he took them completely on
their own level. It was a wonderful exhibition of
popularity and power, but there was a coarse jaunti-
ness in his way of treating the attacks on Cleveland

that disgusted me. . . . Still Beecher is Beecher, at his best and worst."

Yet politics did not exclude other public interests: —

"May 2, 1885.

"I had a very good time speaking on Total Abstinence to an excellent audience of young men at Sanders Theatre with Mrs. Livermore, who appeared admirably. It was a rainy evening but we had a much better audience than Phillips Brooks who preached at St. John's Chapel."

A curious result of this meeting was the arrival at our home, on the same evening, of six bottles of wine labelled "For a man who has the courage of his convictions."

There happened to be in Worcester in this very year a reunion of the Company which Colonel Higginson had recruited. "It was a bewildering evening and night," he wrote, "living back 21 years in an hour. The youngest member of the Company who enlisted at 17 is far grayer than I. All night I could hardly get back from the strange resurrection of my first army experiences — so intense and utterly absorbing — now so inconceivably remote."

It was always a pleasure to Colonel Higginson to live over his dreams by relating them to his family. As early as 1844, when a theological student, he recorded this one: —

"I was mingling in the concerns of life as usual and suddenly became aware of the presence of a red haired wife and two children with large gray eyes; I remember distinctly my utter astonishment and dismay at finding myself so emphatically in for it without any personal consciousness or accountability; what steps I took on the matter I don't know, but I have certainly got rid of the incumbrances this morning much to my relief."

And when he was eighty-five he wrote: —

"I find that my dreams grow more interesting all the time because they have more material in them from the 'hoarded memories of the past,' as Browning says."

In the summer of 1886, he wrote the story, "The Monarch of Dreams." It was his first effort in the story-telling line for many years, and he exclaimed: — "It is a great and almost unexpected delight to me to find that I can really write an imaginative story." This tale did not prove acceptable to magazine editors and was finally published as a booklet at the author's own expense. "The Monarch of Dreams" was, however, translated into French and was always a favorite of the author's. His relatives fancied that this weird little tale had a morbid tinge, and in answer to their solicitudes, he wrote: —

"I am sorry I printed it, if it troubled you, but I never can be sorry that I wrote it, for it is the first strong bit of purely imaginative work I ever did and I shall always be glad to know that I could do it, and it was a real vacation after so much historical and critical work. . . . I like to do things in order to know that I can do them; and the old spirit of adventurousness still lives in me."

The latter statement was proved when the strike of the street-car employees in Cambridge occurred, and he wrote in his diary in March, 1887: —

"Evening to Cambridgeport to meet procession of strikers — rode through them on platform of car; one stone hit me. Find myself enjoying the little danger as of yore."

After another car-ride he reported: —

"The young trolley conductor told me that he had just taken 'Cheerful Yesterdays' from the library and that it was the third book of mine he had read. He spoke especially of the anti-slavery part and has been sorry not to hear me on Irish wrongs at Town Hall."

In May, 1886, Emily Dickinson died. Her acquaintance with Colonel Higginson began in 1862, when she wrote to him enclosing some poems and asking his opinion of her verse. While he was in camp in South Carolina she wrote again to ask if he would be "her preceptor." Henceforth her letters, in extraordinary script, were signed "your scholar." One summer he made his unseen correspondent a long-delayed visit which he has described in the volume

called "Carlyle's Laugh." He wrote in his diary
after her death: —

"To Amherst to the funeral of that rare and
strange creature Emily Dickinson. . . . E. D.'s face
a wondrous restoration of youth — she is 54 and
looked 30, not a gray hair or wrinkle, and perfect
peace on the beautiful brow. There was a little
bunch of violets at the neck and one pink cypripe-
dium; the sister, Vinnie, put in two heliotropes by
her hand 'to take to Judge Lord' [an old family
friend]. I read a poem by Emily Brontë. How large
a portion of the people who have most interested me
have passed away."

But the sad entries in his journal were infrequent
and presently he recorded: —

"One of these days on which, as Emerson says,
'every hour brings book or starlight scroll.' At
breakfast got letters from England, one from W.
Sharp about sonnets of mine for his book of American sonnets — another from —— asking about my
literary methods for his pupils. Then came the
copies of Italian version of my history and finally
(next day) Mrs. Hood's news that she had 'The
Open Garden' ready — her name for illustrations of
'Outdoor Papers.'"

There has always been a confusion in the public
mind between Colonel Wentworth Higginson and
his cousin, Major Henry Higginson, and musicians
sometimes applied to the former for a position in the

Symphony Orchestra. He was wont to say that he
received everything that was intended for his cousin
except cheques. Reporting to his family in their absence various funny stories that he had heard, he
added, "But best of all was the news that several
New York papers have just printed advance puffs of
the Symphony Orchestra headed by my picture."
He wrote to his brother-in-law, in July, 1887: —

"Did you hear that I had been invited to be president of the Handel and Haydn Society? Of course
I refused, but it seemed as if they wanted a good
figurehead with a musical name. 'If it be not Bran
it is Bran's brother,' as the Scotch proverb says."

Yet Colonel Higginson had a great love of music,
and a good, though untrained, tenor voice. He usually sang while dressing in the morning, and often
manufactured his own melodies. He composed music
to Cleveland's "sea-ditty" in Scott's "Pirate," beginning, "Farewell, farewell," and to sundry Scotch bal-
lads. "Lassie come near me," and "We'el may we a'
be," for instance, were put into permanent musical
form by a friend and one of them was published.
The Negro melodies heard in camp, he sang with
our little girl, going through the lively motions and
gestures with great animation.

Many organizations secured Colonel Higginson's
services as president, for longer or shorter periods.

Among these were the Appalachian Mountain Club, the Boston Browning Club, and the Round Table of which he was the first and only president, this office lasting for more than twenty-five years. Of one of the meetings of this club, he wrote to his sister, November, 1891: —

"Lady Henry Somerset was at Round Table and charmed all — short, square-shouldered, with a fine generous face, the simplest and sweetest manner and no cant. It seemed her mission to pour oil on troubled waters. Nothing specially dainty or highbred about her, but no English awkwardness or brusquerie. A most mellow voice of course."

Later the Boston Authors' Club was organized through the efforts of Mrs. Howe and Colonel Higginson, they bearing to it during the former's life the relations of president and vice-president. This association of interests brought to the latter many amusing letters from Mrs. Howe, usually beginning "My dear Vice." One of the members called this club Higginson's "last plaything."

Among the annual public gatherings which he frequently attended was the meeting of the Social Science Association at Saratoga, where he presided over the educational department or gave addresses. He sometimes lectured at Chautauqua which he called "An innocent Saratoga." When he went forth on these expeditions to "scream among his fellows," as an irreverent friend was fond of quoting from Bryant's "Waterfowl," unforeseen difficulties sometimes arose. In such cases a happy versatility saved the day, as when in Bangor, in 1887: —

"Last night I had a good lecture, though I learned just as we went into the church door that the subject was different from what I had supposed, so that I had to switch my thoughts off very suddenly."

In January, 1888, he meditated: —

"It is curious to see how my 64th birthday seems the turning-point for my reputation such as it is. I had a notice of nearly a column with a horrible portrait in a Detroit newspaper and a good many western letters referring to it in one way or another, showing it well advertised. This somewhat tardy repute has the advantage that it comes at a time when my head is past turning."

His interest in public affairs never flagged, and he lent his influence to defeat the bill condemning parochial schools. "Spoke before Legislative Committee," he wrote in his diary for March of the same year, "against the private school bill amid a howling audience of sectarians."

In the same year he went West on a lecture trip and wrote to his sister: —

"KANSAS CITY, June 5, 1888.

"I have got so far, lecturing last night at Lawrence (University), here to-night . . . speaking at

Topeka on Thursday, going Friday morn to Colorado Springs. . . . I have enjoyed the trip greatly. . . . I saw many of the old Kansasers and many of the new; all Kansas is transformed from bareness to a land of trees and hedges, greatly to its improvement and I had a fine reception from the Students."

> "COLORADO SPRINGS,
> "June 11.

"Here I have revelled in flowers and cañons. . . . Nothing disappoints except that the prairies when green are a far paler green than we are used to and Pike's Peak, though it seems to hang directly above the town and is still snow-clad, is far less picturesque and companionable than our New England mountains."

It was impossible not to be drawn into politics and, in the fall of 1888, Colonel Higginson was nominated as Representative to Congress by the Democrats of the Fifth Congressional District. The question whether to accept this nomination required much deliberation. He wrote in his diary September 23: —

"Thinking all day about Congressional proposal and decided to decline it. . . . Wrote accordingly in evening.

"Sept. 24. Felt so dissatisfied and troubled at my decision that I decided to revoke it . . . and substituted another letter. I hope I have at last done right, but it is a risk. I hope some one else will be nominated."

Colonel Higginson was required to do more or less stump-speaking in this campaign and wrote: —

"Nov. 6. Election Day. . . . Globe reporter surprised to find me quietly reading and said that all the other candidates were in rooms at hotels with newspapers, telegraphers, and tables of figures.

"Nov. 7. Learned news of defeat by the morning paper — felt political but not much personal regret, as I have never supposed I should like the life and there is plenty besides to be done."

About the result of the election, he told his sister: —

"I don't doubt that many who at first meant to vote for me decided at last to stick by their party; and this is not strange, as one vote may determine the majority in the House. . . . The defection of the colored people's Club in Boston at the last moment was rather unexpected. . . . But on the whole the Irish-Americans stood by me well and so did some of the colored people. . . . M. volunteered the use of Dapple [a small Shetland pony] all day yesterday for bringing up voters."

In another letter to his brother-in-law he reported: —

"The Election was really on pretty strict party lines. . . . I don't feel that I have wasted time and strength; it has done me no apparent harm and made me feel that I am younger and stronger than I thought . . . the morning disappointment already seems a good way off. Margaret dances about and says, 'O papa, I'm so glad you are not elected.'"

Restored to the quiet of his study, he edited, with his friend Mrs. Ella H. Bigelow, a volume of "American Sonnets"; in 1888, wrote his book "Travellers and Outlaws"; and on New Year's Day, 1889, the diary recorded: "Looking forward also to my volume of poems, the fulfilled dream of a life"; and soon adds: "Translated two Camoëns sonnets and revised Rückert's 'Cradle Song' and got them into volume." This was his first volume of verse and was called "An Afternoon Landscape." A little later, he writes: —

"Jan. 29. At printing office — last proofs. I shall miss the fine and delicate pleasure of revising these verses — the flower of my life; a sort of witchhazel."

When a summons came from the Governor in June, 1889, to appear at the State House, Colonel Higginson supposed that the interview would relate to the controversy on parochial schools, but instead he was offered the post of military historian. This offer he at first declined, but being urged to consider it, he decided a few days later to accept. November saw him fairly launched in this new literary enterprise, and he wrote to his sister: —

" . . . I see that I must be very careful and as I now have Margaret in full force upon me ('Papa, I am going to take good sound care of you,') I shall probably be protected. She requires me to go to bed early. . . . I am quite free from extra engagements and cares and shall keep so for the history's sake."

While engaged on this complicated undertaking, which continued for seven years, Colonel Higginson was very active in civic service. For fourteen years he was one of the hard-working trustees of the Cambridge Public Library, and as a representative member of the Citizens' Committee was in frequent communication with Governor Russell and Mr. F. H. Rindge, of California, in reference to the public gifts of the latter to the city of Cambridge (1888). Mr. Richard H. Dana has called attention to the fact that when petitions or documents relating to public movements were brought to Colonel Higginson to endorse, he always carefully considered them and asked searching questions before giving the influence of his name. This scrutiny often resulted, not only in important changes in the text of such papers, but in an entirely different way of presenting the scheme.

When Margaret was eight years old, we spent the summer at East Gloucester. Here Colonel Higginson bought a fisherman's dory and taught the little girl to row. These notes are taken from his diary of that summer (1889): —

"July 6. P.M. . . . to Gloucester and bought things for boat, and then rowed over — enjoying it as much as thirty years ago at Pigeon Cove.

"July 13. Dr. Rogers here, our first meeting for some ten years; enjoyed seeing him, but felt something of that 'secret pain' described in Longfellow's 'Driftwood Fire.' . . . P.M. rowed to Gloucester and back against wind and sea . . . the best pull I have had for years.

"July 28. Rowed to Gloucester and Ten Pound Island — finding the descendants of Francis Higginson's 'sweet single rose.'"

In October Margaret went home before her father, and he thus described a day without her: —

"The day seemed a concentrated solitude and partial death without Margaret and every little starfish and sea urchin she scattered seemed a part of her and too sacred to be touched. It brought home with terrible vividness the possible desolation of a life without her, and by sympathy, more remotely, the blow that it will be to her ardent nature on that day when she must lose me. That is the only drawback on a long delayed parentage — that one cannot as in youth look forward to a long lifetime within reach of a child. For me it may be something that I shall not live to see her with gray hairs — but for her — The more need to love each other while we can."

XV

JOURNEYS

"Do you know that I am going to England?" wrote
Colonel Higginson to a friend in April, 1872. "I look
forward to it with boyish delight. . . . I have got my
best sympathy so far out of the Hawthornes' book —
Mr. and Mrs. — her accounts are delicious I think,
as eloquent as possible, and they make me so long to
see a cathedral and its *close*, those green homes of
peace, but it is queer that neither describes a night-
ingale or a skylark — my first desiderata."

This brief foreign trip included a hurried visit to
Ireland, Scotland, and the Continent. In Dublin,
the traveller went to see R. D. Webb, an old Abolitionist, who received him with delight, and he visited
the house "where Moore was born and lived — still
a grocery and wineshop such as his father kept. . . .
This was my first shrine such as it was and I found it
easy to conjure up the little sweet singer."

A few days later in the "midst of the wonder and
thrill" of London, he exclaimed: —

"I feel as if I had just been born. . . . I do not see
how there can be a place in the world more delightful
than London for one who loves both study and so-

ciety. . . . I am having the most amazing time, per-
fectly overwhelmed with invitations and kindnesses.
After the above I will add that I breakfast with
Froude Monday."

At the Athenæum Club he found Aubrey de Vere,
"my first author. He came gliding downstairs to me
a tall, refined, ascetic-looking man . . . and seemed
and talked like a simple, sweet recluse." It may here
be added that Colonel Higginson spent his first hours
in London by gratifying his curiosity to see certain
regions he had long known by reputation, and which
were usually considered unsafe for visitors. When he
walked through the Seven Dials and St. Giles —
then called the "Den of Thieves" — he was unmolested and perhaps a shade disappointed to find all
London apparently safe. A certain English correspondent of a New York paper gave exaggerated accounts of these rambles and declared that Colonel
Higginson was "protected by his rashness."

In his book called "Carlyle's Laugh" the American author has described a memorable walk which
he took in Hyde Park with Froude and Carlyle. "I
wished," he wrote home, "we could all be photo-
graphed. . . . We three were nearly run over in
crossing the tide [Rotten Row] and dear old Carlyle
had to run for life. I am so glad to have seen him —
he was charming." Not long after, he dined with

Darwin at his home, which he described in his letters as "enlawned."

"Soon enter the philosopher, taller than I, erect, white-bearded, like a kindlier Bryant, looking like his photograph, but more human and sweet — he was most genial, slight as was my claim on him . . . he seemed even a greater man than I had thought him."

The daily record goes on: —

"Heard Tyndall at Royal Institute and saw him afterwards — delightful man — asked me to dine with him. . . . I sat between Tyndall and one whom I supposed a physician but found to be Lord Lyttleton. I remembered luckily a pretty Latin translation by him of a poem of Lord Houghton's and spoke of it. . . . I think the ease with which one steps into a round only too delightful here is amazing. . . . Heard Bradlaugh the great popular orator of England . . . who came and took lunch with me.

"June 5. Met Mr. Gladstone by appointment at 12 — a fine wise keen face, voice like Emerson's without the hesitancy — we talked America and literature and he heard for the first time that his Juventus Mundi was reprinted. He asked me to breakfast for Thursday next, but impossible."

The same day he met Huxley whom he described as "shortish, strong, black-bearded, with blacking-brush style of hair, looks like a scientific shoemaker, but talks to the point."

From Oxford he wrote: —

"Bryce soon came in for me to go and hear Dean Stanley — it was a special service at the Univ. church and the 'Heads of houses' (or colleges) went in procession, with scarlet gowns, and men bearing maces before them. . . . He is a little man, somewhat like Dr. Palfrey, face keener, and a peculiar intoning manner as he preaches, looking up to the sky every few minutes, but never at his hearers."

At another time when Colonel Higginson heard Dean Stanley officiate at Westminster Abbey, he said: —

"Dean Stanley looked old and mediæval, with a black velvet cap on, and wearing the red ribbon and jewel of the Bath, of which he is a sort of Chaplain."

"Everything was done for me at Oxford," the record continues, "by Bryce, the indefatigable, and Dicey; and I made a speech at a great college dinner and again at a students' supper where I was at first introduced as a Confederate officer, but I got round it." This little episode was referred to by Mr. Bryce in a letter to Colonel Higginson, dated 1907: —

"Do you remember being with Dicey and myself at a Sunday dinner in Trinity College, Oxford . . . where you saved a perilous situation with a swift decision worthy of your military experience? One of the dons had fancied you were a Confederate officer!"

In Oxford, also, Colonel Higginson saw Freeman, the historian, Rawlinson, Montague Bernard, "the late 'High Joint,'" and Miss Thackeray, the novelist, "by far the most original and interesting woman I have seen in England. She pressed on me a letter to Tennyson and I expect to go to see him." This visit to the poet at the Isle of Wight is minutely described in "Cheerful Yesterdays," and from the letters only this extract is taken: —

"Presently I heard a clamping step and in walked rather heavily and awkwardly a man, the most singular compound of Sam Johnson and Professor Lovering . . . fine eyes under spectacles! . . . He was quite pleasant though never exactly interesting or agreeable, took me to his smoking room to the top of the house, through some lovely gardens full of roses, then to see Mrs. Cameron his neighbor and crony [the amateur photographer]."

During his stay in London, Colonel Higginson preached for Mr. Conway at South Place Chapel (Unitarian). This sermon was reviewed in an English paper under the title "A Warrior in the Pulpit." The author of the article said some anxiety was felt lest Colonel Higginson, whom he described as "gentle in speech and manner as Colonel Newcome in society," would fail as an effective speaker. These fears were speedily dispelled, for the English writer exclaimed, "Some of his sentences were on fire!" A London paper spoke of the evident delight this American traveller found in England, adding, "Even the climate, he, like most Americans, does not denounce!"

Before sailing for home, Higginson was given a farewell entertainment by the Anglo-American Association. At this meeting, of which Thomas Hughes was president, a letter was read from Professor Tyndall, saying, "The Association desire to express to Colonel Higginson their sense of the services he has rendered to the cause of human freedom, and to wish him God speed as an unofficial messenger of peace between two nations." The last clause referred to the fact that there were then certain treaty complications between the two countries.

In the spring of 1878, Colonel Higginson made a second visit to Europe. He wrote from the steamer:

"When I sailed before I felt a sort of dismay as we left the wharf as if the experiment were wildly dangerous and I had better jump ashore; now I did not feel that, only that fear of having left something essential behind which we often have on setting out for journeys. . . . I found with regret that I could not look on the Irish hills with quite the intense delight they inspired when they were my first glimpse of Europe."

Arrived again in London, in May, he writes: —

"Went to see Prof. Masson at the Athenæum Club and found that I am admitted as a guest through [Sir Frederick] Pollock and Hughes. It is a great satisfaction and honor. . . . As we went through the hall the Archbishop of Canterbury was coming down stairs, Sir Henry Maine, the author was coming from the smoking room, and the three men in the smoking room were Galton, Palgrave and the editor of the Quarterly Review. No building in the world has so many eminent men within its walls from 4 to 6 daily."

Then he records meeting at the Cosmopolitan Club, Anthony Trollope, Lord Houghton, whom he knew before, "brisk, small, and chatty"; and of having "a talk with Galton, author of 'Hereditary Genius.'"

"Heard a lecture from Max Müller at the Chapter House of Westminster Abbey. Afterwards I went up to speak to him and found him as pleasant as possible. He remembered at once my 'Sympathy of Religions' which I had sent him and begged me to come to Oxford and see him. He looks quite English in style, but has a sweet sunny manner and slight German accent, about as much of both as Agassiz."

Colonel Higginson had been appointed a delegate to a Prison Reform Convention at Stockholm, and of a preparatory English meeting in May he said: —

"The one interesting person was Cardinal Manning — such a prepossessing and distinguished man, the very ideal of an ecclesiastic — tall, spare, with noble head above and narrowing to a keen ascetic jaw — eyes and mouth full of mobility and sensitiveness, the most winning voice and manner, as much American as English, and speaking so nobly and sweetly and humanly. I never felt more the power of the Roman Catholic Church than in seeing how it evolves its man and keeps the type.

"May 18. I went to a reception at Mr. Martineau's (James) chiefly his students and parishioners. . . . It was rather stiffish and the person I liked best was a very pleasing young Professor, Knight of St. Andrew's (Scotland) who to my surprise had my Epictetus and knew all about it.

"To the interesting trial of Mrs. Besant's claim to her child — a case between a Christian husband (clergyman) and an atheist wife, to be tried before a Jewish magistrate on the Jewish Sabbath. . . . It was strange waiting in the Court and seeing the wigged barristers come in. Conway says the wig is a survival of the patriarchal idea of seniority, to give a symbolical age to all concerned in administering justice. Several cases came first and I was struck with the conversational tone between judge and counsel (no jury) and the weight and clearness of the judgment. Mrs. Besant sat patiently, a very fine looking young woman of 28 with a strong sweet face. . . . The husband's lawyer treated her very courteously and made no personal imputation or allusion, but claimed the child for the husband because of her avowed atheism and her publication of books which had been condemned. The second lawyer was more vehement, but not discourteous. She argued her own case, in opposition to the judge's advice, and he often interrupted her but not discourteously. She appeared admirably and took his interruptions very sweetly. She is tall and fair and with great ease and clearness of speech, but the effect was marred by Bradlaugh's standing behind her, his face being unprepossessing though intellectual. . . . She admitted all the facts very gently but explained that she had simply abstained from biasing the child's mind, thinking that all religious opinions should be postponed. She made some weak points but on the whole was strong, but the judge ruled strongly against her, though admitting her personal character. . . . After the decision the Court adjourned. The Conways and I spoke to her; I told her I did not agree with her in some things but could not but respect her and feel for her and she took it with sweetness and dignity. A few people waited, about 30 perhaps; several applauded and one or two hissed as she walked away with Bradlaugh. . . .

"Afterwards went by invitation to a meeting of the society for opening galleries on Sunday, a large fine meeting in the great hall of the Freemasons' Tavern. The young Earl of Rosebery presided, he who married the Rothschild, a good-looking smooth-faced youth and a very pleasing speaker, frank and witty, evidently a great favorite and very independent. He said once that he thought the majority should govern, which was applauded. I should say he has a future before him, though they say both families bitterly opposed the marriage. . . . I was

called on late and introduced as from the United
States and very warmly received; could not go on
for some time.

"An evening meeting of Woman Suffrage in London — really good and sensible speaking — Mrs.
Fawcett, Miss Beeker, and others, several members
of Parliament, but no one of rank as at other meetings. . . . I was asked for the 3rd time to make or
second the vote of thanks to the chairman — an in-
evitable English formality; and I spoke briefly.

"I am struck," he wrote, "with the multiplicity of
societies and movements here for all sorts of odd
things. For instance I have just got a note from a
total stranger, inviting me to the platform of a meeting of the society to resist compulsory vaccination
by the state! . . . Now as I never even heard of
Anti-Vaccination I am rather bewildered, and at any
rate can't go.

"I talked to pretty Mrs. H. who knows the pre-
Raphaelite people and confirmed my impression of
a very false and artificial vein among them. She
knows a set of artists who rendezvous at Hampstead
Heath and every evening dress in costumes of the
last century and try to get away from the commonplace present; they go so far as to have numbers of
Addision's Spectator reprinted with modern dates so
as to keep up the atmosphere of Queen Anne's day.
This was almost past believing. She knows Burne-
Jones well and says he is a very simple person.

"Dined with the Edwin Arnolds. . . . She was
Fanny Channing, a tall, elegant, attractive woman
and a most adoring wife of a loving husband. There

is something un-English about Arnold, perhaps from his long life in the East and his poetic nature. He is delightful when not talking politics, but there he is so vehement as to be a little fatiguing though always in a gentle, graceful way. He is a small man with a pleasing face. . . . He is somewhat egotistic about the Telegraph which has brought all England round to it he thinks and perhaps it is true — says 'The Empire of Russia is an anachronism which I hope to destroy.' He claims to be liberal and even radical, but thinks the thing now to be done is to save the colonial empire which only Beaconsfield can do. He thinks that Beaconsfield is not selfish, or vain in a petty way, but 'has a sublime self confidence and thinks he (B.) alone can save this nation of stupid snub-nosed Englishmen' — and A. seems to think the same of Beaconsfield's policy. To save the British Empire from the Russians is to Arnold like saving Rome from the Gauls. Arnold the other day came upon that poem 'He who died at Azan,' read it with delight and finally remembered that he wrote it himself in youth. . . . She (Fanny) showed me his 'Star of India' with pride; but her children with as much [pride].

"Found General Higginson and Henry H. waiting to go to the Guards' Review for Queen's birthday, 'Trooping the colors,' as it is called. There was a great crowd outside, but all the sentries were deferential to Gen. H. their late commander, and he got us a fine place, which he defended against noblemen and ladies for our sake. Henry is as delighted with him

as I and says, 'He's the best Higginson I've seen
yet.' The review was wonderfully beautiful — the
3 guard regiments (Grenadiers, Coldstreams, and
Fusileers) being considered by Englishmen the finest
regiments in the world and their officers ranking
above all others of the same grade. Gen. H. was
Colonel of the Grenadiers and commanded the whole
brigade till his promotion as Major-General, and he
hopes to command it again. The parade was before
the Duke of Cambridge, commander-in-chief, with
whom was the Prince Royal of Prussia, a very handsome blonde soldierly German, in beautiful white
uniform. With them rode many others of high rank.
. . . The mounted bugle corps wears the picturesque
uniform of Charles II's day — black velvet caps and
heavy gold lace coats. All around the open square
the houses were covered with people, and all un-
covered at God save the Queen. Of course there were
showers but nobody minded that. After review the
Gen. said 'our only chance for the music at St.
James' Palace will be to keep close by these fellows'
— so he, Henry and I marched rapidly between the
ranks of the magnificent guards, keeping close to an
officer he knew and just clearing the edge of the
crowd, who pressed close to us. It was deliciously
amusing to me — the audacity of the thing — Gen.
H. striding on, out of uniform, but of distinguished
bearing, then I behind him, and Henry H. behind
me trying to look as if we had a right there which
sometimes the mob at our side seemed seriously to
doubt. However, we got inside the Palace gates,
heard some more fine music and then Henry and I

took our leave of our gallant kinsman, who for the sake of a tie of blood 250 years old had thus given us the position of temporary Guardsmen — in England a very high title."

The latter part of May he went to Beckenham, "to dine and sleep at Mr. Darwin's. . . . Oh! the beauty of Darwin's grounds, just a window looking on a few flower pots for the foreground, but so exquisitely arranged, such bright colors heaped together with a thicket of rhododendrons for a background and a straight path leading away under trees, I never grew tired of it. Mr. Darwin looks older and weaker than when I saw him 6 years ago, less distinguished and commanding, but always kindly and noble. Mrs. Darwin stouter and also kind and intelligent — two younger sons at home. . . . I was assigned to a large room looking on the lovely flower-beds . . . inside an old-fashioned 4-post bed of the largest size with curtains and feather bed. To my dismay the servant had unpacked my small bag and neatly laid its hastily assorted contents on the dressing table. I do hate this waiting upon. . . . Mr. Darwin has a great desire to come to America, but never will, because of the voyage.

"Lunched with Miss Anna Swanwich the translator of Æschylus, with F. W. Newman translator of Homer, a quaint small long-faced man, with an American look. Afterwards went to meet Browning at the Athenæum Club — one of the desires of my former visit, unfulfilled then."

Of this meeting, which is fully described in "Cheerful Yesterdays," Colonel Higginson said that

Browning "was very cordial, yet I felt it more the
general temperament of the man than from any personal interest.

"Then I went into a Coöperative meeting for a
while — working men, who all dropped their H's,
but spoke much to the point. . . . Later, I walked
through Pall Mall, all illuminated for the Queen's
birthday, and crowded with people. . . . I saw one
fight and stopped it to the displeasure of the crowd
so I decided not to interfere any more. . . .

"I saw Herbert Spencer. He was playing billiards
as he does every afternoon. Prof. Bain introduced
me and he went back to his game, apologizing, but
afterwards came to me in the library and we had
some talk. I liked him better than I had been told I
should. He looks like his pictures and like a Unitarian minister. He is rather small, with large head,
bald forehead and spectacles, bad figure and walks
awkwardly, manner quite pleasant and cordial with a
little that effect of whim and isolation more common
with Englishmen than with us. He said billiards were
of great value to him as his only recreation and
form of activity, and spoke of the great danger of
overwork to all. He seemed to have the common impression (English) that there is less freedom of
thought in America than here, which seems to me
quite untrue. He thought any seeming shrinking on
the part of Tyndall and Huxley due to their wives'
influence, the only thing he said reflecting on women, nor was he cynical as I had heard. He seemed
pleased at the reception of his books in the United
States, but said he should never go there as he could

not stand the loss of sleep in the voyage, which seemed to me a queer view. I have always felt incredulous as to his being a really great man and this interview did not remove it, but I liked him more than I expected. . . .

"Found Justin McCarthy and his pleasant wife and children at home, real Irish hospitality. . . . It was after 12 and they had just come down to breakfast. He and his son both work for morning papers and are up late. Then appeared at the door a great cheery handsome ruddy face with a mass of light gray hair standing out wildly all about it — this was Mrs. M. They are much with all the literary people, Rossettis, etc., and confirmed what I had heard that there is a strong reaction against Dickens — it is not the thing to admire him, his subjects are thought commonplace and his sentiments forced. Walt Whitman among their set is the American poet; the taste for Miller has passed by and though he is here his poetry is forgotten. He was thought original and characteristic and when he came to parties with trousers thrust in his boots, he was thought the only American who dared do in England as he would do at home. Whittier was unknown they said, and Lowell only through the 'Biglow Papers.' Swinburne calls him no poet but a critic who tries to write poetry.

"(13–14 June) I spent in Conway's Convention which was very interesting and called out strong character and ready speaking. I was on the committee too to draft the Constitution which differs somewhat from our Free Religious Association (as does the name 'Association of Liberal Thinkers'). The best known people in it were Voysey (a small and narrow soul who got alarmed and withdrew), Leslie Stephen (who married Miss Thackeray), Stuart Glennie (who wrote the account of Buckle's Eastern travels), G. J. Holyoke (veteran radical), Mr. Blyden of Liberia (black and Mohammedan who has written on that subject in Fraser), Mrs. Rose (formerly of N.Y.), A. J. Eyres the philologist, and various Unitarian ministers. I spoke several times and twice succeeded in allaying incipient contests by suggesting phrases that reconciled different opinions, so that one speaker proposed to send me as arbitrator to reconcile the strikes now going on at the North, and they all laughed and applauded."

In June Colonel Higginson was in Oxford on Commemoration Day and lunched with "the new D.C.L's and their wives and other notabilities, a grand affair in the beautiful hall of All Souls College. I sat between Bryce and Mrs. Spottiswode, wife of one of the new D.C.L's, and opposite a young Lord Donoughmore, whose name delighted me because I thought of the statues of

'Haythen goddesses most rare
Homer, Venus and Nebuchadnezzar
All standing naked in the open air.'

The song says of them farther that they are 'all second cousin to My Lord Donoughmore' and here was the real youth."

Here he met Dr. Pattison, author of "Essays and Reviews," who "spoke warmly to me of 'Atlantic

Essays' which he got in consequence of an extract in a review. He said, 'You must have given great attention to the matter of style'; and afterwards, 'Do you find an audience in America for such critical refinement of style? I fear there would hardly be in England.' I told him I thought Americans when well educated cared more for refinement of style than English and he said he knew they formerly did but thought their style had grown more 'rough and ready' as the English certainly had. He quoted one or two of my stories and said he had often repeated them. . . .

"Waked early with regret from my last night in College. I can't imagine anything more rejuvenating than the way these men come back here and enter, as of right, on their old privileges. H—— for instance still has a right here as A.M. and can come back and claim a parlor and bedroom for these days if any one is vacant, and be served from the kitchen paying only very moderate fees. We have nothing like it. College is with us a passing experience — for them a lifelong home."

Scotland came next and he reported: —

"Going North I had for companion the Professor of Poetry of yesterday, Principal Sharp of St. Andrews, whose books have been printed in America, 'Poetic Interpretation of Nature,' etc. — he is a thin Scotch looking man, recalling Eliot Cabot. I did not at first fancy some things about him but about the time we crossed the border we got acquainted. He soon said, 'Did you ever hear of Yarrow?' I could

hardly help laughing and . . . told him every educated American knew every place mentioned in
Scott, Burns or the Border Minstrelsy.

"July 2. Edinburgh. Had a delightful trip by
coach to Roslin. Nobody can be disappointed in
Roslin Chapel. . . . I longed for hours of peace
there.

"July 3. Dined with the Massons — his talk
about Edinburgh was very interesting. He came
here to the University from Aberdeen and says that
three of the professors, Wilson (Chr. North) Chalmers and Sir Wm. Hamilton were the three most
striking men in appearance that he ever saw.
Wilson's hair was yellow, Chalmers's white and
Hamilton's very dark — Wilson was a giant, and his
statue does not exaggerate his lion like port; Chalmers's face was large and heavy and seamed — he
had but little book knowledge but wonderful origi-
nality and power. Hamilton had great hold upon
young men collectively though not individually.
When Dickens first came here, Wilson said of him
'How could that puppy have written such books.'
Masson says Dickens' imagination was so active his
narratives had very little value. . . . The Massons
knew Alexander Smith and Sydney Dobell the two
young poets, both of whom have died and both interested me. . . . I praised Dobell's ballad of 'Ravelston' so much that Mrs. M. ordered a carriage and
drove me there in the dark leaving at 9 and returning
at 11. . . . The house is quaint and old and is the
original Tully-Veolan of Waverley — Scott used to
go there as a boy. . . . Dobell used to pass the house

daily almost and the ballad wrote itself I suppose —
but the Massons did not know it and it seemed
so strange and weird that an American from afar
should go wandering about the old place, for the love
of a ballad which perhaps the Keiths of Ravelston do
not know."

Returning to London in July, he went "to a
charming garden party. . . . The company was distinguished — Huxley, Spencer, Galton, my friend and
reader Mark Pattison from Oxford, Sir Rutherford
Alcock, Walter Crane and his wife and others. . . .
Huxley . . . was very cordial. . . . Walter Crane is
quite a young man, modest and retiring and has a
nice young wife of the same stamp who seemed
pleased at hearing how well he was known in
America. . . .

"In the evening went to meet a few Women Suffrage people and Mrs. Livermore at Peter Taylor's
M.P. — the author. . . . I saw people there who are
quite American in their sympathies — Miss Helen
Taylor, Mill's adopted daughter, being most interesting and more French than English in the grace
and sweetness of her manners."

At the Voltaire Centenary in Paris, Colonel Higginson heard Victor Hugo speak and was much
struck with the storm of enthusiasm which greeted
him. Another interesting event of this visit to
France was a fortunate meeting with Tourguénieff;
and he found Louis Blanc "a most delightful little
man." His impressions of these distinguished men

are preserved in "Cheerful Yesterdays." At a
French Prison Reform meeting he found he "could
get on in the general French Committee work well
enough, but as for two excited Frenchmen talking to
one another, it is like interpreting heat lightning."
But Colonel Higginson had a natural aptitude for
acquiring languages, and on his first arrival at Paris
he wrote: "French came to me like a flash and I
interpreted for stray Englishmen at the custom-
house!" During this second visit he strolled into the
suburbs of Paris and walked from Scéaux to Chate-
nay, and "bought vin ordinaire in the very room
where Voltaire was born."

To continue the extracts: —

"Paris, Monday, July 22. I dined at Mr. Hitt's
(American Sec'y of Legation) to meet Stanley the
explorer. . . . I sat next to Stanley who is a very queer
combination — much smoothed and softened they
say but a Herald reporter still — not of distinguished look but with a resolute air — accent neither
English, American nor French — talks of course
about himself mainly but not in a specially conceited
way — and seems perfectly incapable of a joke. . . .
He gave an amusing description of his intense delight at finding the queer little old man [Livingstone]
but as the natives were all looking on they repressed
it all and he and Dr. L. met as if in Piccadilly, perfectly coldly. Then he went on to complain and

scold most tediously at the way he was disbelieved
and attacked and finally advised everybody *not* to go
to Africa. When the only Englishman present pro-
tested against what Stanley had said, the latter replied: 'What I complain of in the English is that
they got my girl away from me,' at which nobody
could help laughing — it seems that his betrothed
was convinced that the first Livingstone letters were
forgeries and so dropped him. . . . Afterwards I had
an almost equally amusing scene with one of the
American jurors, who said, 'I am glad to meet you,
Col. H., I have been so interested with what you
have accomplished in *New Caledonia;* your name has
often been before us in the jury of honor.' I knew as
much of New Caledonia as Stanley at first of Livingstone, but recalled some English Higginson who had
been in the papers as connected with copper mines
there and it seems he is called Colonel too. What a
chaos of Colonels! I said if it was necessary to patriotism that I should take the credit, I'd do my
best."

Of his further doings in the French capital, he
wrote: —

"This was the day of the 'Congrès Internationel de
Droit des Femmes.' . . . Mrs. Howe read a paper in
French . . . the language seemed to give a clearness
and precision to her ideas and kept her from the
clouds and she read with much dignity and sweetness."

At the Théâtre Français he "for the first time
saw acting! . . . Sarah Bernhardt seemed the legiti-

mate successor of Rachel and Ristori — a blonde
Rachel, tall and slender and stately and fearfully ill
like her — but oh! such power, such expression by
a glance, a whisper, a motion of the hand and such
utter absence of the visibly histrionic."

Normandy was the next country to be visited, and
there Colonel Higginson stayed with friends, going
thence to Germany.

"Le Manier, Penne de Pie near Honfleur, Normandy. Here I am at this perfectly charming place
. . . wonderfully silent and deep, and delightful after
Paris, and it was pleasant to go to sleep and not
know what the morning would reveal.

"I was waked by the bells for early mass in the old
church opposite, 800 years old. My windows look
upon the sea. . . . Once a day an old man comes
with the mail, and once a day the omnibus goes by
each way between Honfleur and Trouville, — that
is all.

"I got here this morning," he wrote from Cologne,
"leaving beautiful Normandy and dear friends with
difficulty. . . . I shall not feel solitary on the Rhine,
having Bettine's correspondence with me and meaning to visit some of her places."

Apropos of Bettine, these passages occur in one of
the diaries: —

"Just now I am reading Günderode with ever-new
delight: I wish there were a million volumes. Really
there is not an author in the world, save Emerson

and Shakespeare, from whom I have had so much and so fresh enjoyment as from the perennial Child, Bettine. Her effervescence always intoxicates me with delight; though her life flowed prematurely away in it, like champagne left uncorked.

"Bingen, Aug. 7. Hard at work on the castles with intervals of my dear Bettine Brentano on whose tracks I now am. . . . My main object just here is Bettine and I made a long dreamed of pilgrimage to her best loved haunt, whence many of her letters were written, the ruined chapel of St. Roch. . . . I found with dismay that the beautiful little ruin which Bettine describes as recently destroyed has been rebuilt but what was my delight to go round it and find a little ruin of two arches and a wall still remaining, with an altar and a stone crucifix, grim and battered, apparently the very one up which she climbed to stick a bunch of wild flowers in the top. I could have done the same in continuing her work for there were harebells like ours and heather in bloom all around, but just as I sprang down, a fair young priest such as she would have rejoiced in came reading his breviary round the corner and it was well to be discreet. He also cooled my ardor a little by saying that this little ruin was of a second chapel to St. Michael which also stood there — still I dare say it was the same crucifix. She used to write to Goethe there and kept his letters buried there and has an exquisite description of going to sleep there in the moonlight on the wall and having to sleep there all night. She planted grapevines and honeysuckle and lilies there and she says 'all sorts of plants,' but

there were only some ivy roots of which I took one
and shall try to make it grow.

"Aug. 8. From Bingen to Frankfort. O, what a
charming day! wandering along the Rhine with
Bettine in my hand, studying out all the scenes of
the letters I have always enjoyed so much. First I
crossed by ferry to Rudesheim and tried to fix the
spot where Günderode was found dead. . . . Bettine
landed at Rudesheim that day and ran straight up
Ostein, a mountain a mile high she says. . . . I went
up the same hill. It is a steep paved vineyard path.
The valley was utterly still and bathed in heat, it
seemed, as B. writes elsewhere, as if the leagues of
ripening grapes sent up an incense. Along the path
grew yarrow, tanzy and succory, just as in New England; the present emperor loves succory flowers
especially and they always bring him bunches of it
on public days. . . . At two I went on by train to
Winkel — Bettine's regular summer home. . . . I
staid long on the shore [of the Rhine] and the nearly
70 years since 1809 seemed nothing — the two girls
were still young to me. I think I found the place
where Günderode died. . . . I walked back through
the long villages again. It was very hot. I had an
hour at the station and lay down on a bench and
slept as Bettine would have done. . . . It is such a
delight to have an ideal object, especially in travelling alone.

"Aug. 9. Frankfort. Here still was Bettine, but
lost in the greater stream of Goethe. The Goethe
house was my chief interest. . . . Below were his
magnificent mother's rooms . . . portraits of her . . . in

the very room where she used to sit and chat with Bettine and they were (as the latter says) the only two people *alive* in Frankfort or anywhere else."

At Nüremberg he saw Albert Dürer's house, scene of "The Artist's Married Life," which interested him profoundly; and at Dresden he "penetrated into the holy of holies where the Sistine Madonna is. It quite fulfils the hopes I had fixed on that picture for so many years; and familiar as I was with the copies, it is really that event in my life that I imagined it to be. . . . The Sistine Madonna, [the] Venus of Milo — they really fulfil the ideal like cathedrals."

After the traveller's return he wrote: —

"The sojourner in a foreign country, while away from the safeguards of home has a peculiar feeling of safety in another sense — a sort of wall of defence around him in the fact of his own insignificance. To go among a people who know neither you nor your kin is like going about invisible, those who see you take no account of you, you are simply one stranger more, unimportant as a fly. When I look back on my life in Paris, I seem to have carried about with me a moving wall of seclusion, which is now exchanged for the glare of publicity."

The following year, after his second marriage, Colonel Higginson received, through Professor Longfellow, this letter from members of Mr. Conway's parish, accompanied by fifty dollars: —

"LONDON, April 13, 1879.

"Some few of us who retain a grateful recollection of your presence amongst us last summer were glad of the opportunity your marriage afforded us to approach you with some slight offering of our regard, feeling quite sure that you would interpret aright the significance of the act. Whatever form the memento may take I trust, my dear Sir, it will ever speak to you of the disimprisoned spirits; and ever stimulate you to use your rare and noble gift of persuasive eloquence in the cause of truth and freedom."

Colonel Higginson went abroad twice more, in 1897 and 1901, on both of these occasions taking his family with him. From Tintern, England, one of the party wrote: —

"Wentworth is too soft-hearted to travel in Europe. He has discovered great holes in the roofs of some of the cottages near us, and heard that one old woman has to put up an umbrella in the night when it rains, and this makes him unhappy."

The 1897 visit brought us to London at the time of the Queen's Jubilee, and Colonel Higginson wrote: —

"London seems so confoundedly empty to me without the circle of great men whom I met twenty years ago. . . . You can have no conception of the absolute absorption of everything in the forthcoming

Queen's festival or the millions of people who are pouring into the city."

During his wanderings abroad, it was always assumed by strangers that Colonel Higginson was an Englishman. An Englishwoman said to him one day, "Then you have been in America?" and he replied, "Very much so." At another time a respectable housekeeper said to him, "Are you an American gentleman, sir? You don't speak like one. I should have taken you rather for English." He said, rather severely, "I suppose you mean that for a compliment, but I don't consider it one." "Ah," said she, "but you must admit they have a twang, a kind of accent-like." He said, "That's what we say of the English"; and she laughed. He wrote in his diary: —

"We pick up lots of Americans we never heard of at home and learn a great deal that is new about our own country. . . . An Englishman watched me through a knot hole for some Americanism. Said he detected a good many in Holmes."

One of his English friends, Rev. W. Garrett Horder, has written down for this memoir his impressions of Colonel Higginson. From an English point of view no praise could be higher: —

"I think he was the tallest, most erect, most aristocratic in his bearing of any American we had known. While as to his speech, it was difficult to believe that he had been born and lived all his days

across the Atlantic. . . . But more important than
his manner of speech was the spirit that expressed
itself not only in his words but in his actions and
bearing. I have never seen in any other man so perfect a union of the most democratic (I use the word
in our British sense) convictions and the most aristocratic bearing. That to me was the most striking
feature, and one very, very rarely found."

A memorial sermon was preached by this clergyman after Colonel Higginson's death from the text,
"A man shall be as an hiding place from the wind
and a covert from the tempest," and reported in the
London "Times." In this address Mr. Horder called
his subject a "perfect English gentleman, adding
thereto the freshness of the American."

An interesting chance acquaintance was made at
the South Kensington Museum, when the American
author was examining the original manuscripts of
Coleridge. He was talking with the custodian of
these treasures about Hartley Coleridge and quoting his poems, when his listener suddenly remarked,
"My name is Hartley Coleridge!" and explained that
he was a grandson of Samuel Taylor Coleridge. This
new and congenial friend was full of interesting anecdotes about Coleridge, Southey, and Lamb. Higginson wrote: —

"July 20. Lunched with E. Hartley Coleridge at
Oxford and Cambridge Club. . . . Coleridge does not

recall his grandfather but [remembers] well his great
aunt Mrs. Lloyd a most superior woman at 90, reading Horace, etc. His aunt Mrs. H. A. Coleridge
quoted her uncle Southey a great deal. . . . He says
we must go to Torquay where his sister Christobel
(!) lives."

To continue the extracts from the foreign journals
and letters: —

"LONDON, July 27, 1897.
"Yesterday I went to Parliament and heard a
rousing debate on Africa by Chamberlain, Harcourt,
Balfour, Hicks-Beach, Labouchere and the leaders
generally; they hit quite as hard as our congressmen.
To-day I am going to meet Swinburne.

"Our reception at the Channings [Francis Channing, M.P., now Lord Channing of Wellingborough]
was a great success, two-thirds of the invited coming.
The crowd in London was even worse than the day
before and some people spent nearly two hours in
their cabs, much of the time stopping perfectly still.
Mrs. James Bryce gave up the attempt and went
home.

"At British Museum — Dr. Garnett a quaint person. Found almost all my books and even pamphlets
there."

The trip of 1897 included many delightful visits at
English country-houses. One of these was at General
Sir George Higginson's summer home on the Thames,
where we saw the Henley regatta. In his description
of this house, the American visitor said, "The high

hall was lined with old cuirasses and bayonets, the latter all picked up on the field of Inkerman, where Sir George, then a lieutenant, was engaged." The hospitality of English houses was fully appreciated, but the formalities made Colonel Higginson a little impatient. He amused his family by reporting after a London luncheon that he had been "swamped in Lords and Ladies." From Oxford he wrote: —

"Great and prompt is the kindness of these English people. Already invitations of some kind for almost every day, before we have been here twenty-four hours. . . . The librarian of the great Bodleian library remembered me twenty-five years ago and says I ought to have had a degree of D.C.L. in place of some of the Colonial premiers."

He spent a Sunday at Stratford and wrote: —

"I went to Shakespeare's church, a lovely place, and there was a very ritualistic service, a great deal of signs of the cross, etc. The rector presently announced that he would have a prayer service of thanks for an American party saved from danger at sea. After the service I was suddenly surrounded by American Librarians. It proved that they were the party, the Cephalonia having broken a shaft."

And this is his family's account of that Sunday morning: —

"Wentworth sat through the service unhappily, watching the people cross themselves, and then

352 THOMAS WENTWORTH HIGGINSON

walked home between the bishop and vicar, each of
them claiming him as an old acquaintance!!!"

An annoying incident happened on our way to
Stratford in the loss of luggage which prevented
Colonel Higginson from attending a dinner given
near London by the Omar Khayyám Club. There-
upon an amusing squib appeared in the "Morning
Post" in which "incidents connected with the late
Shah of Persia and the present Colonel Wentworth
Higginson" figured.

At Salisbury, he encountered a favorite novelist:—

"This morning we discovered (through a tell-tale
letter directed to him) that a man staying here was
Thomas Hardy. Hardy is small with a keen thin
face, head nearly bald and little gray moustache. He
is very simple and pleasant, willing to talk about
his own books, the scene of which is mostly laid in
this region, and which portray manners now passing
by. He is reputed shy, but when caught in this retired place is very easily approachable. His wife is
sturdy and bicycles. . . . We have been very lucky in
stumbling on people unexpectedly and have really
seen the novelists I most care to see — Hardy, Anthony Hope, Mrs. Ward and Mrs. Alexander — the
latter peculiarly dignified and attractive. . . . He
[Hardy] surprised me by saying that all the dialect
of his peasants (who are perfectly Shakespearean in
quaintness and vigor) is from the memory of his
childhood, and that he never in his life wrote down

a sentence after hearing it. I had always imagined
him with a note-book."

In Paris Colonel Higginson said the best thing he
did was to go to the top of the Eiffel Tower. The
little *pension* which sheltered us was Victor Hugo's
old house, and the salon, which opened into a very
pleasant garden, was his study. In September the
record says: —

"We had a delightful run through Switzerland.
... The Protestant service in the cathedral [at
Basle] seemed to me a glimpse of Puritanism of 200
years ago, even to the gown and band of the preacher
and the tythingmen who stood up to keep the boys
in order."

In the journey of 1901, we sailed direct for Italy,
and from Castellamare Colonel Higginson wrote: —

"Our visits to Madeira, Gibraltar, Tangier and
Granada were perfectly successful and each of them
worth crossing the ocean for."

At Granada "we lived close to the Alhambra and
found it more beautiful even than we had imagined,
especially the ceilings of the rooms which were
carved and colored like a celestial bee hive. . . .

"We are spending a week at this beautiful place.
Vesuvius is only a few miles away; between us and it
stretches a beach of exquisite curve, with a slight
line of surf. Behind it lies a level plain and a long
row of grayish houses, and this is Pompeii. Think of
seeing Pompeii at last!"

From the same place his family reported: —

"He suffers very much from not being allowed to tip everybody; but after being suppressed all the time in Tangier, on our way to the boat there a handsome little Moorish girl smiled on him, and walked along with him smiling still, and the guide was n't looking, and he was lost."

We were detained at Castellamare for several weeks on account of an illness of our daughter Margaret. A letter, dated April 19, says of the invalid: —

"She is drinking a kind of local mineral water, prescribed by Pliny!! Some one suggested that a later endorsement might be valuable! We have to superintend the goat's milking morn and night and we do it from an upstairs window. The goat bleats, and then we go. Angelo stands by her with a silver tray, the 'fat boy' (son of the former head-waiter who was murdered by the former cook) helps hold her contrary head, and the owner milks into a little pitcher."

When convalescence came, the interesting Swedish doctor and author, Münthe, advised us to go to Sorrento and then to Capri where he said Andrews and Coleman (American author and artist) would take care of us till he came. Dr. Münthe had a villa there, but just then was in Rome in charge of the future King of Sweden. "At Sorrento," wrote Colonel Higginson, "we called on Marion Crawford the novelist who has a perfectly beautiful villa and grounds. Mrs. Crawford begged us to come over this afternoon and see the children dance the Tarantella (national dance) in honor of their father."

Removed to the bracing air of Capri, the record continued: —

"Found a very pleasant circle of English and American men. I enjoyed also meeting Wm. Wordsworth, grandson of the poet and himself a minor poet, — a most distinguished looking man, a handsome likeness of his grandpapa."

And later: —

"To tea at William Wordsworth's, returning on donkeys. W. W. is the favorite grandson of the poet."

The next extract is from a Florence letter: —

"May 23. To-day I lunched with the Marchesa Peruzzi de Medici. She is the daughter of Story the sculptor. She lives in a narrow street. You come up a fine stairway into a series of dark high rooms, with some quaint old furniture, frescoed walls and many traces of Story's sculpture work. Out of one parlor opens a small private chapel. I waited a while and heard a door open softly and in glided a little elderly woman, quiet as possible, and putting out a shy soft hand to me. I was quite bewildered by her being so much older in appearance and more unworldly than the brilliant society woman I had expected; and when she sat down with an anxious look and seemed to wait for me, I reverted to the subject which led me there and said, 'I was very sorry that Mr. Waldo

Story was not in Rome when I was there, that I might see him' — to which she said, still timidly, 'Ah.' Then she said breathlessly under her voice, 'I never was in Rome but twice in my life,' and looked to me for sympathy. Inasmuch as my hostess was born and bred there, this was rather bewildering; and at this moment in came hurriedly a fine-looking woman of the world who said eagerly to me, 'Oh, I must apologize for being so late'; and then looking at her said, 'I must present you to Miss Browning.' It was Browning's sister, companion, and amanuensis who still survives him at 88!! Then came in a younger man, short, round-faced and round-headed, looking like a capable business man and he was the present Mr. Browning, the son of two poets. This was he whom I used to hear of in youth as Penini (from Apennines, a nickname given by his mother). . . . We of course talked poetry and Browning more or less, and we spoke of my favorite complaint of his alterations in his published works; and Miss B. said, 'He used to say that of course he wished to be understood and if people could understand better in one way than another the words make little difference.' She spoke of his horror of being lionized and how he shuddered on some public occasion when a lady was selected to sit next to him (he was told) because she was 'used to sitting by poets.' He said, 'She will wish to give me my tea with a spoon!' and managed to have the arrangement changed, and an unprofessional neighbor substituted. Both she and the son spoke strongly of the practical character of Browning and said he was always ready to help

every one, while Tennyson lived more in the clouds;
but they testified to the unbroken friendship between the poets."

In July we were back in England, dipping into
Wales and exploring the Lake region. From Gras-
mere Colonel Higginson wrote: —

"My wife and I drove out to Rydal Mount,
Wordsworth's later home, and as we stood looking
through the gate a very pleasing man came from
among the rosebushes and asked if we would not like
to see the place. As we entered I told him that I had
heard with pleasure that Rydal Mount was again occupied by some of the Wordsworth family. When I
said that I had heard it from the present William
Wordsworth at Capri my host became quite interested and said that his wife was the niece of my Capri
friend. He showed us over the place where Wordsworth used to walk up and down and declaim his
verses aloud before going to have his sister 'pick 'em
up for him' as an old woman said in describing the
process. He showed us also the particular rocks he
had made his theme and the tree where the wren's
nest was. . . . She [our host's wife] was quite ready
to talk about her uncle, and then took us into the
house and showed us some memorials of the poet,
though most of the original furniture was sold by
auction after his widow's death; but some things were
left, e.g., the cuckoo clock out of which he made a
poem and which struck, just in time for us to hear,
the cuckoo peeping out just in time to inspect us.
What interested me most in the house was a really

remarkable painting of Wordsworth by Haydon, a painter who always interested me by his tragic career; a picture of which the engravings give no adequate impression, and which brings out the shape and bearing of his head quite superbly."

"Keswick, Aug. 10. We have done a good deal 'between drops' and had a delightful companion in Canon Rawnsley the antiquarian and factotum of the whole region who has taken us everywhere . . . but for all literary associations this whole region is quite unequalled; it is *Concord* on a much larger scale."

From Windermere, Colonel Higginson wrote to the Reverend Reuben Kidner, whom he facetiously called his pastor and to whom he bore the fictitious relation of warden: —

"DEARLY BELOVED PARSON: —

"In my wanderings through foreign countries I have of course taken a (sometimes unappreciative) part in religious services in various tongues, especially in Rome where the Higher Intelligences are understood to communicate mainly in Latin. They were less obstructive to my mind however than when, at the close of an early service in the Church of England at Bettws-y-coed in Wales I heard a language at once rattling and melodious and found that a service was proceeding in Welsh. I remembered the school-poem by Thomas Gray called 'The Bard' which begins

'Ruin seize thee, ruthless king
Confusion on thy banners wait,'

and felt that confusion had prevailed in the Welsh language ever since. It suggested inquiring whether the word Welsher as applied, I am told, on the English race-course to any swindler, grew out of this early bewilderment in the use of words. . . .

"I learned on inquiry that the medical profession at least if not the clerical suffers through this confusion of tongues. The only physician in Bettws-y-coed, a spot known by the irreverent as Betsy Coit, told us that the only Welsh sentence which he had yet mastered was the phrase ordering a patient to put the tongue out, which he rightly thought essential to his practice. Having employed this with success on an elderly peasant woman, it occurred to him too late that he had not yet learned in Welsh the request that should have followed — to put it in again — so that it is not quite clear whether the good woman is not still standing with that useful member protruded. This was a confusion of tongues indeed; and since the tongue is clearly the banner of health it may be the very disaster which Gray's bard predicted.

"Such are the anxieties of the wanderer; and when I think how many opportunities I have missed of attending a prescribed worship in Dublin, N.H., I feel that I may have erred in wandering too far and must next year confine my sober wishes to Dublin.

"Ever faithfully, in any one dialect,

"Your Warden."

A London letter written in August reports: —

"The Colonel and Margaret had a delightful afternoon with Swinburne. The house where he and Watts-Dunton live is full of Rossetti's pictures. Swinburne devoted himself to Margaret and showed her many treasures."

The rest of our time was spent in the south of England. From Wells, Colonel Higginson went to Glastonbury partly "to see Mrs. Clarke, John Bright's daughter, whom I saw in America, a strong reformer and Anti-Imperialist."

At Ottery St. Mary, he enjoyed taking tea at Lord Coleridge's house which was full of interesting portraits and other memorials of the Coleridges. In Lord Coleridge, who was a radical, the American reformer found a congenial spirit. For this was at the time of the South African war and although he ordinarily felt under bonds to keep silence, all of Colonel Higginson's sympathies were with the Boers. "Nothing," he wrote, "ever revives my innate republicanism better than coming to England."

The next step was to Winchester, the capital of the ancient kingdom of Alfred the Great, "to what they call the 'millenary' celebration (1000th anniversary of King Alfred's death), probably so called because they all go in finery and I am to represent Harvard, by President Eliot's appointment."

A London letter thus described this event: —

"I enjoyed greatly my trip to Winchester . . . a speech of my own was received most warmly by the English delegates and officials, and was more effusive than is my wont. It is hard not to be so here, for no one in America can appreciate the warmth and width of the feeling in England about the President's [McKinley] death. No European sovereign's death has ever called forth so much, they say — meetings and mourning, flags in all churches, on the streets, and in the smallest villages. . . .

"I did not know there was to be any speaking but the mayor came when lunch was half through and asked if I would respond for the delegates when he gave the toast, the only speech to be made; it was very sudden, but I did. It was most warmly received and people kept coming to me afterwards to thank me. I told them frankly that I was an anti-imperialist both at home and here and one of them said that this cleared the speech from all sound of flattery. . . .

"Instead of the military part being the most showy as with us, the splendor was in the public officials, especially the mayors of a dozen cities who all wore costumes of rich furs, velvet, silk, and gold or jewelled necklaces. You cannot imagine anything odder than to see those plain and common men, often awkward or fat or thin, or stooping or spectacled become transformed to something wholly gorgeous in the robing room before my eyes. Then the academic men wore robes of black and purple or scarlet, I wearing the robes and scarlet hood of a Cambridge

(England) LL.D., hired for 10/6 from a dealer in London."

Colonel Higginson's credentials, in the shape of a letter from Harvard University, commended him "as one whose experience as a teacher, soldier, author, and historian has fitted him to appreciate the character and services of the great king."

Rev. Mr. Horder writes of this event: —

"It was never my good fortune to hear the Colonel speak, but I met with fine and quite unbiassed testimony as to the charm of his public utterance in connection with the unveiling of the Alfred Statue at Winchester where he represented his old University of Harvard. A little time afterward I was visiting the Mayor of Winchester and describing the Alfred celebration, he said, 'There was an American named Higginson who made quite the speech of the occasion,' and he added, 'Rosebery and he were the speakers, and the rest were nowhere.'"

This record of journeys would be incomplete without some account of two visits to the Southern States. In the winter of 1878, while Colonel Higginson's home was still in Newport, he revisited his old haunts at the South.

He wrote to his sister that their Virginia cousins "gave such interesting accounts of their war life, when the two sides alternately occupied Culpeper; and when either [garrison] left, they hurried to the camp for boxes of hard-bread or salt left behind.

They liked to have a garrison there, for they always lived better and the soldiers almost always behaved well. They were months without bread — living on potatoes, squashes and milk and sometimes even wild onions and garlic and boiled clover."

"It was so strange," he wrote from Florida, "to touch at Jacksonville as a quiet passenger, where I could once have burned the city with a word. However, greatness is always appreciated and a man came on board with a message for the steamboat Captain and insisted on delivering it to *me*. I have n't had such an honor since my little nephew took me (in uniform) for a policeman. . . . Colored church in evening with just such 'shouting' as we used to have in my regiment — I feared it was all gone. Things are so little changed to the eye, it is almost incredible that fifteen years have passed.

"I have been down to Jacksonville for the day," he wrote from Magnolia. "I said in my 'Army Life' that I should feel like a Rip Van Winkle who once wore uniform — but it went beyond my dreams in that way. The city I had last seen deserted and in flames, I found made over into a summer paradise. . . . I was alone with my ghosts of fifteen years ago and got a horse and went wandering round, searching for my past. The forts we built were levelled, only a furrow here and there in the ground. Where we made a lookout in a steeple, there was the church, but with a new spire. The house where I sat all night on the doorsteps waiting for an attack was burned long since. The house I had for headquarters, then the pride of the town, is now an old house and in poor condition. The railroad along which we used to skirmish is torn up and I traced its line with difficulty to the woods that formed our debatable ground; they were the same, [but] where once was a dangerous ford, was now a bridge and fine road. Nothing was wholly unchanged but the exquisite climate and the budding spring. I began to feel fearfully bewildered, as if I had lived multitudes of lives. An individual seems so insignificant in presence of the changes of time; he is nothing, even if his traces are mingled with fire and blood."

Here the former Colonel met one of his old sergeants, and "we agreed to have some others of the men come and meet me there next Tuesday, and with their warm hearts, I can let the past take care of itself. One curious thing I should mention is that as it was Washington's birthday, guns were being fired all the while, so like those remote days."

A second visit in the spring of 1904 gave Colonel Higginson an opportunity to see the wonders of the "New South." At this time he was a guest of Mr. Robert Ogden on his educational trip through the Southern States. On account of Colonel Higginson's war experience, he felt a little doubtful as to his reception by Southerners. To find that he was known through his books, — many of which were in Southern libraries — rather than as leader of a black regiment was a delightful surprise. "People hardly seem to remember the war at all," he wrote. "Never in my life have I been received so warmly and everywhere I have found my books well known, one private school even using my 'Young Folks History,' and one schoolmaster in South Carolina holding my Epictetus to be next to the Bible."

To find that certain Southern libraries had been sadly injured in the Civil War appealed to Colonel Higginson's sense of justice; and he interested his friends in replenishing the vacant shelves, contributing many books from his own library.

Both white and colored schools were visited on this trip, but Booker Washington's Institution at Tuskegee and the Calhoun school, of which Colonel Higginson was a trustee, were of especial interest to him. At Calhoun, which is in the "Black Belt," the colored people came from twenty miles around, many walking this distance barefoot, and gathered in a grove to listen to addresses, one of which was made by Colonel Higginson. It was a striking scene, this mass of jet black faces all eagerly upturned to the speaker, and responding to his words with sympathetic nods and ejaculations. The objective point of the "Conference for Education in the South" was Birmingham, Alabama. Here the "Yankee" Colonel was cordially entertained by a man whose father had been in the Confederate army and who was captured at Gettysburg and died in prison.

At the evening opening of the Conference, which was in a large and crowded theatre, Colonel Higginson was one of the speakers. The only colored persons present were confined to an upper gallery and to this small contingent the former commander of a black regiment at once turned his attention and his remarks. That was a tense half-hour for his special friends, who felt as if they were all treading the edge of a volcano. The speaker, who was quite aware of this solicitude, kept skilfully within the danger-line and won the applause of his critical audience. When the meeting broke up, he turned to a stately ex-Confederate officer, saying, "I hope I have said nothing improper!" This old-time Southern gentleman laid a benignant hand on Colonel Higginson's shoulder and exclaimed, "Say what you please!"

On his return from this memorable trip, Colonel Higginson found that he was somewhat criticized by certain Boston colored people, who were antagonistic to Booker Washington, for taking part in the expedition and especially for speaking at Tuskegee. Thereupon, with his usual fearless way of grappling with difficulties, Colonel Higginson requested his critics to meet him at Parker Memorial Hall. With one sympathetic friend, Rev. Edward Cummings, to second his efforts, he talked plainly to his audience of their mistakes and dangers, of their opportunities and responsibilities; and through his talk ran always the warm strain of personal sympathy and affection for the race. He might well have ended this speech with these words uttered on another public occasion:

"Formerly I had no protection around my tent except in the fidelity and courage of black soldiers, and so long as I live, every drop of blood in my veins will beat true to them."

XVI

THE CROWNING YEARS

IN 1889, Colonel Higginson began what proved to be a four years' task of editing, with Mrs. Mabel Loomis Todd of Amherst, Emily Dickinson's poems and letters. Of this work he wrote Mrs. Todd: —

"I can't tell you how much I am enjoying the poems. There are many new to me which take my breath away."

A year later he wrote to her: —

"You are the only person who can feel as I do about this extraordinary thing we have done in recording this rare genius. I feel as if we had climbed to a cloud, pulled it away, and revealed a new star behind it. . . . Such things as I find in her letters! 'The Madonnas I see are those that pass the House to their work, carrying Saviours with them.' Is not that one of the take-your-breath-away thoughts?

"There is much that I never could print, as where she writes, 'Of our greatest acts we are ignorant. You were not aware that you saved my life.' What a unique existence was hers!"

Four years later, he wrote: —

"I feel half sorry to hear that the book is so nearly ready; it will be the last, I suppose, and will not only yield the final news of Emily Dickinson, but take from me a living companionship I shall miss."

After the volume of letters was published, of which Mrs. Todd was the principal editor, Colonel Higginson wrote to her November 29, 1894: —

"Emily has arrived. They sent her to Sever's book store where I rarely go and where she might have hid forever in a cupboard. . . . It is extraordinary how the mystic and bizarre Emily is born at once between two pages . . . as Thoreau says summer passes to autumn in an instant. All after that is the E. D. I knew. But how is it possible to reconcile her accounts of early book reading . . . with the yarns (O! irreverence) she told me about their first books, concealed from her father in the great bush at the door or under the piano cover? Well! what an encyclopædia of strange gifts she was."

During these years of fascinating though strenuous editorial labor, Colonel Higginson was also engaged on various pieces of original work. He wrote in July, 1890: —

"I am now to correct proof of three books — Epictetus, American Sonnets and Emily Dickinson's poems."

And in November: —

"I was about writing the determination never again to have three books on hand at same time, going through the press, when I found myself entrapped into a promise to give the Centennial Oration of Massachusetts Historical Society, having also to prepare an address for 19th Century Club, and the life of Francis Higginson besides my regular work. Too much again."

Yet one day when proofs of several different articles came to him, he said, "I am naturally a glutton of such work and rather enjoy it."

In the spring of that year he visited the battlefield of Gettysburg in connection with his Military History and wrote home: —

"At Gettysburg I rose at 6 A.M. and soon after seven set off with fifty people and two buglers in a series of omnibuses and barouches to drive about, over twenty miles of Union and Confederate lines of battle. At certain places we stopped, were called together by the buglers while Colonel Batchelder who is a sort of professor of Gettysburg battle knowledge told us just what happened, and as we had with us a number of persons who had been in the battle at different points, they often added their reminiscences. One of these was a western physician who had lost his hearing in the battle by the noise of cannon and whenever we stopped and gathered round the speaker, he would run up to the front and stick his long ear trumpet up to Colonel B. and drink it all in with beaming eyes. . . . Squirrels played where once guns had thundered and I saw a great Luna moth quietly reposing against a tree. After all the brightness and beauty, it was a haunting place and day, and I understood a great battle as I never did before."

To Margaret he wrote: —

"The blackbirds and meadow larks were all singing on the farms at Gettysburg and as we drove along our bugler would sometimes make a great noise (toot-toot-toot) with his bugle, and the birds would go flying away. He was a little fat man with a great blue overcoat and his cheeks looked as if he had puffed so much at the bugle that they were all round and swelled and he could not get them back again.

"When we went away from Baltimore to Gettysburg there was a great good-natured old woman, jet black, who bade us all good-bye at the station. She had a large round face and no teeth and a common towel, very clean, pinned round her head and under her chin; and when we came back there she was, all ready to receive us, and saying, 'Got back all safe? Bress de Lord!' And when we got into our carriages again, a lot of little black boys and girls ran along beside us, shouting whenever the bugler played."

After this visit he noted in the journal: "Began anew on history with fresh interest for visiting localities."

The summer of 1890 was spent in Dublin, New Hampshire, which became henceforth a permanent summer home. The little daughter wrote her aunt in Brattleboro: —

"Papa wishes you to know that the castle in the

air has a place on earth. He has just bought an acre of ground beautifully situated above the lake. We begin building this autumn."

These bits of Dublin life are from the diaries: —

"June 12, 1891. Began thoroughly to enjoy the primitive forest feeling. Felt that conscious happiness which Thoreau describes — every little pine needle seeming to stretch toward me. There was a feeling as of late summer in the air and the crickets' incessant chirp seemed saturated with happiness. It was enough simply to live and look round on the trees I love."

Her father always bore an active part in Margaret's birthday celebrations, whether they took the form of climbing the mountain, perhaps getting drenched in the mountain brook on the way, or a picnic in the woods. Later, on her seventeenth birthday, he joined in the Virginia Reel.

About an earlier celebration, he wrote to his sister that the children "played and swung and then came the two young Smiths [Joseph Lindon and his brother] clad in brilliant Japanese costumes who made great fun as they always do. We had tea on a large flat boulder above the road shaded by pines, and this was very merry. . . .

"It is very pretty to see her and Rob [an Irish setter] dancing about together with the butterflies. The birds come quite near her and do not seem afraid, and sometimes, when she whistles to them, they answer her from the forest. . . .

"S. . . . calls me Thomas Ewart Higginson from my devotion to the Gladstonian axe; I am clearing away a good many of the little gray birches which obstruct more valuable trees. . . . I find endless joy in pottering about among trees and shrubs."

"Aug. 7, With Margaret, watching birds, and she climbing trees."

"Sept. 29, First gipsying with Margaret for flowers."

This referred to an autumnal habit of the "happy little couple," as the child called her father and herself, of plundering our friends' flower-beds after their owners had gone.

"Oct. 10, Felt as I strolled about after breakfast that I should be willing to go to sleep for the winter and wake up to find myself here [Dublin] again. There is still woodchopping to be done and I hate to leave it."

Of our neighbors the Abbot Thayers, he said they "live outdoors, know all birds and butterflies, and rear the latter from the chrysalis till they flutter in and out of the great sitting-room as if it were their home."

One summer we had Mark Twain for a neighbor: —

"Called on Clemens. Found him in bed where he prefers to write, a strange picturesque object, in night clothes, with curly white hair standing up over his head. The bed was covered with written sheets which his daughter carried off at intervals, to be copied by her on typewriter, his secretary only writing his correspondence. He often leaves off anything in the middle and begins on something else and goes back to it. He has always worked in this way and likes it."

In our early years at Dublin, the Smiths' outdoor theatre was dedicated and Colonel Higginson read these lines. They are given as a specimen of his gift at impromptu verse, which was often in demand on such occasions. Later he himself took part in a miracle play, "Théophile," written by our neighbor, Henry Copley Greene, for the Teatro Bambino, in which Higginson personated an aged abbot.

"When the Goddess of Dulness would rule o'er this planet
  And bind all amusements, like Samson, with withes,
Fate conquered her scheme, ere she fairly began it,
  By producing one household — a household of Smiths.

"Fate selected the seed of a Rhode Island Quaker
  Its wit and its wisdom, its mirth and its pith,
And brought all these gifts to a Point — one half acre —
  And gave to the product the surname of Smith.

"Though Care killed a cat it cannot hush the Mewses
  Nor reduce all our joys to monotonous myth;
Some gleams of pure fun o'er the earth Fate diffuses, —
  So cheers, three times three, for the household of Smith!"

In those first years of the Dublin life, when the shore of the lake was not wholly owned by summer residents and was still the scene of annual town picnics, Colonel Higginson took a cordial part in those

THE HOUSE AT DUBLIN, N.H.

festivities, and usually made some address to the throng of young and old. He also spoke at meetings of the Farmers' Grange. Men who were then boys still remember their delight in these talks from a man who had "been in the war," who wrote books, and could tell no end of amusing stories. One of these youths, now a college professor, writes of Colonel Higginson: —

"The traits that marked his summer life at Dublin specially appealed to me; his sincere recognition of genuine manhood and womanhood in the townsfolk and his detection of a poetic element in even the grim and seemingly sordid side of country life."

Literary work was continued at Dublin and the author's secretary imported for a time each summer, as this plea to his so-called pastor for the loan of a typewriter shows: —

"REVEREND SIR: —

"A virtuous maid has arrived at this house, for whose spiritual welfare I am bound to concern myself. She is to do certain copying for Goodman Hart and myself on that carnal instrument called a typewriter, which I myself eschew, finding it to savor little of the great Scriptural Types which we are bidden to revere.

"Now the only typewriting machine yet accessible here is that belonging to your neighbor Goodman Cooke, a species of lay preacher, who offers his for the afternoon. Yet I ask myself, Is it meet that this maid, soberly nurtured . . . should perform the office of writing on a Unitarian typewriter and that only? Should she not be kept in the right path, during each *morning*, by a typewriter of sounder views — your own perchance? Pray consider, perpend and reply.

"Your faithful PARISHIONER.

"Written at the breakfast table — hence spots. But what are these, besides spots on the Faith?"

The distinction of being Harvard's oldest graduate Colonel Higginson whimsically coveted. He wrote to his sister in 1890: —

"I am renewing my efforts for the post of oldest living graduate of Harvard and have now only 236 ahead of me, not counting my classmates."

"One curious feeling," he meditated, "about Commencement in growing older is that you do not feel as if you were getting among the oldest, but as if the really old men had grown lazy and stayed away."

The return to Cambridge in the autumn was always delightful to him on account of the tide of young life flowing in at the beginning of the college year. He took a perennial interest in the football games, going to Harvard Square to learn the results long after he was obliged to give up attending the contests. He wrote in his diary of 1901: "Nov. 22. Football game — very exciting. Harvard 22; 0.

When a young man attempts to kick a goal in such a game as to-day's, he has 36,000 pairs of eyes fastened with interest upon him. Is there any other such opportunity in life?"

The students were often sent to Colonel Higginson by their instructors to glean information about the Anti-Slavery period, and he was often asked to talk to them in their own haunts. Many were the times when he was enabled by the generosity of his friends, who were always ready to respond to his calls for money, to give substantial aid to struggling youths and maidens. If these aspirants for an education happened to be colored, they enlisted from him all the more sympathy. Such entries as these in his diary were not uncommon, the second referring to a Radcliffe Commencement: —

"Went with young —— to further his application for Harvard scholarship."

"Was anxious because I could not see my colored protégé [a young girl whom he had helped through college] until actually called up. When she came and had more applause than any, I felt that I would rather give up my degree for to-morrow than that all her efforts and mine should fail."

For in 1898 Colonel Higginson was given by Harvard the degree of LL.D., an honor already conferred upon him by Western Reserve University two years earlier. As he went forward to receive this honor, he was greeted with a prolonged burst of enthusiasm which was almost overpowering. He wrote in his diary, June 26: —

"Received degree of LL.D. somewhat tardily, but glad of delay for the sake of the roar of applause from the audience (beginning with the young men) which greeted it. It was wholly a surprise to me and was something to have lived for."

The secret of Colonel Higginson's popularity was the overflowing fountain of sympathy which pulsed in his veins. Lowell's lines might have been written about him: —

"[He] doeth little kindnesses
Which most leave undone, or despise."

One of these was his invariable habit of writing to young authors whose work had pleased him. A typical instance of the little thoughtful deeds which always seemed to be second nature to him is given the writer by a Yale professor. When a lonely and homesick sophomore at Harvard, he was startled to receive a call from Colonel Higginson with an invitation to attend an interesting meeting in Boston, not open to the public. To this day he does not know how his unexpected visitor discovered him, but he says the incident brought the first real pleasure into his college life.

"You know," one of his early friends, now a well-

known author, wrote to him, "how fully you have
my affection with that of so many others to whom
you have opened great avenues of happiness." It
was easier for him to emphasize a man's good points
rather than his failings, and he was always ready to
make excuses for one who was in any way criticized
— a trait that his impetuous young daughter sometimes found trying. People who were almost strangers unburdened their souls to him as to a father con-
fessor. As he once said, "It is my fortune or mis-
fortune to have one of those temperaments which
have since early youth drawn unexpected and sometimes perilous confidences from others."

Applicants for assistance were never turned away,
even if by helping them pecuniarily he inconven-
ienced himself. Mr. George Higginson (father of
Henry Lee Higginson) once gave his cousin Wentworth an illustration of this family trait. Hailing an
imaginary passer-by, he cried, "Do you want anything?" — at the same time thrusting his hand into
his pocket and bringing it out full of silver. "Here,
take this!" So long as the silver lasted this form of
philanthropy came easily; but the most injurious of
the daily visitors were those who robbed the busy
author of precious time. Expressing one day some
doubt about the advantage of a future life, one of the
family attempted to expostulate. "But I should

have to meet so many people who bore me!" was his quick rejoinder.

A Cambridge young man who was a "checker" at the polls in the fall of 1900 at the same booth where Colonel Higginson voted, received a lesson in citizenship at that time which impressed him deeply. The atmosphere of the booth in question he described as most repulsive; but the story can best be told in the youth's own words, as printed in a local newspaper: —

"The writer, while not particularly finicky, by ten o'clock that morning was heartily sick of his job. At about ten o'clock, however, the door opened, and in stepped Colonel Thomas Wentworth Higginson. I shall never forget his appearance. He was very plainly dressed and had on a rather old looking ulster. . . . His figure, however, was full of dignity. With an air of utmost veneration and respect, such as I have never seen before or since, he removed his hat from his head and then stepped forward to get his ballot. During the whole time that he was casting his ballot he kept his hat in his hand and only put it on when he had stepped out of the door into the street. That is all he did — simply removed his hat — but I can never forget his manner in doing it. . . . No one knew better than he the real value of the privilege of voting and knowing it he treated it with the respect which is its due. . . . Since I saw Mr. Higginson cast his vote, I have never failed to take off my hat when casting mine."

In 1892, Colonel Higginson's devoted sister Anna died, and he wrote, "It was a touching thing thus to close the half century of our family's residence in Brattleboro, where they went in 1842." But the gradual disappearance of early friends never visibly depressed him. He lived in the present, and when disappointed in a contemporary wrote in his diary, "Thank God, there are always children!"

The lecture habit was assiduously pursued, and on the four hundredth anniversary of the landing of Columbus, 1892, he wrote, "I give a Columbus and musical address in New York on October 21, for which I am to be paid $250, twice the biggest fee I ever get for a speech." This celebration took the form of a concert, the handbill stating: "In the course of the proceedings an oration will be delivered by Colonel Thomas Wentworth Higginson."

The author's seventieth birthday came in 1893. It was made an especially festive occasion by his friends, and the little red house was thronged. These celebrations were continued through successive birthdays when flowers, letters, telegrams, and personal greetings made the day a milestone. Although the different eras through which he had passed made him feel as if he had lived several lives, he seldom unless urged spoke of past events in which he had had a share. His athletic training served him well, and until long after seventy he bounded upstairs like a boy, two or three steps at a time. In 1895 and again in 1901, he gave a course of lectures at Western Reserve University, and in one week he records speaking every day. Overwork finally brought its penalty, and in the autumn of 1895 he was sentenced to confinement in his room and a milk diet. This trying illness lasted for a year, during which he wrote his "Cheerful Yesterdays" propped up with pillows. On Christmas Day he wrote to his friends at the Cambridge Public Library: —

"I am moving slowly along and have now held out to me the munificent offer of a raw egg, which seems a whole Christmas dinner after eight weeks of milk-cure! . . . Some people think I write better than formerly, in my horizontal attitude!"

On the cover of the diary for 1896, he wrote: —

"'Now that I begin to know a little, I die.' St. Augustine."

And within the covers are these entries: —

"Jan. 6. For 10 weeks to-morrow I have had absolutely no nourishment but milk. . . . I have done a great deal of reading and writing on this and some talking."

"Jan. 13. Per contra, had to give up the hope of working on the history in bed. I cannot handle the wide sheets or heavy books. It is a great disappointment."

"Feb. 6. Wedding Day celebrated, not unprosaically, by an Easter lily and a cup of mutton broth. Delicious! beyond my dreams! It is almost worth three months of milk alone to get the flavor of that first cup of broth."

"Mar. 1. I still remain with my head in perfect condition, able to write ad libitum. I enjoy life and have adapted myself wonderfully to my recumbent condition."

"Apr. 5. Beautiful Easter Sunday. Choir from church [First Parish] came and sang hymns — an entire surprise and delight."

Colonel Higginson's own physician was confident of his recovery, although most of the profession who knew of his condition thought it impossible that a man of his age could revive. The consulting physician wrote to him the following summer, "I am rejoiced to hear of your favorable progress, which I regard as due largely to a sound mind." In some anxiety as to how he should meet the expenses of this illness, he received what he called "bread upon the waters." Many years before, he had befriended a young man who was convicted of burglary and sentenced to prison, and had given substantial aid to establish him in business when he was released. His own account of this bit of good fortune is found in his diary: —

"May 2. Received from Mrs. —— check for $500

for two notes of her brother for $123 dated about 1859 . . . having long held them as worthless, this being with compound interest at perhaps 4 pr. ct. though the notes were without interest. . . . Great surprise."

In June the invalid was transported to Dublin, and in July made the following note: —

"July 30. Sent to printers first (new) instalment of narrative. ['Cheerful Yesterdays.'] . . . Collapse. . . . This involves putting back on milk diet and cessation of drives for a time. Giving up autumn journey part planned. Giving up (probably) winter lecturing. Giving up (probably) England next year. Very possibly semi-invalidism for the rest of my life. Still this to be quietly faced and recognized."

However, these anxieties proved needless, as the next year saw him sufficiently recovered to embark for Europe.

It pleased him to find that during the year in bed he had earned more by writing than in several previous years. In April of this year (1896) he made a list of books read in the previous six months — forty-two in all. He also noted that in seven years he had read four hundred and seventy-nine books. Giving away books was another source of pleasure, those given to different libraries during his life amounting to ten thousand volumes. He also gave to the Gray Herbarium of Harvard College his botanical notebooks which were pronounced by the professor in charge "a careful chronicle of a vegetation which for this immediate region has largely disappeared forever." His correspondence with and concerning John Brown was given to the Boston Public Library; also collections of Margaret Fuller Ossoli's and Emily Dickinson's letters.

December 1st he recorded, "My office of Military and Naval Historian expired, much to my satisfaction, after seven years and four months." An extension of a year's time without compensation was however granted at Colonel Higginson's request, and the "History" was satisfactorily completed.

These fragments from the diary after his recovery show the continued activity: —

"Oct. 20, 1897. Evening presided at Anthony Hope Hawkins's reading. Had him here afterwards."

"Feb. 12, 1898. Springfield. Spoke at Lincoln dinner after half hour's reception to 100 men."

"March 9. Spent morning at State House — outrageous bill against Sunday Concerts."

"May 31, 1900. Evening, Boer meeting and presided. Got through well, though voice not strong. The three Boer envoys unusually fine looking men."

This was a meeting at Faneuil Hall where envoys from the Boer Republic presented their side of the South African trouble with England. From a newspaper account of a similar meeting in Worcester at which Colonel Higginson presided, this extract is taken: —

"However much the audience sympathized with the Boers, they very much more disliked England, and when the presiding officer undertook to say a word in behalf of England's effort in behalf of humanity, in spite of her wrong attitude toward the Boers, he was greeted with a perfect hurricane of objurgations. The Colonel quietly waited until the riot had ceased when he went on calm and unruffled; and my admiration, always great, sensibly rose as I saw his wonderful command of himself."

"Feb. 15, 1901. P.M. Lectured to Filene's work-people on 'People I have Met.'"

"Mar. 6, 1902. Prince Henry of Prussia here. I spoke at the dinner at the Somerset."

After the "Military History" was off his hands he wrote, "Tales of the Enchanted Islands of the Atlantic," "Book and Heart," and "Old Cambridge." In 1900, he began a "Life of Longfellow" for the American Men of Letters series, and in 1902 wrote a biography of Whittier, recording in July, "Have worked for ten days on Whittier — averaging 1000 words daily."

The French writer, Th. Bentzon (Mme. Blanc), after visiting this country in the nineties, wrote an account of Colonel Higginson which was translated

with the inapt title, "A Typical American." The
1902 diary says: —

"Received proof of 'A Typical American,' by
Madame Blanc; a London translation into English
sent me for revision.

"I regard this as the greatest honor of my life, in a
literary way — to be treated so fully in the 'Revue
des Deux Mondes' by so able and so distinguished a
woman and then to have it fully translated and published in London. Of course it gratified me, even
if sometimes overstated and undeserved, gratified
more than such pleasant personal tributes as those of
Justin McCarthy, Tom Hughes, and others in their
books of reminiscences."

In February of the same year, he writes: —

"It was curious after my seven months' absence
[in Europe] when I wrote nothing for print, to come
back and find the same continuous impulse of hard
work in my study."

"April 3, 1902. Evening. E. E. Hale Festival —
a fine meeting, thoroughly worked up and in a good
cause; but I should not wish to have any injudicious
friends try the same thing for me, even on a smaller
scale, for my birthday. Such occasions are carnivals
of flattery, no discrimination, no one venturing to say
the exact truth. Should it ever be attempted for me,
I wish to be painted as I am."

"Aug. 4. Early this morning I read over some of
the opening chapters of my 'Cheerful Yesterdays,' and
it seemed like another world, though a deeply inter-

esting and picturesque one, and I wondered whether it might be permanently read by students as a living picture of that period. Without the slightest feeling of old age I am drifting, I suppose, toward another sphere of existence, even more strange and interesting, I dare say, than this one has been."

His admiration of the Shaw Monument by Saint-Gaudens, on Boston Common, led him often to revisit it; and on one of these occasions he wrote the following lines in his notebook: —

"Ever before mine eyes the beautiful pageant is passing,
Colonel and dusky braves, who are marching onward forever,
But for some inches of space, one trivial turn of Fate's arrow,
I had been riding there, foredoomed to Shaw's glory immortal."

"Written beside the monument
"Jan. 25, 1902."

Several of Colonel Higginson's poems were set to music, "Sixty and Six," "Vestis Angelica," and "The Trumpeter," a poem he wrote after hearing the first two lines sung in a dream. "Waiting for the Bugle" had two different settings. One of his most musical poems written for special occasions was the unpublished one read at a small dinner given in Boston to celebrate Josephine Preston Peabody's engagement to Lionel Marks, Professor of Engineering at Harvard College. He called it "'The Go-Abroad' (Sequel to 'The Stay at Home,' by

Josephine P. Peabody)"; and these are the first two
stanzas: —

> "We have waited, we have longed —
>   We have longed as none can know,
> While this winter smiled with sun
>   And the spring came in with snow,
> Waiting till some hour serene,
> Bridegroom worthy should be seen,
>   For Josephine.
>
> "Softly has time glided on —
>   Love, that wondrous engineer,
> Who the hopes of youth and maid
>   Brings together, far or near,
> Drew these closer, till there fell
> Potent hands that bound her well
>   To Lionel."

In 1899–1900 Colonel Higginson gave a course of
lectures before the Lowell Institute upon "American
Orators and Oratory," and recorded the fact in his
diary: "Nov. 15. My first Lowell lecture (of course,
extempore) and enjoyed it much. Audience fine and
cordial." In 1902–03, he gave a second course of
Lowell Lectures on "American Literature in the
Nineteenth Century"; and in the winter of 1905
he delivered a third course on "English Literature
in the Last Half of the Nineteenth Century." At
these lectures, he was always greeted with crowded
houses.

"Dec. 23, 1902. Much pleased to find that I could
still speak without notes and without forgetfulness

or confusion. I had been a little anxious about this and have therefore written out my Lowell lectures in full."

"Jan. 5, 1903. The lecture was considered a great success. All standing room occupied and almost everybody stayed through. I found reading to be far easier than speaking without notes (as I have done so long) and almost as effective; it seemed like beginning a new career and my voice served me well."

Of the third course, in 1905, he wrote: —

"Feb. 28. First Lowell lecture (Wordsworthshire). A great success — an unexpectedly fine voice."

"March 7. Second Lowell lecture. Carlyle, Ruskin, Froude, Hunt."

"March 28. Fifth Lowell lecture. Dickens, Thackeray and reading Tennyson's poems."

"April 4. Last Lowell lecture. Considered very successful and was pronounced by John Lowell the best he ever heard in that hall."

In May, 1903, he spoke at the Concord Emerson celebration: —

"Meeting good and my address successful. After it, Senator Hoar turned to me and said, grasping my hand, 'What I have to say is pewter and tinsel compared to that.'"

His position as chairman of the Harvard Visiting Committee on English Literature he resigned in 1903, having served on this and other Visiting Com-

mittees for sixty-odd years. In the latter part of that
year he wrote in the journal, "I always keep on my
desk 'Sunset and Evening Star' [Tennyson's 'Crossing the Bar'], and am ready for whatever comes."
On the eve of his eightieth birthday, in 1903, a reception was given to him by the Boston Authors' Club,
when Judge Robert Grant read his inspiring verses
written for the occasion, and afterwards printed in
the "Atlantic Monthly," beginning: —

> "Preacher of a liberal creed,
> Pioneer in Freedom's cause;
> Ever prompt to take the lead
> In behalf of saner laws,
> Still your speech persuasive flows
> As the brooks of Helicon.
> You have earned a fair repose,
> Thomas Wentworth Higginson!"

This poem Colonel Higginson called "one of the
greatest laurels I ever won." He thus alluded in his
diary to the celebration: —

"Dec. 21. Evening — an unexpected and elaborate reception by the Authors' Club. There was a
series of flattering speeches, of a more headturning
description than anything I ever had addressed to
me, but they left me happy and humble."

After one of the receptions given him by the Grand
Army Post which bore his name, he wrote, "Reception by T. W. H. Post Sons of Veterans — much enthusiasm making me feel quite humble."

These notes from the journals show the intellectual and physical activity of the remaining years: —

"Old Colored Women's Home. A jolly spectacle, those old ladies at their tea-table; some of them with white fleecy hair, very becoming, and good features."

"Feb. 23, 1904. Evening reception from the colored people in Boston, with warm speeches and poetry, etc. It is long since I have been in so close relations with them and their hearts are as warm as ever."

"Mar. 15, 1904. Lecture South Boston (People I have Met) Church of the Redeemer . . . a remarkably interesting audience — mostly teachers, mechanics and children, very attentive and sympathetic; and greeting me with much personal ardor. It was in an Episcopal chapel hall, but included many Roman Catholics, which I like."

"June 26, 1905. Began work in earnest on life of my grandfather [Stephen Higginson] and enjoyed it."

"June 28, 1905. To Rochester, N.Y. to give a Phi Beta Kappa address and felt no harm from it."

"July 6. First proof from 'Part of a Man's Life.'"

This was in a manner a continuation of "Cheerful Yesterdays," although more fragmentary.

In 1905, Margaret was married, with her father's cordial approval, to a young Boston physician. The ceremony took place in the village church at Dublin, and Dr. Robert Collyer officiated. Fortunately his

views about the "heathen obey" coincided with
those of the bride's father. This clergyman was wont
to relate in his own amusing way the beginning of his
friendship with Colonel Higginson. When living in
Chicago, he heard Higginson speak on physical
training and utter an impressive warning against
the use of mince pie. Dr. Collyer's curiosity was
excited, and after the lecture he invested in one of
the condemned viands. The consequence was, he
declared, that his larder was ever after stocked with
mince pies. This reverend gentleman and Colonel
Higginson were born in the same year, and the
latter once wrote these humorous lines for the
clergyman's birthday: —

> "I entered glad on life's wide fold,
>   But soon my hopes grew colder;
> How could I e'er seem wise or bold
>   With him a fortnight older?
>
> "I never could be blithe as he
>   Since he was always jollier:
> So I'll his faithful collie be
>   With him forever Collyer."

It is said that Higginson's opposition to church organization lessened in later life. He said himself, "I
am not sure of any change of attitude, though doubt-
less old age makes one more equable in general attitude." At any rate he considered it his duty to
attend church semi-occasionally, both summer and

winter. His family rallied him for sleeping through the sermon, but in such cases it always happened that he had remembered more of the discourse than any of those who criticized him.

The 1906 diary records: —

"Feb. 12. Evening at North End school — very turbulent — Italian boys, but I enjoyed talking to them, until I read from Army Life which was a mistake. Never read before children."

"Mar. 12. Boston before legislative committee at State House, with 8 old soldiers against me."

This meeting was to consider the erection of a statue to General Butler, which Colonel Higginson opposed.

"Mar. 19. At Binghamton, N.Y. P.M. Lecture and had good audience of perhaps 250 in hard storm."

"June 28. Phi Beta Kappa. At meeting, gave notice of amendment next year in regard to women's admission to dinner."

Two grandchildren came to cheer these later days, the first a boy named Wentworth born in 1906, of whom he wrote: —

"The beautiful and happy baby makes my health or illness a secondary trifle — if I can only pass quietly away without those melancholy intermediate days or weeks when I may be only a burden."

And at Ipswich, two years later, he thus announced the arrival of a second little Margaret: —

THE GRANDCHILDREN

"One of the happiest days of my life, in the birth of a beautiful girl baby with abundant black hair and fine health."

He wrote in November, 1906: —

"I may be relied on to keep on working here to the last, for my own pleasure if for nothing else, but the silent and gradual withdrawal from the world in which I was once so active does not trouble me at all. Nor have I the slightest fear of death, whether it be that something or nothing lies beyond it. The former seems to me altogether the more probable."

These lines of Walt Whitman's were quoted by him with deep emotion, and he once said that he would like to have them engraved on his memorial stone: —

> "Joy, Shipmate, joy!
> (Pleas'd to my soul at death I cry)
> Our life is closed, our life begins,
> The long, long anchorage we leave,
> The ship is clear at last, she leaps,
> She swiftly courses from the shore,
> Joy, Shipmate, joy!"

December 21, 1907, he wrote: —

"This being the last day of my 84 years, I laid out some pleasant work during the coming year. As I have succeeded so with my postponed volume of my grandfather's memoir, I decided to carry out another old project and one very good for elder years, viz.: to translate from the Greek the 'Birds of Aristophanes' . . . I enjoy life, love and work but should hardly care to be a nonagenarian."

"Dec. 22. Beautiful day begun with much surprise at my own advanced years, as there is very little inward change and it is generally thought I carry them well externally."

In the summer of 1908, he was attracted by an article in the "Dial" called the "Grandisonian Manner," and wrote this letter to the author: —

"DEAR SIR OR MADAM: —

"You will pardon me for thus addressing you, when I tell you that I have just finished the whole series of Richardson's writings, including Diderot's commentary and all, having come upon them in one of the very best of the Massachusetts Public libraries in this attractive rural town [Ipswich]. All my life I have wished for time to renew Sir Charles, as I heard him read aloud by my mother in Cambridge in early boyhood; and as I am now fast approaching my 85th birthday it is a delight to find the book quite reviving the old affection and the old associations of humor. The sense of personal nobleness about Sir Charles is renewed and also the wonderful and quite unique creation . . . of Miss Grandison."

In 1908 and 1909, short newspaper and magazine articles kept him busy, and he began a record of the Higginson family. In the latter year the collection of papers called "Carlyle's Laugh" was published. "Perhaps," he wrote, "my last book, when nearly eighty-six." In 1910, he finished the editorship of the "Higginson Genealogy," revised his "Young

Folks' History," and noted, May 13, "Work almost at an end, perhaps for life." Still his pen never rested. He had, as he laughingly declared, "got into the habit of living," and there were always thoughts to be uttered either about live issues or departed contemporaries. Various lectures and addresses were given during this year. The diaries again furnish the record: —

"Feb. 18, 1909. Evening — delightful and unexpected singing from a party of colored singers. They came unseen by me and sang on the stairs, 'Marching thro' Georgia!' They took me by entire surprise; also bringing flowers."

"May 4, 1910. To meeting of officers at American House. Drove in alone. Was treated with curious deferential attention and made a speech."

"May 12. Pleasant and successful memorial meeting for Margaret Fuller Ossoli, 100th birthday. It was held in the house of my birth, the parlors crowded. Perhaps it was my last public meeting."

"May 17. To Concord, Mass., to funeral of Judge Keyes [a classmate]."

This excursion to Concord was violently opposed by his family, for he was obliged to go alone, his "natural guardian" being absent; but he was inexorable; delighted to escape from feminine control; and came back triumphant.

"May 26. At the notice of an hour or so prepared a talk on Theo. Parker for F.R.A."

"May 27. To Boston for lunch of Free Religious Association at which I spoke for the last time. Afterwards at Mrs. Howe's birthday reception."

"May 30. [Decoration Day.] To exercises in morning, marched with G.A.R. to chapel."

"June 10, 1910. Closing the care and labor of nearly two years [Genealogy] — my last literary work properly so called. I am now the sixth on the list of Harvard graduates."

One of the reforms which interested Colonel Higginson in later years was Simplified Spelling. It must be confessed that he did not attempt to remodel his own way of writing, but he defined the movement as an effort to save the time of the busy world; and he believed that to simplify "our great chaotic language" would make life easier for the stranger within our gates.

His attitude toward Socialism, that word of many meanings, is indicated in the diary of 1908. "Foolish and exaggerated paper on me in Boston 'Post,' announcing me as a Socialist." To a friend, he wrote in the same year: —

"I have for many years had some leaning toward Socialism, I suppose, but the thing for which I joined the College Association was because I thought it very undesirable that colleges should ignore the very *word* as they almost uniformly did then; Harvard being almost the only one which allowed it even to be mentioned. . . . As for the name 'Socialist,' I never either claimed or disclaimed it, regarding it as merely a feeler in the right direction and refusing any prominent place in the movement. I remember that Dr. Edward Hale and I both took this same position in a similar organization formed by Edward Bellamy in his time."

His social creed, as stated in a letter dated 1859, would have equally fitted the succeeding years: —

"Every year makes me, at least, more democratic, with less reverence for the elect and more faith in the many."

During the winter of 1911, strength gradually failed, though interest in the affairs of life never flagged. In February, he read a paper on Dickens, with all his old spirit, before the Round Table, and in April, he attended a meeting of the Authors' Club in Milton. His last thoughts and directions were for others, and his last days painless and serene. On the evening of May 9, while soft spring airs lifted the curtains of his windows, his visible presence was quietly withdrawn.

The farewell service was held by his own wish in the First Parish Church in Cambridge which claimed his allegiance from early association and from his warm regard for the pastor, Dr. Samuel M. Crothers, whom he had named, many years before, "the youth with the radiant brow."

The escort to the church was furnished by the Thomas Wentworth Higginson Post. The Loyal Legion conducted the military part of the service and the casket was borne up the aisle, to the sound of muffled drums, by young Negro soldiers. His verses, "Waiting for the Bugle," and his hymn, "To Thine Eternal Arms, O God," were sung, the large gathering of friends, which included all classes of the community, joining in the latter. Aldrich's "Monody on the Death of Wendell Phillips," beginning, —

> "One by one they go
> Into the unknown dark," —

was read, this being a poem for which Colonel Higginson had deeply cared. His ashes were deposited in the Cambridge Cemetery by the side of the little grave where he had strewn flowers on Decoration Day for thirty years. Of this spot, overlooking the Charles River Valley and commanding a view of the city of his birth, he had written: —

> "Shadows come and shadows go
> O'er the meadows wide;
> Twice each day, to and fro,
> Steals the river-tide;
> Each morn with sunrise-glow
> Gilds the green hillside."

On the bright May morning of 1911, when we stood there sorrowing, Dr. Crothers recalled a thought which had come to him in the church when he heard the bugle sounding "Taps" and the distant response. "I thought," he said, "of the passing of Mr. Valiant-for-truth in 'Pilgrim's Progress.' 'So he passed over, and all the trumpets sounded for him on the other side.'"

BIBLIOGRAPHY

THIS bibliography, based on a manuscript notebook of Thomas Wentworth Higginson, was originally compiled by the Cambridge Public Library, in 1906, in honor of the author's eighty-third birthday. This list has been revised and brought up to date by Colonel Higginson's private secretary. It does not aim to include all of his writings, but only the more important ones.

In the following list the place in parenthesis under the year indicates where Higginson resided during that time.

Def. I, II, etc., after a title refers to the volume in the definitive edition (1900) in which that title also appears.

CHRONOLOGICAL LIST

1843

(CAMBRIDGE)

A History. [Poem.] (In *Christian Examiner*, Nov.) Signed H.
Mrs. Child's Letters from New York. (In the *Present*, Nov. 15.)
La Madonna di San Sisto. [Poem.] (In the *Present*, Dec. 15.) Def. VI.
    Same. (In *Our Book*. [A Salem Fair publication.] Sept., 1844.)
    Same. (In Longfellow. *Estray.* 1846.)

1845

(CAMBRIDGE)

Lay of the Humble. [Poem.] (In New York *Tribune*, Oct. 1.)
Tyrtaeus. [Poem.] (In *Harbinger*, Nov. 1.)
    Same. (In *Liberator*, Nov. 7.)
Articles. (In *Christian World*, Jan., Feb.) Signed H.

1846

(CAMBRIDGE)

Four hymns. (In Longfellow and Johnson. *Book of Hymns.*)
The Railroad. [Poem.] (In *Harbinger*, April 4.)
Holiness unto the Lord. [Sonnet.] (In *Harbinger*, June 20.)
Hymn of Humanity. (In *Harbinger*, June 27.)

Hebe. [Poem.] (In *Harbinger*, July 4.)
A Word of Hope. [Poem.] (In *National Anti-Slavery Standard*, Sept. 3.)
Sonnet to William Lloyd Garrison. (In *Liberty Bell*.)
(*Tr.*) A Cradle Song, from the German of Rückert. (In *Harbinger*, July 4.)
Same, entitled *Nature's Cradle Song*. Def. vi.
Two articles on licentiousness. (In *Chronotype*.)

1847
(CAMBRIDGE — NEWBURYPORT)

Hymn. (In *University of Cambridge Exercises at the Thirty-first Annual Visitation of the [Harvard] Divinity School*, July 16.) Pph. Def. vi.
Ordination Exercises, Sept. 15, with letter about ecclesiastical councils. Pph.

1848
(NEWBURYPORT)

"Man shall not live by bread alone": Thanksgiving Sermon, Newburyport, Nov. 30. Pph.
Fugitives' Hymn. (In *Liberty Bell*.)

1849
(NEWBURYPORT)

The Twofold Being. [Poem.] (In Peabody, Elizabeth P., *ed.* *Æsthetic Papers.*)

1850
(NEWBURYPORT)

Address to the Voters of the Third Congressional District of Massachusetts. Pph.
Birthday in Fairyland. Pph.
Same. (In Phillips. *Laurel Leaves for Little Folks*, 1903.)
The Tongue: Two Practical Sermons. Pph.
(*With* C. Cushing *and* F. L. Dimmick.) Address to the Citizens in Behalf of the Public Library [Newburyport]. Broadside.

1851
(NEWBURYPORT)

Merchants: a Sunday Evening Lecture, Jan. Pph.
Same. (In *Hunt's Merchants' Magazine*, Oct.)

Newbury School Committee Report, 1850–51. Pph.
Newburyport Free Evening School Report, 1851. Pph.
To a Young Convert. [Poem.] (In *Liberty Bell*.)
    Same. (In his *Afternoon Landscape*. 1889.)

1852

(NEWBURYPORT — WORCESTER)

Things New and Old: An Installation Sermon, Sept. 5. Pph.
Address for Freedom Club, Worcester. Broadside.
Address to the Citizens of Worcester. (Young Men's Library Association.) Broadside.
Elegy without Fiction: Sermon, Oct. 31, suggested by the deaths of Webster and Rantoul. Broadside.
Man and Nature. (In *Christian Examiner*, July.)
(*Tr*.) Forward. [Poem], from the German of Hoffman von Fallersleben. (In *Liberty Bell*.) Def. VI.
    Same. (In *Sword and Pen*, Dec. 17.)

1853

(WORCESTER)

Thalatta: A Book for the Seaside.
    Ed. anonymously by Higginson and Samuel Longfellow. Contains three of Higginson's poems.
Address on the Operation of the Anti-Liquor Law, Boston, Jan 21. (State Temperance Committee Report.) Pph.
Unitarian Autumnal Convention: A Sermon. Pph.
Remarks before the Committee of the Constitutional Convention on the Qualification of Voters, June 3. Broadside.
Am I my Brother's Keeper? Sermon. (In *Liberty Bell*.)
Vindication of the Lord's Supper. Sermon. Pph.
Conscience in the Counting-Room. (In *Hunt's Merchants' Magazine*, Jan.)
Speech at Anti-Slavery Convention. (In *Liberator*, Feb. 11.)
Woman and her Wishes: An Essay inscribed to the Massachusetts Constitutional Convention. (Several editions and reprinted in London.) Pph.
    Reprinted in London; originally written for the *Una*.
November; December. [Poems.] (In *Putnam's Monthly Magazine*, April.) December. (In his *Afternoon Landscape*. 1889.)
Moral Results of Slavery. (In *Hunt's Merchants' Magazine*, June.)

The Lovers. [Poem.] (In *Putnam's Monthly Magazine*, Sept.)
Odensee. (In *Putnam's Monthly Magazine*, Nov.)
  Same. (In Longfellow, *ed. Poems of Places*.)
A Day in Carter Notch. (In *Putnam's Monthly Magazine*, Dec.)
Sermons to Children. (In *Sunday School Gazette*.)
Speech at the Legislative Temperance Society. (In *Life Boat*.)
(*Ed*.) Whole World's Temperance Convention Report. Pph.

1854
(WORCESTER)

Does Slavery Christianize the Negro? (Anti-Slavery Tract, no. 4.)
Massachusetts in Mourning: A Sermon preached in Worcester, June
  4. Pph.
Scripture Idolatry: A Discourse. Pph.
  Same. (In *Liberator*, Oct. 6.)
    Reprinted in London.
Letter. (In Hartford Bible Convention. *Proceedings*. Appendix.)
Sermon on the Nebraska Bill. (In *Liberator*, Feb. 17.)
Speech at Abington, Aug. 1: Celebration of West Indian Emancipa-
  tion. (In *Liberator*, Aug. 11.)
African Proverbial Philosophy. (In *Putnam's Monthly Magazine*,
  Oct.)

1855
(WORCESTER — WINTER IN FAYAL)

Worcester School Committee Report, Dec. 31, 1854.
Speech at New England Anti-Slavery Convention. (In *Liberator*,
  June 8.)
Anti-Slavery Colporteurage. (In *Liberator*, Sept. 7.) Signed H.
Speech at Anniversary of Boston Mob Convention. (In *Liberator*,
  Nov. 2.)

  At Fayal began a book, the *Return of Faith*, of which only one chapter
  was afterwards published as the *Sympathy of Religions* (1871).

1856
(WORCESTER — TRIP TO KANSAS)

Speech at Anniversary of West Indian Convention. (In *Liberator*,
  Aug. 8.)
Going to Mount Katahdin. (In *Putnam's Monthly Magazine*, Sept.)
  Purporting to be written by one of the ladies of the party.

Portugal's Glory and Decay. (In *North American Review*, Oct.)
Letters from Kansas to New York *Tribune*.

> Published later as an anti-slavery tract (no. 20), under the title *A Ride through Kansas*, and also published independently.

1857

(WORCESTER)

Speech. (In State Disunion Convention, Worcester, Jan 15. *Proceedings*.) Pph. and Broadside.
Speech at Twenty-fifth Anniversary of the Massachusetts Anti-Slavery Society. (In *Liberator*, Jan. 16, and a Broadside.)
Statement on Spiritual Manifestations, April 15. Broadside.
The New Revolution: A Speech before the American Anti-Slavery Society, May 12. Pph.
Circular Letter, July 8, calling for State Disunion Convention. Leaflet.
Call for a Northern Convention at Cleveland, Oct. 28–29. Leaflet.

1858

(WORCESTER)

Woman in Christian Civilization: New York Address. (In *Religious Aspects of the Age*. By various authors.)
Saints and their Bodies. (In *Atlantic Monthly*, March.) Def. VI.
Speech at Fifth Anniversary of the New York Anti-Slavery Society. (In *Liberator*, May 28.)
Mademoiselle's Campaigns. (In *Atlantic Monthly*, July.) Def. VII.
Waterlilies. (In *Atlantic Monthly*, Sept.) Def. VI.
Physical Courage. (In *Atlantic Monthly*, Nov.)
> Same. (In his *Outdoor Papers*. 1863.)

Romance of History. (In *Liberty Bell*.)
(*Comp. with* Mrs. Lucy Stone.) Woman's Rights Almanac for 1858.

1859

(WORCESTER)

The Rationale of Spiritualism. Pph.
The Results of Spiritualism: A Discourse, New York, March 6. Pph.
Ought Women to learn the Alphabet? (In *Atlantic Monthly*, Feb.) Def. IV

> Also published as a tract. Boston, 1870, and Manchester, Eng., 1873, and as Woman's Suffrage Tracts, No. 4, Boston, 1871.

Letter to a Dyspeptic. (In *Atlantic Monthly*, April.)
Same. (In his *Outdoor Papers*. 1863.)
A Charge with Prince Rupert. (In *Atlantic Monthly*, June.) Def. VII.
Murder of the Innocents. (In *Atlantic Monthly*, Sept.)
Same. (In his *Outdoor Papers*. 1863.)

1860
(WORCESTER)

A Visit to John Brown's Household in 1859. (In Redpath. *Public Life of Captain John Brown*.) Def. II.
Maroons of Jamaica. (In *Atlantic Monthly*, Feb.)
Same. (In his *Travellers and Outlaws*. 1889.)
Maroons of Surinam. (In *Atlantic Monthly*, May.)
Same. (In his *Travellers and Outlaws*. 1889.)
Theodore Parker. (In *Atlantic Monthly*, Oct.) Def. II.
Fayal and the Portuguese. (In *Atlantic Monthly*, Nov.) **Def. VI.**

1861
(WORCESTER)

Barbarism and Civilization. (In *Atlantic Monthly*, Jan.)
Same. (In his *Outdoor Papers*, 1863.)
Gymnastics. (In *Atlantic Monthly*, March.)
Same. (In his *Outdoor Papers*, 1863.)
April days. (In *Atlantic Monthly*, April.) Def. VI.
Denmark Vesey. (In *Atlantic Monthly*, June.)
Same. (In his *Travellers and Outlaws*. 1889.)
Ordeal by Battle. (In *Atlantic Monthly*, July.)
Nat Turner's Insurrection. (In *Atlantic Monthly*, Aug.)
Same. (In his *Travellers and Outlaws*. 1889.)
My Outdoor Study. (In *Atlantic Monthly*, Sept.)
Same. (In his *Outdoor Papers*. 1863.)
A New Counterblast. (In *Atlantic Monthly*, Dec.)
Same. (In his *Outdoor Papers*. 1863.)

1862
(WORCESTER — ENLISTED IN SEPTEMBER)

Worcester Public Library, Second Annual Report. Pph.
Snow. (In *Atlantic Monthly*, Feb.) Def. VI.
Letter to a Young Contributor. (In *Atlantic Monthly*, April.)
Same. (In his *Atlantic Essays*. 1871.)
Same. (In his *Hints on Writing and Speech-Making*. 1887.)

Health of Our Girls. (In *Atlantic Monthly*, June.)
Gabriel's Defeat. (In *Atlantic Monthly*, Sept.)
  Same. (In his *Travellers and Outlaws*. 1889.)
Life of Birds. (In *Atlantic Monthly*, Sept.) Def. VI.
Procession of the Flowers. (In *Atlantic Monthly*, Dec.) Def. VI.

1863
(WAR)

Outdoor Papers.
The Puritan Minister. (In *Atlantic Monthly*, Sept.)
  Same. (In his *Atlantic Essays*. 1871.)

1864
(WAR — NEWPORT)

Regular and Volunteer Officers. (In *Atlantic Monthly*, Sept.)
A Night in the Water. (In *Atlantic Monthly*, Oct.) Def. III.
Leaves from an Officer's Journal. (In *Atlantic Monthly*, Nov., Dec.)
Book Notices. (In *Atlantic Monthly, Friend of Progress*.)

1865
(NEWPORT)

Leaves from an Officer's Journal. (In *Atlantic Monthly*, Jan.)
Bequest of Spiritualism. (In *Friend of Progress*, Feb.)
Herbert Spencer. (In *Friend of Progress*, March.)
Up the St. Mary's. (In *Atlantic Monthly*, April.) Def. III.
Fair Play the Best Policy. (In *Atlantic Monthly*, May.)
Frances Power Cobbe. (In *Friend of Progress*, July.)
Up the St. John's. (In *Atlantic Monthly*, Sept.) Def. III.
Our Future Militia System. (In *Atlantic Monthly*, Sept.)
(*Tr.*) Works of Epictetus.
  Same. Revised. 2 vols. 1890.
  Same. (In *Cambridge Classics*.)
Book notices and editorials. (In *Atlantic Monthly, Commonwealth,
  Friend of Progress, Independent*.)

1866
(NEWPORT)

Children's Books of the Year. (In *North American Review*, Jan.)
(*Ed.*) Harvard Memorial Biographies. 2 vols.

Same. Another edition. 2 vols. 1867.

13 of these biographies were written by Higginson.

Book notices and editorials. (In *Atlantic Monthly, Independent.*)

1867

(NEWPORT)

Newport Free Public Library. [Circular calling the attention of the community to its history, needs, etc.] Pph.

Nonsense of it. Leaflet.

Replies to arguments against woman suffrage.

A Plea for Culture. (In *Atlantic Monthly*, Jan.)

Same. (In his *Atlantic Essays.* 1871.)

Charlotte P. Hawes. (In *Radical*, Jan.)

A Driftwood Fire. (In *Atlantic Monthly*, Feb.) Def. v.

Out on Picket. (In *Atlantic Monthly*, March.) Def. III.

The Haunted Window. (In *Atlantic Monthly*, April.)

Same. (In his *Oldport Days.* 1873.)

Oldport in Winter. (In *Atlantic Monthly*, May.) Def. v.

Negro Spirituals. (In *Atlantic Monthly*, June.) Def. III.

An Artist's Dream. (In *Atlantic Monthly*, July.)

Reprinted in Def. v, under the title *An Artist's Creation.*

Up the Edisto. (In *Atlantic Monthly*, Aug.) Def. III.

Sunshine and Petrarch. (In *Atlantic Monthly*, Sept.) Def. v.

Literature as an Art. (In *Atlantic Monthly*, Dec.)

Same. (In his *Atlantic Essays.* 1871.)

Articles. (In *Independent, Nation.*)

1868

(NEWPORT)

Newport Free Library, President's Report, 1867-68. Pph.

Lydia Maria Child; Margaret Fuller Ossoli. (In *Eminent Women of the Age.* By various writers.)

Oldport Wharves. (In *Atlantic Monthly*, Jan.) Def. v.

The Pedigree of Liberalism. (In *Radical*, March.)

The American Lecture System. (In *Macmillan's Magazine*, May.)

Same. (In *Littell's Living Age*, June 6.)

(*Adapted.*) Child Pictures from Dickens.

Book notices and editorials. (In *Independent.*)

The book notices include a series, *Live Americans*, giving accounts of Longfellow, Lowell, and others.

1869

(NEWPORT)

Malbone.
Same. (In *Atlantic Monthly*, Jan.–June.)
Ought Women to vote?
Memoir of Dr. Thaddeus William Harris. Pph. Def. II.
Reprinted from *Harris's Entomological Correspondence.*
Preface. (In Erckmann-Chatrian. *Mme. Thérèse.* Tr. by C. L. Forten.)
Immortality: An Address [Boston], Feb. 21, 1869. (In *Radical*, March.)
Greek Goddesses. (In *Atlantic Monthly*, July.) Def. VII.
Tr. into French in the *Revue Britannique*, Oct., 1869, and also into modern Greek.
Letters to Country Boys. (In *Hearth and Home.*)
Book notices and editorials. (In *Atlantic Monthly, Independent,* New York *Tribune.*)

1870

(NEWPORT)

Army Life in a Black Regiment. Def. III.
Same. Tr. into French under the title *Vie militaire dans un régiment noir.* Paris, 1884.
Decoration Day Address, Mount Auburn, May 30. Broadside.
Same. (In Reed *and others,* eds. *Modern Eloquence,* vol. 8. 1901.)
Americanism in Literature. (In *Atlantic Monthly*, Jan.)
Same. (In his *Atlantic Essays.* 1871.)
A Shadow. (In *Atlantic Monthly*, July.) Def. VI.
Footpaths. (In *Atlantic Monthly*, Nov.) Def. VI.
Our Menagerie. (In *Our Young Folks.*)
Swimming. (In *Atlantic Almanac.*)
Book notices and editorials. (In *Atlantic Monthly, Independent, Index,* New York *Tribune, Woman's Journal.*)

1871

(NEWPORT)

Atlantic Essays.
Madam Delia's Expectations. (In *Atlantic Monthly*, Jan.)
Same. (In his *Oldport Days.* 1873.)
The Sympathy of Religions. (In *Radical*, Feb.) Def. VII.
Published as a pamphlet, Boston, 1871; reprinted, London, 1872, and Boston, enlarged, 1876; reprinted in *Unity Church-Door Pulpit,*

Chicago, June 16, 1885; reprinted in *World's Parliament of Religions*, vol. I, Chicago, 1893; tr. under the title, *L'affinité des religions*, by Mrs. Maria E. MacKaye, Paris, 1898.

Plutarch's Morals. (In *Radical*, March.)

Unpublished Letters from Theodore Parker. (In *Radical*, May.)

Buddhist Path of Virtue. (In *Radical*, June.)

Sappho. (In *Atlantic Monthly*, July.) Def. VII.

An Evening with Mrs. Hawthorne. (In *Atlantic Monthly*, Oct.) Def. II.

On an Old Latin Textbook. (In *Atlantic Monthly*, Oct.) Def. VII.

Book Notice of *Verses*, by "H. H." (In *Atlantic Monthly*. Recent Literature.)

Editorials. (In *Independent*, *Index*, New York *Tribune* (including letters from Newport and from Harvard College), *Woman's Journal*.)

1872
(NEWPORT)

A Day of Scottish Games. (In *Scribner's Monthly*, Jan.)

In a Wherry. (In *Atlantic Monthly*, Feb.) Def. V.

Character of Buddha. (In *Index*, March 16.)

Hawthorne's Last Bequest. (In *Scribner's Monthly*, Nov.)

Editorials. (In *Index*, *Woman's Journal*.)

1873
(NEWPORT)

Oldport Days.

Are you a Christian? Pph.

Same. (In *Index*, Jan. 25.)

Higher Education of Woman: A Paper before the Social Science Convention, May 14. Pph.

Intercollegiate Scholarships. (In *Scribner's Monthly*, Jan.)

Editorials. (In *Index*, *Woman's Journal*.)

1874
(NEWPORT)

The Baby of the Regiment. (In Whittier, *comp. Child Life in Prose*.)

Reprinted from *Army Life in a Black Regiment*. 1870.

How the American Revolution Opened. (In *Oliver Optic's Magazine*.)

Same. (In *Young Folks' History of the United States*. 1875.)

Charles Dudley Warner. (In *Scribner's Monthly*, Jan.)

Decoration. [Poem.] (In *Scribner's Monthly*, June.) Def. VI.

Old Dutch Times in New York. (In *St. Nicholas*, Sept.)
   Same. (In *Young Folks' History of the United States*. 1875.)
Editorials. (In *Independent, Woman's Journal*.)

1875
(NEWPORT)

English Statesmen. (Brief Biographies of European Public Men Series.)
   Edited the 3 other volumes in this series.
Young Folks' History of the United States.
   Tr. into French (2 editions), Paris, 1875; into German, Stuttgart,
   1876; into Italian, 1888.
Questions on Higginson's *Young Folks' History of the United States*.
   For the use of teachers. Pph.
Life of Emerson. (In *Johnson's Universal Cyclopædia*.)
The Word Philanthropy. (In Free Religious Association. *Freedom
   and Fellowship in Religion*.) Def. VI.
Introductory Address, Free Religious Association. Pph.
The Gymnasium and Gymnastics in Harvard College. (In Vaille and
   Clark, *comp. Harvard Book*, vol. 2.)

1876
(NEWPORT)

History of the Public School System in Rhode Island. (In *History of
   Public Education in Rhode Island*, 1636–1876.)
A Moonglade. (In *Laurel Leaves*. Pub. by W. F. Gill.) Def. V.
Speech at memorial service for Dr. S. G. Howe. (In Howe, Mrs. Julia
   Ward. *Memoir of Dr. Samuel Gridley Howe*.) Def. II.
(*With* Thomas H. Clarke.) A Sketch of the Public Schools in the City
   of Newport. (In *History of Public Education in Rhode Island*.)
Childhood's Fancies. (In *Scribner's Monthly*, Jan.)
Lowell's *Among my Books*. Second Series. (In *Scribner's Monthly*,
   March. Culture and Progress.)
Story of the Signing. [Declaration of Independence.] (In *Scribner's
   Monthly*, July.)
   The paper *Provençal Song* mistakenly attributed to Higginson in
   Galaxy, April, was by Mrs. Maria E. MacKaye.

1877
(NEWPORT)

[Education in] Rhode Island. (In Kiddle and Schem. *Cyclopædia of
   Education*.)

Intercollegiate Literary Association Report. Pph.
(*Comp.*) A Book of American Explorers. (In *Young Folks' Series.*)
Book notices and editorials. (In *Nation, Woman's Journal.*)

> A portion of the book notices in the *Nation* were called Poetry of the Month, later entitled Recent Poetry. The reviews were continued to Feb., 1904.

1878

(CAMBRIDGE — TRIP TO EUROPE)

Speech at Conference of Liberal Thinkers, London, June 13. Pph.
Letter on Physical and Intellectual Habits. (In Holbrook. *Hygiene of the Brain Nerves.*)
R. G. White. (In *Atlantic Monthly*, May. Contributors' Club.)
Some War Scenes Revisited. (In *Atlantic Monthly*, July.)

> Reprinted in Def. III under the title *Fourteen Years After.*

Saxe Holm's Botany. (In *Atlantic Monthly*, July. Contributors' Club.)
An Irish Heart. (In *Scribner's Monthly*, Dec.)
Editorials. (In *Woman's Journal.*)

1879

(CAMBRIDGE, FROM THIS TIME)

Short Studies of American Authors.

> First published in the *Literary World.*

Intercollegiate Literary Association: Its History, Aims, and Results. Pph.
Speech at Frothingham Festival, New York, April 22. Pph.
Joseph Cook. (In *Atlantic Monthly*, March. Contributors' Club.)
New England Life. (In *Atlantic Monthly*, June. Contributors' Club.)
Recent Essays. (In *North American Review*, July.)
Speech at Library Convention in Boston, June–July. (In *Library Journal*, Sept.–Oct.)
(*With others.*) Other Side of the Woman Question. (In *North American Review*, Nov.)
Editorials. (In *Woman's Journal.*)

1880

(IN LEGISLATURE)

From the Death of Winthrop to Philip's War. (In Winsor, *ed. Memorial History of Boston*, vol. I.)

A Revolutionary Congressman on Horseback. (In *Scribner's Monthly*, Jan.)

Same. (In his *Travellers and Outlaws*, 1889.)

Dwelling-Places. [Poem.] (In *Scribner's Monthly*, March.) Def. VI.

The Reed Immortal. [Poem.] (In *Atlantic Monthly*, Aug.) Def. VI.

Two Anti-Slavery Leaders. [William Lloyd Garrison and Levi Coffin.] (In *International Review*, Aug.)

Howells's *Undiscovered Country*. (In *Scribner's Monthly*, Sept.)

A Search for the Pleiades. (In *Atlantic Monthly*, Nov.) Def. VI.

Editorials. (In *Harvard Register, Woman's Journal*.)

1881

Common Sense about Women.

> Reprinted in London, 1890, 4th ed., with some omissions. Tr. into German from the English ed. under the title *Die Frauenfrage und der gesunde Menschenverstand*, by Eugenie Jacobi, 1895.

Young Folks' History of the United States. 2d ed.

> Printed in raised type by the Howe Memorial Press, Perkins Institution and Massachusetts School for the Blind.

French and Indian Wars. (In Winsor, *ed. Memorial History of Boston*, vol. II.)

Address at the Celebration of the Battle of Cowpens, Spartanburg, South Carolina, May II. Pph.

Same. (In Reed *and others, eds. Modern Eloquence*, vol. 8. 1901.)

Oration. (In *Exercises in Celebrating the 250th Anniversary of the Settlement of Cambridge, December 28, 1880*.)

French Radical Eloquence. (In Reed, *ed. The City and the Sea, with other Cambridge Contributions in aid of the Hospital Fund*.)

Memorial Ode [May 30]. (With Long's *Oration*.) Pph. Def. VI.

> Also printed separately.

Notice of Benjamin Peirce. (In King, *comp. Memorial Collection*.)

Carlyle's Laugh. (In *Atlantic Monthly*, Oct.)

> Reprinted in *Carlyle's Laugh and Other Surprises*, 1909.

Sellar's *Roman Poets of the Republic*. (In *Atlantic Monthly*, Oct.)

Short March with the Guard. [Verses.] (In *Sword and Pen*, Dec. 9.)

Book notices and editorials. (In *Christian Register, Literary World, Woman's Journal*.)

1882

Young Folks' History of the United States. New ed., with additional chapters.

Speech at Rev. Samuel Johnson's funeral. (In *Samuel Johnson: A Memorial.*) Pph.
(*With Others.*) Testimony on Charles River Railroad, Feb. 13. Pph.
The Brook Farm Period. (In *Demorest's Monthly*, July.)
First Americans. (In *Harper's Monthly Magazine*, Aug.)
Visit of the Vikings. (In *Harper's Monthly Magazine*, Sept.)
Spanish Discoverers. (In *Harper's Monthly Magazine*, Oct.)

> The last three articles were published later in Higginson's *Larger History of the United States* (1885), and in Higginson and MacDonald's *History of the United States* (1905).

The Baby Sorceress. [Sonnet.] (In *Century Magazine*, Nov.) Def. VI.
Editorials and other articles. (In *Index, Nation, Woman's Journal.*)

1883

Dedicatory Address at unveiling of the statue of John Bridge, Sept. 20, 1882. (In *Cambridge City Document*, 1883.)
Why do Children dislike History? (In *Methods of Teaching History.* Hall's Pedagogical Library, vol. I.)
Report on the Parker Library. (In Boston Public Library. *31st Annual Report.*) Pph.
Old English Seamen. (In *Harper's Monthly Magazine*, Jan.)
French Voyageurs. (In *Harper's Monthly Magazine*, March.)
Negro Race in America. (In *Atlantic Monthly*, April.)
Conway's *Emerson at Home and Abroad.* (In *Century Magazine*, April.)
"An English Nation." (In *Harper's Monthly Magazine*, April.)
The Hundred Years' War. (In *Harper's Monthly Magazine*, June.)
Second Generation of English in America. (In *Harper's Monthly Magazine*, July.)
The British Yoke. (In *Harper's Monthly Magazine*, Aug.)
Dawning of Independence. (In *Harper's Monthly Magazine*, Oct.)

> The foregoing articles in *Harper's Magazine* were published later in Higginson's *Larger History of the United States* (1885), and in Higginson and MacDonald's *History of the United States* (1905).

Lodge's *Webster.* (In *Atlantic Monthly*, Oct.)
Book notices and articles. (In *Nation.*)

1884

[Life of] Margaret Fuller Ossoli. (In *American Men of Letters.*)
Wendell Phillips. Pph. Def. II.

> Reprinted from the *Nation*, Feb. 7, 1884.

Young Men's Party. Pph.
  Reprinted from the New York *Evening Post*, Oct. 4, 1884.
Palmer's *Odyssey*. (In *Atlantic Monthly*, Oct.)

1885

Larger History of the United States.
Oration. (In *Memorial Services in the City of Cambridge on the Day of
  the Funeral of General Grant, Aug. 8.*) Pph.
Reviewed Julian Hawthorne's *Nathaniel Hawthorne and His Wife*. (In
  Atlantic Monthly, Feb.)
American Flash Language in 1793. (In *Science*, May 8.)
Lowell in England. (In *Literary World*, June 27.)
"H. H." (In *Critic*, Aug. 22.)
Mrs. Helen Jackson, "H. H." (In *Century Magazine*, Dec.) Def. ii.
(*With others*) Is Boston losing its Literary Prestige? (In *Brooklyn
  Magazine*, Dec.)
  Began a series of articles, entitled Women and Men, in *Harper's Bazar*.

1886

The Monarch of Dreams. Def. v.
  "A German translation of this story appeared in the New York *Freie
  Zeitung* of Aug. 18, 1889, the translator being Louis Wägele and
  the title *Der Monarch seiner Träume*. It is said to have also ap-
  peared in French, but no particulars are known."
William Lloyd Garrison. (In *Atlantic Monthly*, Jan.) Def. ii.
Grant. (In *Atlantic Monthly*, March, Sept.) Def. ii.
How I Was Educated. (In *Forum*, April.)
  Same. Pph.
  Republished in 1887 in a volume entitled *The College and the
  Church*.
To the Memory of "H. H." [Sonnet.] (In *Century Magazine*, May.)
  Def. vi.
Reminiscences of Helen Jackson. (In *New Princeton Review*, July.)
Old Salem Sea-Captains. (In *Harper's Monthly Magazine*, Sept.)
  Same. (In his *Travellers and Outlaws*. 1889.)
E. P. Whipple. (In *Atlantic Monthly*, Sept.)
  Same. (In his *Short Studies of American Authors*.)
Mr. Hamerton on Literature in a Republic. (In *Harvard Monthly*,
  Dec.)
Articles. (In *Critic, Independent, Good Cheer, Harper's Bazar,
  Nation*.)

1887

Hints on Writing and Speech-making.
Women and Men.
> Reprinted from *Harper's Bazar*.

For Self-Respect and Self-Protection: Speech at the Annual Meeting of the American Woman Suffrage Association, Phila., Nov. 1. Pph. and leaflet.

Preface. (In Stevens. *Around the World on a Bicycle.*)

Speeches, letters, etc., 1853–87. (In Stanton *and others, eds. History of Woman Suffrage.* 4 vols.)

Unsolved Problems in Woman Suffrage. (In *Forum*, Jan.)
> Reprinted later as a pamphlet.

Mr. Hamerton on Literature in a Republic. (In *Harvard Monthly*, Jan.)

Hayne, Paul Hamilton. (In *Chautauquan*, Jan.)

Lanier, Sidney. (In *Chautauquan*, April.)

A Missent Letter. (In *Strawbridge and Clothier's Quarterly*, vol. 6, no. 2. Summer no.)
> Same. (In *Woman's Journal*, Aug. 27.)

Sub Pondere Crescit. [Sonnet.] (In *Century Magazine*, Sept.) Def. VI.

A June Migration. (In *Appalachia*, Dec.)

Articles. (In *Harper's Bazar, Independent.*)

1888

Short Studies of American Authors. Rev. and enl.

Address. (In *Reunion of the Free-Soilers of 1848–1852*, Boston, June 28.) Pph.

John Brown. (In Appletons' *Cyclopædia of American Biography.*)

English Sources of American Dialect. (In American Antiquarian Society. *Proceedings.* New series, vol. 4.)

Howell's *Modern Italian Poets.* (In *Nation*, Jan. 5.)

A Precursor of Hawthorne [William Austin]. (In *Independent.* March 29.)

English and American Manners. (In *Forum*, July.)

Speech. (In *Protest against the Majority Report on the Employment and Schooling of Children, and against any Legislative Interference with Private Schools, Massachusetts House Document, No. 19.*) Pph.

1889

The Afternoon Landscape: Poems and Translations.
Travellers and Outlaws.

Three Outdoor Papers. (Riverside Literature Series.) Pph.
Lowell in Cambridge. (In *Critic*, Feb. 23.)
Vestis Angelica. [Poem.] (In *Scribner's Magazine*, March.) Def. VI.
Nils's Garden. [A story.] (In *Century Magazine*, July.)
Ode to a Butterfly. [Poem.] (In *Century Magazine*, Nov.) Def. VI.

1890

In a Fair Country: Essays from *Outdoor Papers*. Illustrated by Irene E. Jerome.
Cambridge Public Library: Plan reported to the Book Committee. Pph.
Cambridge: Literature. (In Hurd, *comp. History of Middlesex County*, vol. I.)
Opening Address. (In Browning Society of Boston. *Memorial to Robert Browning*, Jan. 28.)
A World Literature. (In *Century Magazine*, Jan.)
Letter Relating to the Cambridge Public Library. (In *Cambridge Tribune*, March 15.)
Richard Henry Dana. (In *Cambridge Tribune*, Dec. 20.)
(*Ed. with* Mrs. Ellen H. Bigelow.) American Sonnets. Preface by Higginson.
(*Ed. with* Mrs. Mabel L. Todd.) Poems, by Emily Dickinson. Preface by Higginson.

1891

Life of Francis Higginson. (In *Makers of America*.)
On the Steps of the Hall (University Hall, Aug. 28, 1837). Privately printed. Leaflet.
Poem inscribed to the class of 1841, Harvard University.
Address at the 100th Anniversary, Jan 24. (In Massachusetts Historical Society. *Proceedings*.)
Landmarks of Progress. Address at the 40th Anniversary of the National Woman's Rights Convention. (In *Woman's Journal*, Feb. 14.)
Rabiah's Defence. [Poem.] (In *Atlantic Monthly*, Sept.) Def. VI.
Emily Dickinson's Letters. (In *Atlantic Monthly*, Oct.)
The Two Lessons. [Sonnet.] (In *Century Magazine*, Dec.) Def. VI.
Glimpses of Authors. (In *Brains*, Oct. 15–Jan. 1, 1892.)
(*Ed. with* Mrs. Mabel L. Todd.) Poems, by Emily Dickinson. 2d series.
(*Ed. in part.*) The Rindge Gifts to Cambridge. [City publication.]
Articles. (In *Harper's Bazar, Independent*.)

1892

Concerning All of Us.

The New World and the New Book: An Address delivered before the Nineteenth Century Club of New York City, Jan. 15, 1891, with kindred essays.

Literature in a Republic: A Lecture. (In Reed *and others, eds. Modern Eloquence*, vol. 5.)

Tribute to Lowell. (In Massachusetts Commandery of the Loyal Legion. *In Memoriam.*) Pph.

    Same. (In *Cambridge Tribune*, Feb. 20.)

Youth and Literary Life. (In *Lectures to Young Men*, New York.) Pph.

English Ancestry of the Higginson Family. (In *New England Historical and Genealogical Register*, April.)

An Egyptian Banquet. [Sonnet.] (In *Scribner's Magazine*, April.) Def. vi.

The Sleeping Car. [Poem.] (In *Century Magazine*, May.) Def. vi.

School, College, Library. (In *Cosmopolitan Magazine*, May.)

A World Outside of Science. (In *New World*, Dec.)

    Same. Pph.

    Same. (In his *Book and Heart.* 1897.)

(*With* Mrs. Florence W. Jaques.) List of battles and casualties of Massachusetts regiments during the war of the Rebellion. (In *New England Historical and Genealogical Register*, Jan.)

Articles. (In *Nation*.)

1893

Cambridge Public Library Report. Pph.

Straight Lines or Oblique Lines? (In *Woman Suffrage Leaflet*, Nov.)

(*With* Mrs. Mary T. Higginson.) Such as They Are: Poems.

(*With* Edward Channing.) English History for American Readers.

Speech on the Turning-Point in the History of the Parliament of Religions. (In *World's Parliament of Religions*, vol. 1.)

Articles. (In Boston *Evening Transcript, Nation, Public Opinion*.)

1894

Cambridge Public Library Report. Pph.

Note [to] *Books and Reading*, by Sir John Lubbock. (In *Woman's Book*, vol. 2.)

Introduction. (In *Speeches and Addresses of William E. Russell*.)

How to Use a Public Library. (In *Golden Rule*, Sept. 27.)

The Prospect Union and the Public Library. (In *Prospect Union Review*, Oct. 24).

How to Read Magazines. (In *Golden Rule*, Nov. 15.)

1895

Massachusetts in the Army and Navy during the War of 1861–65. Vol. 2.

The Fairy Coursers. [Poem.] (In *Cambridge Sketches*, by Cambridge authors.)

The Woman who Most Influenced Me. (In *Ladies' Home Journal*, Oct.)

A Young Girl's Library. (In *Ladies' Home Journal*, Nov.)

Articles. (In Boston *Evening Transcript, Harper's Bazar, Nation, et al.*)

1896

Massachusetts in the Army and Navy during the War of 1861–65. Vol. 1.

Prefatory note. (In Aspinwall. *Short Stories for Short People.*)

The School of Jingoes. (In *Essays from the Chap-Book.*)

Life in Cambridge Town. (In Gilman, ed. *Cambridge of 1896.*)

Octavius Brooks Frothingham. (In *New World*, March.)

A Keats Manuscript. (In *Forum*, June.)

   Same. (In his *Book and Heart.* 1897.)

The Romance of a Brown-Paper Parcel. (In *Century Magazine*, Aug.)

A Bookshelf in the Kitchen. (In *Ladies' Home Journal*, Nov.)

Cheerful Yesterdays. (In *Atlantic Monthly*, Nov.–Dec.) Def. 1.

Early Free Churches. (In *Free Church Record*, April.)

(*Comp.*) Rough list in manuscript of his Galatea collection of books, in the Boston Public Library, relating to women. With newspaper scraps, printed titles, and a supplementary accessions catalogue.

   A comment on the Galatea collection may be found in the Boston *Evening Transcript*, Feb. 18, 1896.

(*Comp.*) Scrapbook of periodical articles, newspaper cuttings, and portraits relating to James Russell Lowell.

   Presented to the Cambridge Public Library, 1896.

Articles. (In Boston *Evening Transcript, Harper's Bazar, Harper's Weekly, Independent, Nation, Outlook, Youth's Companion, et al.*)

1897

Book and Heart.

Procession of the Flowers, and kindred papers. Def. VI.

The Biography of Browning's Fame. (In Browning Society of Boston. *Papers*.)

Educational Conditions and Problems. [Speech at the Annual Meeting of the Harvard Teachers' Association, March 6.] (In *Educational Review*, May.)

Cheerful Yesterdays. (In *Atlantic Monthly*, Jan.–May.) Def. I.

Colored Troops under Fire. (In *Century Magazine*, June.)

Göttingen and Harvard Eighty Years Ago. (In *Harvard Graduates' Magazine*, Sept.)

Literary London Twenty Years Ago. (In *Atlantic Monthly*, Dec.)

Articles. (In *Nation, et al.*)

1898

Cheerful Yesterdays. Def. I.

Cambridge Public Library Report. Pph.

Tales of the Enchanted Islands of the Atlantic.

(*With* Edward Channing.) English History for Americans.
New edition of their *English History for American Readers*. 1893.

Harriet Beecher Stowe. [Preface.] (In Stowe. *Uncle Tom's Cabin*. New ed.)

[Sketches of] Brown, Cooper, and Thoreau. (In Carpenter, *ed. American Prose*.)

Literary Paris Twenty Years Ago. (In *Atlantic Monthly*, Jan.)

On the Outskirts of Public Life. (In *Atlantic Monthly*, Feb.)

The First Black Regiment. (In *Outlook*, July 2.)

Anti-Slavery Days. (In *Outlook*, Sept. 3.)

Articles. (In *Nation, Outlook, et al.*)

1899

Contemporaries. Def. II.

Contents:

    Ralph Waldo Emerson.
    Amos Bronson Alcott.
    Theodore Parker.
    John Greenleaf Whittier.
    Walt Whitman.
    Sidney Lanier.
    An Evening with Mrs. Hawthorne.
    Lydia Maria Child.
    Helen Jackson ("H. H.")
    John Holmes.
    Thaddeus William Harris.
    A Visit to John Brown's Household in 1859.

William Lloyd Garrison.
Wendell Phillips.
Charles Sumner.
Dr. Howe's Anti-Slavery Career.
Ulysses Simpson Grant.
The Eccentricities of Reformers.
The Road to England.

Old Cambridge.
Contents:
    I. Old Cambridge.
    II. Old Cambridge in Three Literary Epochs.
    III. Holmes.
    IV. Longfellow.
    V. Lowell.
"Where Liberty is *Not*, there is My Country." (Anti-Imperialist Leaflet, no. 19.)
    Reprinted from *Harper's Bazar*, Aug. 12, 1899.
(*With* William Taggard Piper.) Cambridge Public Library Report. Pph.
Wendell Phillips. (In *Encyclopædia Britannica*.)
My Literary Neighbors. (In *Outlook*, Feb. 4.)
His Brother's Brother [John Holmes]. (In *Atlantic Monthly*, Aug.)
The Road to England. (In *Atlantic Monthly*, Oct.)
Articles. (In *Nation, Outlook, et al.*)

1900

[Writings. Definitive ed.] 7 vols.
Vol. 1. Cheerful Yesterdays.
    Chapters first printed in the *Atlantic Monthly*.

2. Contemporaries.
    Most of the sketches previously printed.

3. Army Life in a Black Regiment.
    Previously printed.

4. Women and the Alphabet.
    Chiefly articles printed in *Harper's Bazar*.

5. Studies in Romance.
    Includes Malbone. — The Monarch of Dreams. — Oldport Days [part of].

6. Outdoor Studies.
    Mostly previously printed essays and poems.

BIBLIOGRAPHY

7. Studies in History and Letters.

Most of these essays previously printed.

The Alliance between Pilgrim and Puritan in Massachusetts: An **Address** delivered before the Old Planters' Society, Salem, June **9,** 1900. Pph.

Reasons for Voting for Bryan. Leaflet.

Reprinted from the Springfield *Daily Republican,* Sept., 1900.

(*With* W. L. Garrison *and* G. S. Boutwell.) How Should a Colored Man Vote in 1900? Leaflet.

Reprinted from the Boston *Herald,* Oct. 11, 1900.

The Reoccupation of Jacksonville in 1893. (In Mass. Commandery of the Loyal Legion. *Civil War Papers,* vol. 2.)

Addresses and Remarks. (In Free Religious Association. *Proceedings,* 1867–1900.)

Octavius Brooks Frothingham. (In *Prophets of Liberalism: Six Addresses before the Free Religious Association of America.* Pph.)

Education and the Public Library. [Typewritten.] (Boston Public Library. Free Lectures, 1900.)

Articles. (In *Independent, Outlook.*)

1901

American Orators and Oratory: Being a Report of Lectures delivered at Western Reserve University.

The edition is limited to 500 copies.

(*With* William J. Rolfe.) Cambridge Public Library Report. Pph.

Childe Roland to the Dark Tower Came. (In *Poet-Lore,* April–June.)

Articles. (In Boston *Evening Transcript, Independent, Outlook, et al.*)

1902

[Life of] Henry Wadsworth Longfellow. (In *American Men of Letters.*)

[Life of] John Greenleaf Whittier. (In *English Men of Letters.*)

Horace Elisha Scudder: A Memorial. (In American Academy of Arts and Sciences. *Proceedings.*) Pph.

Speech at Winchester, Eng., Sept. 18, 1901. (In Bowker. *King Alfred's Millenary.*)

American Genius and Life. (*With others.*) (In The Most American Books, in *Outlook,* Dec. 6.)

(*Ed.*) Story without an End. By F. W. Carové; tr. by Sarah Austin. Preface by Higginson.

(*Ed.*) Walks with Ellery Channing. [Extracts from manuscript diaries

of Ralph Waldo Emerson. Introduction by Higginson.] (In
Atlantic Monthly, July.)
Reviewed Scudder's Life of Lowell. (In *Harvard Graduates' Magazine*,
March.)
Articles. (In *Independent, Outlook*.)

1903

James Elliot Cabot: A Memorial. (In American Academy of Arts and
Sciences. *Proceedings*.) Pph.
(*With* Mrs. Margaret Higginson Barney.) [Papers.] (In *Heath
Readers*.)
(*With* Henry Walcott Boynton.) Reader's History of American Litera-
ture.

> Based upon a course of lectures, "American Literature in the Nine-
> teenth Century," given by Higginson at the Lowell Institute, Bos-
> ton, 1903. They were reported in part in the Boston *Evening Tran-
> script* under the following titles and dates: American Literature,
> Jan. 6; The Philadelphia Period, Jan. 9; Irving and Cooper, Jan. 13;
> Boston Takes the Lead, Jan. 16; Concord Litterateurs, Jan. 20;
> Influence of the South, Jan. 23; Writers from the West, Jan. 27;
> Our Literary Obstacles, Jan. 30.

Personality of Emerson. (In *Outlook*, May 23.)
Address. (In *Centenary of the Birth of Ralph Waldo Emerson, Concord*,
May 25.)
(*Tr.*) Fifteen Sonnets of Petrarch.

> The introduction is based essentially upon *Sunshine and Petrarch*
> (1867), which originally included most of the sonnets in this vol-
> ume. This edition consists of 430 numbered copies.

Articles. (In *Christian Endeavor World, Independent, Outlook, Success*.)

1904

Address on Decoration Day in Sanders Theatre [Cambridge], May 30.
Pph.
The Sunny Side of the Transcendental Period. (In *Atlantic Monthly*,
Jan.)
English and American Cousins. (In *Atlantic Monthly*, Feb.)
Books Unread. (In *Atlantic Monthly*, March.)
Aristocracy of the Dollar. (In *Atlantic Monthly*, April.)
Intensely Human. (In *Atlantic Monthly*, May.)
Butterflies and Poetry. (In *Atlantic Monthly*, June.)
Articles. (In Boston *Evening Transcript, Encyclopædia Americana*,

Nation, Outlook, The Reader, Sunday Magazine, [Wanamaker's] Book News.)

1905

Part of a Man's Life.

George Frisbie Hoar. (In American Academy of Arts and Sciences. *Proceedings.*) Pph.

Letter Relating to the Intercollegiate Socialist Society. Leaflet.

Reprinted from *Harper's Weekly*, July 14.

(*With* William MacDonald.) History of the United States.

Enlarged ed. of Higginson's *Larger History of the United States.*

Introduction. (In Capen. *Country Homes of Famous Americans.*)

Introduction. (In Sinclair. *The Aftermath of Slavery.*)

American Audiences. (In *Atlantic Monthly*, Jan.)

The Close of the Victorian Epoch. (In *Atlantic Monthly*, March.)

English Literature in the Last Half of the Nineteenth Century: lectures delivered at the Lowell Institute, Boston, 1905.

Not published, but reported in part in the Boston *Evening Transcript* under the following titles and dates: A Few English Poets, March 1; Carlyle, Froude, Ruskin, March 8; Darwin's Domesticity, March 15; Landor and his Class, March 22; Recent English Letters, March 29; Browning and Tennyson, April 5.

Letters of Mark. (In *Atlantic Monthly*, April.)

Wordsworthshire. (In *Atlantic Monthly*, July.)

William James Rolfe. (In *Outlook*, July 22.)

Literature as a Pursuit; An Address before the Harvard Ethical Society, Cambridge, Mass. (In *Critic*, Aug.)

History in Easy Lessons. (In *Atlantic Monthly*, Sept.)

The Cowardice of Culture. (In *Atlantic Monthly*, Oct.)

The above six papers in the *Atlantic Monthly*, together with the six published in the same periodical for 1904, form the volume "Part of a Man's Life."

Garrison and Whittier. (In *Independent*, Dec.)

The Place of Whittier Among Poets. (In *The Reader's Magazine*, Feb.)

(*Ed.*) The Hawthorne Centenary Celebration at the Wayside, Concord, Mass., July 4-7, 1904.

Contains Higginson's address, July 4, as presiding officer of that day.

Articles. (In *Christian Endeavor World, Critic, Independent, Nation, Outlook.*)

1906

Address delivered at the celebration of the 275th anniversary of the founding of Cambridge. Dec. 21, 1905. [Pamphlet, reprinted from the *Proceedings* of the Cambridge Historical Society, 1.]

Introduction. (In Braithwaite, *ed. Book of Elizabethan Verse.*)
A Great Poet in her Prime: Elizabeth Barrett Browning. (In [*Wanamaker's*] *Book News*, March.)
A Reunited Anglo-Saxondom. (In *Critic*, April.)
"Gentlemen by Profession." (In *Independent*, April 12.)
(*With Others.*) The Creative Spirit in Literature. (In *Outlook*, Nov. 24.)
Mrs. Howe and her Commentator. (In Contributors' Club, *Atlantic Monthly*, Oct.)
Cambridge Eighty Years Since. (In *Proceedings* of the Cambridge Historical Society, vol. II.)
Reminiscences of John Bartlett. (In *Proceedings* of the Cambridge Historical Society, vol. I.)

1907

Life and Times of Stephen Higginson.
Massasoit. (In *Massasoit Memorial.*) Pph.
Julia Ward Howe. (In *Outlook*, Jan. 26.)
The Early Days of Longfellow. (In *Book News Monthly*, Feb.)
The Youth of Longfellow. (In *Independent*, Feb. 21.)
Literature (1857–1907). (In *Atlantic Monthly*, Nov.)
John Greenleaf Whittier. (In *Independent*, Dec. 19.)
Literature at Off Tide. (*With others.*) (In Literature or Life, in *Outlook*, Nov. 23.)
Address at Longfellow Memorial Meeting. (In *Proceedings* of Cambridge Historical Society, vol. II.)
Edward Atkinson. (In *Proceedings* of American Academy of Arts and Sciences, vol. XLII.)
Louis Agassiz. (In *Proceedings* of the Cambridge Historical Society, vol. II.)
(*Ed.*) Discourse of Matters Pertaining to Religion. By Theodore Parker. Preface by Higginson.
Articles and addresses. (In *Christian Endeavor World, Cambridge Tribune*, Boston *Evening Transcript, Youth's Companion.*)

1908

Things Worth While. (In *Art of Life Series*, Griggs *ed.*)
Most of the sketches previously printed.
Religious Progress in the Last Two Generations. Pph.
Address at the Fiftieth Anniversary of Cambridge Public Library. (In *History of the Cambridge Public Library.*)
Edmund Clarence Stedman. (In *Independent*, Jan. 30.)

Edmund Clarence Stedman. (In *Atlantic Monthly*, March.)
Edward Everett Hale. (In *Book News Monthly*, Aug.)
Republican Aristocracy. (In *Harper's Monthly*, July.)
First Steps in Literature. (In *New England Magazine*, Oct.)
Emerson's "Footnote Person [Alcott]." (In *Putnam's Monthly and The Reader*, Oct.)
Charles Eliot Norton. (In *Outlook*, Oct. 31.)

1909

Carlyle's Laugh, and Other Surprises.
  Most of the sketches previously printed.
Preface to *A Mother's List of Books for Children*, by Gertrude Wild Arnold.
Old Newport Days. (In *Outlook*, Apr. 17.)
The Future Life. (In *Harper's Bazar*, May.)
  Afterwards, 1910, in a book (*with others*) as *In After Days*.
Edward Everett Hale. (In *Outlook*, June 19.)
(*Ed.*) White Slaves in Africa. (In *North American Review*, July.) Preface.
(*Ed.*) A Poem of the Olden Time, by his Aunt Nancy. Note by Higginson.
Articles. (In Boston *Evening Transcript*.)

1910

(*With others*.) In After Days: Thoughts on the Future Life.
Introduction. (In Austin's *Peter Rugg, the Missing Man*.)
William J. Rolfe. (In *Emerson College Magazine*, Nov.)
(*Ed.*) Descendants of the Reverend Francis Higginson. (Genealogy.)
Articles. (In *Congregationalist and Christian World*, Boston *Evening Transcript*.)

1911

Dickens in America. (Appeared after Col. Higginson's Death in *Outlook*, May 20.)

INDEX